Femme Fatalities

Femme Fatalities

Representations of Strong Women in the Media

Rikke Schubart & Anne Gjelsvik (eds.)

NORDICOM

Femme Fatalities
Representations of Strong Women in the Media

Editors:
Rikke Schubart & Anne Gjelsvik

ISBN 91-89471-25-3

Published by:
Nordicom
Göteborg University
Box 713
SE 405 30 GÖTEBORG
Sweden

Cover by:
Roger Palmqvist
Printed by:
Grafikerna Livréna i Kungälv AB, Sweden, 2004

Contents

III. From the Margins

Foreword

The origin of this book lies in the two sessions 'Representations of Strong Women in the Media I and II' chaired by Rikke Schubart at Crossroads Conference in Tampere the summer of 2002. The interest at the Conference convinced us that the topic of strong women in the media was a research field in growth, but in want of literature and research. In the last decade women in popular media emerged as an expanding field of research. After the groundbreaking studies by Carol Clover (*Men, Women and Chainsaws*, 1993) and Yvonne Tasker (*Spectacular Bodies*, 1993, *Working Girls*, 1998) new aspects are rapidly developing. Together with articles based on papers from the conference we have collected new articles focusing on this up-to-date theme.

Courses on the representation of women in media are taught widely at universities and we hope this anthology represents new insights for researcher and students to discuss. The anthology is aimed at undergraduate and post-graduate students as well as teachers within the field of gender studies, film and media studies, cultural studies and anyone working with gender and media aspects.

Finally we would like to thank The Research Council of Norway and The Danish Humanistic Research Council for financial support and Nordicom and Ulla Carlsson for publishing the anthology and thereby making this book possible.

Odense and Trondheim in October 2004

Rikke Schubart   *Anne Gjelsvik*

Acknowledgments

We would like to thank Taylor & Francis for permission to reproduce Yvonne Tasker's "Soldier's Stories: Women and Military Masculinities in *Courage Under Fire*" which first appeared in *Quarterly Review of Film and Video*, vol. 19, 2002.

We are grateful to the following for permission to reproduce copyright material: Sandrew Metronome/Warner for *Addicted to Love* and *Practical Magic*, Angel Films *Lola Rennt*, for Le Studio Canal/ Pan Européenne Production for *Baise-Moi*, Paramount Home Video for *Tomb Raider*, and Dinamo Story for *Salige er de som tørster*.

Thanks also to The Danish Film Institute/The Danish Film Museum for help in finding the illustrations.

Introduction

Babes, Bitches, Dominatrixes
and Teen Witches

Rikke Schubart & Anne Gjelsvik

During the nineties strong women have moved to the fore in media fictions. In the cinema, in television series and in computer games we find heroines in leading roles that used to be occupied by men. Female doctors now run their own medical drama series, women star in action and suspense computer games, and women even write and direct feminist avant-garde movies employing elements from 'male' genres such as the road-movie and the pornographic movie. The success of strong women is beyond discussion; we find them everywhere from popular television series such as *Buffy the Vampire Slayer* and *Xena: Warrior Princess* to blockbuster movies such as *Charlie's Angels* and *Lara Croft: Tomb Raider*. It is, however, not entirely clear how we should regard such heroines. Are they positive role models for a female audience? Or are they merely new versions of the old pin-up, refashioned in new outfits, new flesh and new roles to cater to a new taste in a postmodern media age?

The representation of strong women raises complex questions related to issues of gender and genre, identity and identification, pleasure and violence. First, do these heroines appeal to women at all? If so, what kind of pleasures do they offer us? And if intended for a male audience, is it possible to kidnap a male fantasy and turn this figure into a feminist icon, thus turning an object of sexual pleasure into an active subject?

The relation between the new strong women and gender politics, media products, consumerism and heterosexual cultural politics is not a simple one, as research in this new field has shown. In the last decade, film and media researchers have been divided in their evaluation of strong women. Carol Clover in her groundbreaking study *Men, Women and Chainsaws: Gender in the Modern Horror Film* (1992) made it clear that the Final Girl of the slasher movie (who kills the monster and saves herself) should *not* be read as a feminist development: "To applaud the Final Girl as a feminist development, as some reviews of *Aliens* have done with Ripley, is (..) a particularly grotesque expression of wishful thinking" (p. 53). Other researchers, however, have taken another view on strong women in media fictions. Yvonne Tasker in her *Working Girls: Gender and Sexuality in Popular Cinema* (1998) is open to the ambivalences inherent in images of beautiful women playing cowgirls, action heroines or detectives, entering 'male' territory, yet submitting to the traditional aesthetics of the pin-up and the narrative subplots of rape, prostitution and domestication through romance.

Recent research suffers from the very same ambivalence that Tasker identifies in the media products. Sarah Projansky in her *Watching Rape: Film and Television in Postfeminist Culture* (2001) is thus dismissive of the new wave of rape-revenge heroines, whereas Jacinda Read in her *The New Avengers: Feminism, Femininity and the Rape-Revenge Cycle* (2000) views the very same cultural products as progressive and postfeminist. The editors of *Reel Knockouts: Violent Women in the Movies* (2001), Martha McCaughey and Neal King, even suggest that images of strong women in fiction may prevent women from becoming victims of male violence in the real world: "We like the threat that women's movie violence presents to the all-important divide between women and men. We wonder what effect such images would have on men who assault women partly because they're so confident that they'll win the fights" (p. 6). So, is Lara Croft merely a "sergeant-major with balloons stuffed up his shirt", as Germaine Greer has called her? Or is she an image of a woman, who can and will fight back? Is Ilsa from the infamous *Ilsa, She-Wolf of the SS* "the first true feminist" as actress Dyanne Thorne coined her? Or is she a sexual display of perverse male desire?

Such questions of representation and interpretation are complex, and answers cannot be simple. One thing, however, is certain: From the early seventies women have been steadily invading more 'male' media territory within film and television genres and computer games. Today we find female protagonists in traditional male roles, female Hollywood stars have postfeminist star personas, and computer game heroines are gaining cult following among both male and female players. We may like or dislike the strong women in the media, suspect them of foul play or reject them as fake products of a patriarchal and consumerist society, but they are here to stay!

This anthology brings together twelve original essays on the representations of strong women in film, television and computer games. It traces women from the cultural margins of exploitation and avant-garde cinema, across the mainstream and into the real lives of audiences, critics and game players. Subjects of the essays vary from sadistic torturess Ilsa in the *Ilsa*-series to synthespians, consumerist teen witches and lesbian audiences. Although all essays are informed by a feminist view, the theories applied vary from textual analysis and feminist critical theory to reception studies and postfeminist aesthetics. And just as subjects and theories differ, so do the evaluations of the strong women; some of the contributors analyze the strong heroine as a consumerist product, others investigate her feminist potentials and some discuss her as a postfeminist sign created out of ambivalence, contradictions and multivocality. Taken together, the essays in this anthology are representative for a postfeminist approach to culture in the sense, that none of them provide simple answers to complex questions. They do not take a normative stance, regarding for instance low culture as 'bad', men as 'evil' or feminist politics as 'good'. Instead, they all search for new meanings arising out of the gaps between consumer culture and popular pleasure, between silicone breasts and subversive audience reactions. This is where the strong women live and flourish: between guilty pleasure and gender politics. And this is also where we, the editors, find ourselves: caught between taking pleasure in media products that are often debated and condemned by many. "How can you even bring yourself to watch those films!" is a comment often heard in regard to wip-movies. Well, if we wish to understand our culture we cannot judge it beforehand.

The anthology springs from what was intended to be a small session on "Representations of Strong Women in Film and Tv-Fiction" at the Fourth International Conference Crossroads in Cultural Studies in Tampere, Finland, in 2002. It proved so popular that it ended up as a double session with more than eighty delegates at both sessions: Strong women are a hot issue. Our intention with this anthology is not to end the debate stirred by Lara, Buffy, Xena, Ilsa and their sisters, but to qualify it by providing analyses, theoretical discussions and historical perspectives.

● ● ●

The book is divided into three parts. The first part, "New Media and Postfeminist Aesthetics", explores relations between new media, new theory and the archetypical representation of women. The four essays move between close analysis of single texts – the French movie *Baise-Moi*, the Danish movie *Breaking the Waves*, the American movie *Lara Croft: Tomb Raider*, the German movie *Lola Rennt* and the computer game *Tomb Raider* – and general discussions of theory, gender and narrative change in contemporary media. Essays employ varied theories and methods: empirical research (Lindell), audience interviews (Mikula), comparative media analysis (Walden) and postfeminist theory (Mühleisen). The second part, "Genre Fictions", discuss representations of strong women in mainstream film and television fictions. Here we meet the new heroines in television genres such as the medical drama (Pantti) and the teen soap (Deneka), and see how female protagonists tie in with audience pleasures, marketing strategies and audience targeting. Why is vampire slayer Buffy concerned with shopping, and in what way does a female doctor differ from a male? This part also discusses the new wave of Norwegian thrillers with female protagonists (Gjelsvik) and the transition of the femme fatale from film noir into the dark comedies of the nineties (Waltonen). The third and final part, "From the Margins", is dedicated to marginalized strong women. We find here the very first study of the controversial *Ilsa*-series from the seventies (Schubart). Another unconventional figure is warrior princess Xena from the popular television series, who is interpretated by Latino gay and lesbian audiences as a lesbian protagonist

(Alesci). Last is a reading of "the definitive bitch from hell" in *Dolores Claiborne* and a discussion of feminist violence (Tay).

Several contributors draw from a recent development of *postfeminism* or *neofeminism*. In this theoretical discussion we find a differentiation between feminism and postfeminism. Within this debate the expression 'first-wave feminism' refers to the feminist movement in the mid-1800 and the expression 'second-wave feminism' refers to the feminist movement in the 1960ies and onwards. Feminism, whether liberal, radical or Marxist/socialist, is always critical of patriarchy and normative heterosexuality, which is considered oppressive to women and non-heterosexuals (such as homosexuals, transsexuals, transvestites). Postfeminism, on the other hand, differs from feminism in having a positive approach to patriarchy, popular culture and postmodernism. Postfeminism embraces the consumer culture of postmodern society and abandons the essentialism, binarism and macro-narratives often underlying 'modern' feminism. Just as researchers are divided in their evaluation of strong women, they are also divided in their evaluation of postfeminism. Some are positive, such as Read, who in her *The New Avengers* analyzes Catwoman as an example of a postmodernist woman constructing a new strong identity out of feminine as well as masculine traits and clichés (the latex costume and superhero narrative). Others are negative, such as Clover rejecting the feminist potentials of the Final Girl, or Projansky rejecting the subversive potential of the female rape-avenger. Projansky even locates postfeminism within the 'backlash' against the women, famously termed so by Susan Faludi in her *Backlash: The Undeclared War against American Women* (1991).

In her article "*Baise-moi* and feminism's filmic intercourse with the aesthetics of pornography" Wencke Mühleisen draws on postfeminist theory and aesthetics from a positive perspective. In her use of postfeminism this term embraces a range of ambiguous aesthetical expressions, it shares queer-theory's criticism of traditional categories of gender and sexuality, and it also challenges 'the woman as victim position'. The French art- and road movie *Baise-moi* (*Fuck Me*, Virginie Despentes/Coralie, 2000) is an illustrative example of this aesthetic strategy where female directors criticize patriarchy by employing male genres such as pornography. A sexualization of people, lifestyles and everyday surroundings is central in mainstream entertainment and *Baise-Moi* forces such sexualization to the extreme by using porno-actors, hard-core pornographic aesthetic, and the point-of-view of the female protagonists. Mühleisen discusses how this can be understood in a postfeminist perspective.

Next, Ingrid Lindell's essay "Over and over again: The representation of women in contemporary cinema" examines the representation of women in cinema. Based on an empirical survey of the film repertoire in Swedish cinemas during 1996, the essay compares mainstream to avant-garde movies and asks whether avant-garde movies contain alternative or subversive representations or not. Lindell compares her Swedish findings to other surveys of the representations of women in mainstream film for a discussion of the term 'strong' in relation to women. Analyzing the avant-garde film *Breaking the Waves* (Lars von Trier, 1996) the essay focuses on the ambiguous representation of its heroine Bess. The author argues that the impression of this movie takes on new meaning when viewed against the repetitive and stereotypical meta-structures of gender in the surrounding film flow.

Maja Mikula also engages with postfeminism in "Lara Croft, between a feminist icon and male fantasy". Lara Croft, a widely popular computer game superwoman and recently also the protagonist of the blockbuster film *Lara Croft: Tomb Raider* (Simon West, 2001), has animated feminist polemics since her creation in 1996. Independent, strong, determined and fearless, Lara is viewed by some as a desirable role model for present-day women, her violence a welcome counter-balance to the submissiveness of traditional female stereotypes. Others object that her Barbie-like body and the moans she generates when engaging in demanding physical stunts, makes her an object of desire and the Cyber-goddess of the average adolescent male computer game player. The original cinematic concept of the computer game meant to reduce the possibility of transference or identification of the player with the character. However, Mikula argues that in both the game and the film, Lara's violence is controlled by the male gaze, thus leaving little room for any shift in traditional gender stereotypes.

It has been asserted that cinema responds to the challenge of new media forms by appropriating their styles and absorbing them into its cultural domain. The final essay of the first part, "Run, Lara, run! The impact of computer games on cinema's action heroine" by Kim Walden, argues that this is also the case with the computer game. Through an examination of *Lola Rennt* (*Run Lola Run*, Tom Tykwer, 1998) and *Lara Croft: Tomb Raider*, Walden examines how cinema is influenced by computer games and considers how they influence representations of the action heroine. Drawing on recent theories of remediation (Bolder and Grusin) the paper analyzes the 'new' action heroine in two areas: First it shows how films mobilize the narrative conventions of the computer game to 'play' with female roles. Secondly, the essay discusses the body as erotic spectacle, locating characters like Lara Croft within the aesthetic traditions of Japanese manga and animé and the Hollywood studio pin-up.

The second part of the anthology now turns to the 'old' media of film and television, which despite their age must develop rapidly to keep up with the media landscape and new audience tastes. In the first article in this section, "Soldier's stories: Women and military masculinities in *Courage Under Fire*", Yvonne Tasker draws the attention towards a major masculine genre, the war movie. Tasker argues that masculinity is important for the understanding of contemporary representations of women, thereby aiming to come to terms with the critical slippage that occurs between talking about gender as a set of qualities or characteristic culturally aligned with men or women, and the way filmic images transgress these borders. With the focus on *Cour-*

age Under Fire and military officer Karen Walden (Meg Ryan), Tasker expands the notion of masculinity and femininity, and argues that military woman in modern genre movies are normalized *through*, and not *against* discourses of masculinity. Investigating the female solider as both female masculinity and as being both ordinary and butchy, Taskers article throws new light on issues central to mainstream representations in film and television as such.

The link between stars and fashion is as old as cinema itself, and this link is continued by today's television stars. In "Iconic eye candy: *Buffy the vampire slayer* and designer peer pressure for teens" Deneka McDonald discusses the interaction between pulp culture programs such as *Buffy the Vampire Slayer* and popular media campaigns directed specifically toward teen audiences. Informed by a postfeminist view, Deneka is ambivalent about the feminist potential of the star playing Buffy, Sarah Michelle Gellar. Deneka finds a discrepancy between on the one hand Buffy as a feminist and a sexually inexperienced teenager and, on the other hand, the star Gellar who is in her twenties, is a model for Maybelline cosmetics and plays the stereotypical 'ditzy blonde' in *I Know What You Did Last Summer* and *Scream 2*. McDonald is caught in the gap between pleasure and popular culture, between feminism and consumerism: Can you be a feminist and at the same time advertise traditional feminine looks?

Such ambivalence does not resonate in the essay by Karma Waltonen, "Dark comedies and dark ladies: The new femme fatale", about the femme fatale in contemporary cinema. On the contrary, Waltonen describes the very 'backlash' that the pessimistic (or negative) view on postfeminism is afraid of. According to Waltonen the fatale is still found in neo-noir and thrillers, but her most intriguing reappearance is definitely in recent Hollywood romantic dramas and comedies such as *Practical Magic* (Griffin Dunne, 1998) and *My Best Friend's Wedding* (P.J. Hogan, 1997). With the femme fatale the antiquated message of film noir – be beautiful, be lethal and seductive, and be killed in the end – is brought back disguised in the feminist coding of the nineties. The heroines of the dark dramas and comedies are strong, independent, and definitely dangerous. As they exist outside of dark fantasy, however, they are not punished with violence or death, but with romance. Waltonen argues that a female audience is encouraged to internalize the patriarchal values, which ultimately conquers any threat to heterosexual love.

During the late nineties Norwegian cinema saw a wave of thrillers with female protagonists. A recurring characteristic was the central role of a woman on both sides of the camera; two movies were based on novels by Norwegian writers Anne Holt and Karin Fossum, and three were directed by female directors. In her essay "A woman's gotta do what a woman's gotta do" Anne Gjelsvik analyzes three of the movies: *Cellofan – med døden til følge* (*Cellophane*, Eva Isaksen, 1997), *Evas øye* (*Eva's Eye*, Berit Nesheim, 1999) and *Salige er de som tørster* (*Blessed Are Those Who Thirst*, Carl Jørgen Kiøning, 1998). Firmly grounded within a feminist perspective, Gjelsvik discusses the 'realistic' representations of modern working girls in view of the conventions of the thriller. While the Norwegian thrillers follow the generic conventions and classical narration of the Hollywood thriller, they add aspects relating to women's everyday experiences. Central to the article is an analysis of the 'private life' of the heroines and the relation between private experience and the choices the women make. Dwelling on the 'right' and 'wrong' of these choices (for instance the use of violence, the role of revenge after rape and so forth) the audience is invited to participate more in the ethical judging of actions than in most mainstream movies. As director Berit Nesheim said about *Eva's Eye*: "I like that the focus is on 'the why' and not 'the who' in Fossum's crime stories." Drawing on recent theories of audience engagement (Smith, Caroll) Gjelsvik show how extensive focus on character development creates a strong involvement in these movies, thus opening for feminist readings of an otherwise male genre.

Ending the second part of the anthology is the essay "'Must-see medicine women': Breaking borders of genre and gender in *ER*" by Mervi Pantti. In the sixties women only had supporting roles in medical drama series because TV programmers believed a starring woman would create rating problems. The first show with the name of a female doctor in the title, *Julie Farr, M.D.*, was cancelled in 1978 after only four episodes. In 1986 CBS had another medical drama with a female doctor, *Kay O'Brien*, a show that lasted eight weeks. Recent prime-time medical dramas, however, have many female doctors; *E.R* has five and *Strong Medicine* has two female stars. Comparing one season of *E.R.* with one season of *Strong Medicine* Pantti examines how female doctors are represented and targeted to audiences in the two shows, one of which has a mixed gender cast and is targeted to a heterogeneous audience, the other which has only female protagonists and is targeted to a female audience. Through readings of the two shows Pantti discusses the role of female doctors in present television series and the development of the female doctor from a historical perspective.

Women-in-prison-films – wip-films – have been dismissed by film critics as perverse, misogynist pictures where women are maltreated to the enjoyment of a male audience. Such a conclusion is not wrong. However, in her essay "Hold it! Use it! Abuse it! *Ilsa, She-Wolf of the SS* and male castration" Rikke Schubart argues that the pleasures of the *Ilsa*-films are less obvious and more ambivalent and polysemic than recognized until now. The pleasures of wip-films are assumed to be male and sadistic. In this wip-series, however, men are tortured, caged, castrated (literally) and killed. To understand what pleasures a male audience derives from such a spectacle, Schubart links these scenes to male masochism and reads the male protagonists as not Final Girls, but instead as Final Boys, suffering punishment at the hands of Ilsa, performing as a beautiful dominatrix. Schubart is feminist rather than postfeminist in her stance on Ilsa as a strong woman: Ilsa is neither progressive nor regressive; she should be understood as an element in the initiation rites of adolescent men, thus being part of a phase in the development towards the 'normal' mature masculinity of a patriarchal society. In the debates over feminism in a patriarchal society we often forget that masculinity is not a monolithic social construction, but rather a heterogeneous and contradictory thing. Most men will agree that being male is not a simple matter.

In fact, Walter Alesci's essay *"Xena: Warrior Princess* out of the closet? A melodramatic reading of the show by Latin American and Spanish lesbian and gay fans"* analyzes exactly the complexity of gender construction. Alesci looks at the interpretations of *Xena: Warrior Princess* (1995-2001) by Latino lesbian and gay fans and problems related to these interpretations. The conflicts raised by its protagonists in the American series are used to explore the impact of a 'subtextual' interpretation found in the creative productions from Latino fan communities in "Xenaverse" on the Internet. The essay discusses both the discourse of the series and the external discourse surrounding the program, whose producers were quite aware of Xena's gay and lesbian fans. Alesci shows that the gender performance of Xena is clearly lesbian, but that her performative character of gender has to remain hidden within the patriarchal structures of a heterosexist, homophobic and discriminatory culture. Because of this Xena cannot come out of the closet.

The final essay of the anthology, "Sustaining the definitive bitch from hell: The politics of *Dolores Claiborne* within a feminist genealogy" by Sharon Lin Tay also discuss paternal politics; or rather, a revolt against paternal politics. Tay takes a postfeminist stance, drawing on female anger as a valid response to repression and male violence. In this way the women in *Dolores Claiborne* are not chastised for doing away with husbands, instead the narrative of the film confirms the need to kill off male patriarchs abusing women and – in the case of the protagonist, Selena – daughters. Drawing on Deleuze's theory of the flashback and Halberstam's suggestion that female cinematic violence challenges the hegemonic linking of might and right under the sign of masculinity, Tay analyzes time, neo-gothic space and the recuperation of lost memory. In true postfeminist spirit, Tay suggests we follow in the footsteps of the forgiven female killers of *Dolores Claiborne* and do away with Freud and Lacan, the male patriarchs haunting feminist film theory. A suggestion which most of our contributors have indeed taken to heart.

References

Bolter, Jay David & Grusin, R. (1999). *Remediation*. London: MIT.

Clover, C. (1992). *Men, women and chain saws: Gender in the modern horror film*. London: BFI.

Faludi, S. (1991). *Backlash: The undeclared war against American women*. New York: Crown.

Halberstam, J. (2001). Imagined violence/queer violence: Representations of rage and resistance. In M. McCaughey & N. King (Eds.), *Reel knockouts: Violent women in the movies*.

McCaughey, M. & King, N. (2001). *Reel knockouts: Violent women in the movies*. Austin: University of Texas Press.

Projansky, S. (2001). *Watching rape: Film and television in postfeminist culture*. New York: New York University.

Read, J. (2000). *The new avengers: Feminism, femininity and the rape-revenge cycle*. Manchester: Manchester University Press.

Tasker, Y. (1998). *Working girls: Gender and sexuality in popular cinema*. London: Routledge.

I. New Media
and Postfeminist Aesthetics

Baise-moi and Feminism's Filmic Intercourse with the Aesthetics of Pornography

Wencke Mühleisen

How and why is the aesthetics of pornography as a condensed western narrative of sexuality of interest from a feminist perspective? The French road movie *Baise-moi* from 2000 can serve as a filmic case study for this issue, since it appears to reiterate for 77 minutes that gender, sex, violence, and power are closely interconnected phenomena, which, incidentally, is a view that some 'hardcore' feminists have held for quite a long time. Therefore, the question is which aesthetic and gender political meanings this film generates – a movie in which the aesthetics of violence and pornography are presented by female directors and female porn actors. Is this a speculative, nihilistic film, as some critics claim, or are these effects used to problematize heteronormative sexual power relations and conventional representations of women and sex in film?

During the summer and autumn of 2002, Norwegian publishers released pornographic classics and fictional and factual literature on pornography, and the American performance artist Annie Sprinkle visited Norway. Pornography became a hot issue in the Norwegian public debate during this period. The debate has been less predictable than earlier debates, which were pure pro and con debates, and it demonstrates a new sensibility towards the aesthetics and thematics of pornography in relation to gender, sexuality, and power in literature and film.

This trend is very much inspired by the French neo-pornographic wave from the late 1990s. What characterizes this trend, and also is the source of the massive attention it has generated, is that we are witnessing a host of female writers and directors with explicit feminist intentions that include pornographic elements as part of their artistic forms of expression. In literature we have seen works in which sexuality and pornographic features play a major part, for example Claire Castillon's Claire *Le Grenier* (2000) and Catherine Cusset's *Jouir* (1999). The latter can be classified as a literary road movie which incorporates representations of fairly rough sexual experiences. In the novel *La Nuit l'apres-midi* (1995) by C. Lamarche, the female protagonist responds to a sex ad, and out of pure curiosity, she becomes involved in sadomasochistic sex. In this context we can also mention the respected art magazine editor Cathérine Millet, who published her sexual memoirs in *La Vie Sexuelle de Cathérine M.* (2001).

Several French female film directors have made movies with explicit pornographic depictions, such as for example Laetitia Masson with *A Vendre* (1998), Virginie Wagon with *Le Secret* (2000), Claire Denis with *Trouble Everyday* (2001), and Catherine Breillats with *Romance* (1999) and *A ma Soeur* (2001). This article focuses on the film *Baise-moi* (2000) by director Virginie Despentes and the porn movie director Coralie TrinhThi which has attracted much attention and debate.

In other words, the aesthetics of pornography in some form of feminist or post-feminist wrapping appears to have gained ground. We are therefore witnessing a shift from the early feminist frostiness in relation to pornography as an aesthetic form of expression. However, pornography as a *social* and societal problem has – in particular in the US – been a subject for both research and debate. Pornography as an aesthetic genre has received less attention in literary and media research. Susan Sontag's classical essay *The Pornographic Imagination* from 1976 in many ways served to legitimate the research interest in the representational system of pornography. This cultural analytic essay investigates the shared aesthetic features in pornography and devices in *highbrow* classic literary texts.

The pornographic *popular* or *mainstream culture*, however, has to a lesser degree been a research topic. Mainstream pornography is usually relegated to sex shops and video stores and thereby avoids being the subject of the general public cultural critical debate through criticism, reviews, and research. In the US both public debate and research are often divided between a pro censorship (e.g., Dworkin 1979, Griffin 1981, Kappeler 1986, Mac Kinnon 1993) or no censorship (e.g., Carter 1978, Ellis m.fl.1986, Kuhn 1982, 1985, Straayer 1996, Sobchack 1999) approach among feminists.

Within gender and media research the American film historian Linda Williams broke the silence related to mainstream pornographic films and videos with the book *Hard Core. Power, Pleasure and 'the Frenzy of the Visible'*, first published in 1989. Williams' main concern is to show that filmic hardcore pornography has a special system of representation with a unique history that depicts historical changes in gender relations. Central to this history is the increased problematization of the apparent natural and universal nature of sexuality. Sexuality understood as making visible what purports to be completely natural is the primary fiction of hardcore pornography. Could it be the case that pornography as a genre wants to have to do with sex, but that it on closer inspection always turns out to have more to do with gender? The problematics and raw material of gender difference certainly appear to be at stake in pornography (Williams 1999:268).

In what follows, I will give a summary of *Baise-moi* and call attention to certain filmic features, by pointing to differences and similarities between *Baise-moi* and the road movie *Thelma and Louise*. Further I will discuss briefly the film's incorporation of lowbrow pornographic aesthetics into an art film project and some of the reviews of the movie. I will have a special focus on the pornographic devices of *Baise-moi* and their gendered interpretations in a feminist perspective. Finally I will focus on the utopian aspect of the film, a feature it shares with the genre of pornography, but my question is whether queer articulations are also at stake.

Plot Summary

Baise-moi is an adaptation of Virginies Despente's award-winning and bestselling novel of the same title. The film was originally released for regular distribution in France. However, after three days of showing the movie ended up in the high court, and the film was banned from regular cinema distribution after complaints from conservative groups, led by a campaign from the French political right-wing party Front National.

The literal English translation of *Baise-moi* is *Fuck me,* and the fact that the film ended up with the title *Rape me* – a title which is misleading, to say the least – in English distribution is very telling, but it is pertinent to ask if this is a more politically correct female invitation than 'fuck me'. *Baise-moi* is the story about two women, the porn actress Manu (Rafaëlla Anderson) who lives in a multicultural suburban hell, and the prostitute Nadine (Karen Bach). Manu becomes the victim of a gang rape together with a friend who is a drug addict. Here we recognize the theme of the rape revenge movie and the motivation for the story.[1] Unlike her desperate friend, Manu refuses to accept the expected role of a rape victim, and when her brother accuses her of not having resisted the rape and calls her a whore, she shoots him and takes off with the money that she finds in the cash register of her brother's coffee shop. At the same time Nadine is in conflict with her moralizing live-in partner and strangles her. Nadine finds her best friend and drug supplier shot dead, whereby she runs to the underground and meets Manu, who is also on the run. They find each other and this is where the road movie in the shape of an excessive orgy of violence and sex through France begins. The victims are often simply at the wrong place at the wrong time, such as e.g. the first victim, a women who is shot dead cause the anti-heroines are broke and steal her credit card. However, most of the victims seem to be men with gender political or physically unfortunate strategies, such as the random passer-by who asks: "Wanna feel my balls slapping your ass?" or the guy who insists on having safe sex by using condoms. Nevertheless, the protagonists also find partners with which they share apparently pleasant sexual experiences. The excess of violence ends in a sex club where all the guests are executed while they are in the middle of various sexual activities. The movie ends with Manu getting shot by a shop-keeper during a robbery. Nadine, grieving the loss over her friend, tries to commit suicide but is stopped by the police.

Cinematic Strategies

The film keeps close to the conventions of realism, shot by the use of digital video, a hand-held camera and low lighting. The plot and the dramaturgy is disorderly and partly illogical, energetic and potentially provocative. The narrative only hints at the characters' psychology or motivation, and thereby represents a break with the personal and psychological *Bildungsreise* of the road movie. The two protagonists in *Baise-moi* do not cry, they do not whine, and neither do they psychologize or reflect very much; at one point in the road movie, they comment: "The more you fuck, the less you think and the better you sleep."

However, although *Baise-moi* is different from the traditional road movie genre it is also an explicit gesture to *Thelma and Louise* (1991). The parallels between the two movies are obvious: In both movies, rape is the introduction to and the motivation for the escape/journey. Both movies involve two female protagonists that stand in place of women's traditionally stationary passivity in the genre of the road movie (Bjurström and Rudberg 1997:19) and depart from a number of conventional ideas concerning women's freedom and possibilities for agency in relation to sexuality and violence. In both movies the women develop a close friendship and their escapades are only rewarded, if ever, in heaven. The female anti-heroines die, and although Nadine in *Baise-moi* survives, it is against her will.

The differences between the two movies are, however, equally obvious: The protagonists in *Baise-moi* belong to a different class and have a different ethnic background than the protagonists of *Thelma and Louise*. Manu and Nadine are a porn actress and a prostitute respectively and they live in an extreme urban lower-class environment, and are socially much more marginalized than the characters in *Thelma and Louise*. *Thelma and Louise* has a star-studded cast, while the actresses in *Baise-moi* are from the porn industry and unknown to both the general cinema audience and the art film audience. *Thelma and Louise* constructs a psychological realism related to the motivations and emotional reactions and relations of the protagonists, and this ensures the audience's empathy and identification with the protagonists. The partial lack of logic in the plot of *Baise-moi* (in contrast to the classical dramaturgy of *Thelma and Louise*) and the lack of psychological staging of the protagonists in *Baise-moi*, in addition to their seemingly unbridled exercise of sex and violence, do not guarantee our sympathy with the protagonists. The acts of violence in *Thelma and Louise* are first of all relatively 'harmless', and in the end they are portrayed to be righteous and justified, while the acts of violence in *Baise-moi* are beyond any sense of justice, realistic motivation or explanation. The violence is one single cinematic excess which is markedly deprived of any narrative direction or psychological meaning. Therefore, the ending of *Baise-moi* is all the more tragic. Thelma and Louise choose death and seal their pact with a kiss before they hang suspended over the abyss; the image freezes,

Baise-moi (Coralie, Virgine Despentes, 2000) Le Studio Canal +
and Pan Européenne Production.

and who knows, maybe they are on their way to heaven. In *Baise-moi* the girls are not even able to stage their own suicide. Besides, *Thelma and Louise* carries every hallmark of the polished Hollywood movie regarding the quality of the production and the quality of American cinematography, while *Baise-moi* appears as a problematic confusion of genres with low-brow connotations and the ambition of the art movie. I will return to this issue below.

Baise-moi is neither a horror movie nor a conventional porn movie, and this is perhaps a problem for the film. The pornography in the movie is hardly satisfying for a traditional porn audience, and neither does it meet the requirements of violent effects in horror movies. The violent scenes have a theatrical and amateurish effect, and are thus reminiscent of amateur or homemade pornography. Among the things that are unusual in *Baise-moi* is the mixture of documentary porn scenes and fictional, unrealistic violence: the mixture of *authentic* pornographic phantasms and *simulated* violence (Williams 2001:16).

The movie possesses self-conscious meta-attitude towards the cinematic tradition. Its nihilistic ethics are matched with many intertextual references to its predecessors. This includes features of so-called exploitation cinema; American off-Hollywood productions about tabooed topics from the 1930s and 40s, references to *Bonnie and Clyde* (1967), and the afore-mentioned gestures to *Thelma and Louise*. In addition there are more complex references to exploitation cinema by way of references to the reincarnations of the form from the 1990s. When the girls in *Baise-moi* hold up a gun store, Nadine is dressed in a black tight-fitting suit and a wig in the style of Uma Thurman's in Quentin Tarantino's *Pulp Fiction* (1994). After having shot two men in a sex club, Manu forces a man to stand on all fours and grunt like a pig before she fires a gun through his rectum. This scene has a reference to the infamous scene in John Boorman's *Deliverance* (1972) and its parody in Tarantino's film. The intertexual 'greetings' of *Baise-moi* all point to sexualized violent scenes as direct expressions of forms of power that show the norms for constructions of gender through the discourse of heteronormativity. The film operates within the framework of a film context that comments by its references to a series of historical as well as current discourses on gender, sexuality, feminism and film. *Baise-moi* comments on its own trash aesthetics as the protagonists complains about their own lack of Tarantinoesque humour after having shot the owner of a gun store to get hold of handguns:

Manu: Fuck, we're useless. Where are the witty lines?
Nadine: We've got the moves. That's something. We're not that bad I think.
Manu: I mean people are dying. The dialogue has to bee up to it; good an crucial like!
Nadine: We can't write it in advance.
Manu: You're right. That's totally unethical. Let's grab some drink.

Art Film or Trash Movie?

What happens when one uses lowbrow film aesthetics with explicit pornographic depictions? The lowbrow porn aesthetics of the movie is one of the main reasons why the film was censored or not released for regular distribution. According to critics, the film does *not* confirm to the aesthetics of the French art film because of the punkish and brutal form of expression and the inclusion of elements from hardcore porn aesthetics (Vik 2002). In other words, the most startling aspect of this movie is the use of the conventional hetero-pornographic lowbrow aesthetics in a movie that has art film ambitions, not to mention the use of two female protagonists as maniacs acting out sexual and violent inclinations. Has the lowbrow, popular culture placed itself in a highbrow aesthetic and has the feminine placed itself in the culturally defined masculine position in this film?

It is pertinent to ask whether explicit and direct cinematic depictions of sexuality today give rise to similar discussions as violence and gore elements did in the 1970s. There seems to be a parallel to the discussions about violent movies and aesthetics in the exploitation cinema of the 1970s such as *Texas Chainsaw, Massacre, Last House on the Left* and *I Spit on your Grave.*[2] The new 'sex on film' trend with down-to-earth, direct, and porn-connoted depictions of sexuality stands in contrast to the eroticising, metaphoric imagery of the Hollywood movie. In the new films, sexuality is no longer a liberating or harmonizing solution to anything. It seems like a brutal departure from the dreams of liberation and a better society of the 1960s generation, in which sexuality represented some kind of utopian focus point. From sexuality as inherently unnameable, which both poetically and perversely was sublimated and fetishized on the screen, it appears that sexuality in the neo-pornographic trend is reduced to a brutish, physical act. The heterosexual intercourse is displayed in all its concrete bodily awkwardness, difficulty and/or pleasure. The sexual representations that some female directors are currently working with within the genre of the art film were formerly relegated to commercial filmic pornography and not subject to public criticism and discussion.

The inclusion of elements from lowbrow genres such as hardcore porn movies, exploitation cinema, horror movie effects and the rape revenge movie in the film in focus here, together with numerous references to film history, have become a problem for the reception of the film. This stands in contrast to for example Catherine Breillat's movies. Her film *Romance* conforms to the discourse of the art film aesthetically and – importantly – it firmly lodges female sexuality in conventional bourgeois and psychoanalytically inspired ideas of masochism, self-renunciation and self-hatred. While the radical feminist and Marxist inspired opposition between men as oppressors and women as eternal victims reaches its apparent cinematic and heteronormative climax in *Romance, Baise-moi* is far more unsettling and problematic in its representation of female subject positions.

Postfeminist Aesthetics

In relation to the main question of this article, that is, which possible interpretations are created in the feminist or postfeminist incorporation of the aesthetics of pornography, I wish to emphasize the *queer* or *queer utopian* aspect, where humanity, love and the suggested same-sex relationship are ensured by the two female protagonists – I will return to this issue below.[3] Aggression, violence, sexuality, and marginalization in a postmodern urban environment constitute a persistent and pressing theme in *Baise-moi*. This aesthetic, which self-reflexively enters into dialogue with the gender stereotypes and clichés of popular culture, has been labelled a postfeminist or neofeminist aesthetic (Krewani 1995, Gade 2000, Mühleisen 2002).

Postfeminist aesthetics is related to both *postmodern feminism* and *postfeminism* as phenomena. Postmodern feminism both designates an era and includes or entails a form of *contemporariness* – of both poststructuralist feminist positions *and* a criticism of poststructuralism. At the same time, we may claim that it includes the modern feminist position *as well as* a criticism of or reflection over the modern feminist position. This creates several tensions. If we have as open a concept of postmodern feminism as I suggest here, and if we insist on the concurrency of contrary positions and the tensions that this creates, we will be able to see some interesting parallels to the current media world. In the media we see representations of gender and sexuality that purportedly are based on the modern feminist focus on the shared interests of women and emphasis on the difference between men and women. Concurrently, there are representations that seem to knock the bottom out of any unified understanding of what gender or sexuality may mean. These representations often coexist in a concurrency within the same expression (Mühleisen 2003).

There is another term lingering in the background here, and this term is postfeminism, a concept that refers to popular cultural expressions, and which often is associated with phenomena like the Spice Girls, Madonna, and popular TV series with female protagonists such as *Ally McBeal*. The term postfeminism is in itself a media-created phenomenon from the early 1980s, and initially its connotation was to a kind of cheerful liberation from an apparently hopelessly outdated feminist movement. However, in parts of feminist research, postfeminism is used in a negative manner. For example, in the book *Material Girls* (1995) the American sociologist Suzanna Danuta Walters equals postfeminism with *antifeminism* and American *backlash* tendencies which deprive feminism of a mutual and definable womanhood and solidarity. In other words, there is a prevailing scepticism toward what is conceived of as the sexualized superficial game of postfeminism, in close connection with popular culture, subculture and mainstream media. Other researchers focus on postfeminism's potential for deconstructing the binary oppositions that have been characteristic of modern feminism – for example the tension between the feminine and the feminist, or between liberation and oppression (McRobbie 1997, Krewani 1995, Brunsdon 2000, Hollows 2000, Lotz 2001).

The German literary critic Angela Krewani mentions authors such as British Angela Carter and American Kathy Acker as examples of authors who base their writings on a postfeminist aesthetics. These authors perform a cultural criticism by parodically quoting and playing with the gendered cultural clichés and thereby entering into the tradition of postmodern texts (Krewani 1995:165).[4] These authors have repeatedly come into conflict with the women's movement, as some groups within this movement have tended to cling to viewing women as victims. Among Ackers' stated ambitions was to produce pornographic textual elements. This is interesting seen in the light of the above-mentioned feminist frostiness toward the pornographic genre and a representation of sexuality that departs from victim-based representations, or from empathic and psychological depictions of sexual relations. Within feminism, intertextuality has not been discussed to any large extent in relation to the field of sexuality. Pornographic language can however be given a new meaning in the same manner as postmodern aesthetics opens for recitation and recasting of traditional genres and meanings.

Part of the postfeminist aesthetics involves that fictitious characters have almost stopped searching for alternatives to the existing society. Characters are searching for individual niches in a society often depicted as violent. Many of the American literary texts are also located in urban environments.[5] The image of women in so-called postfeminist literature is intuitively more attractive than that in earlier feminist works, as these are nurtured by mass culture clichés from movies, television, and commercials. What fascinates us in this context is the departure from the conventional position of the victim and the pleasurable play with power positions that formerly connoted masculinity. In this respect postfeminist aesthetics borrows certain features from narcissistic possibilities for identification traditionally associated with power positions occupied by men. Postfeminist, postmodern, and queer aesthetics are related to each other both theoretically and aesthetically. These positions all involve a departure from the modernist emphasis on the negative aesthetics of avant-gardism, as well as from socio-psychological realism, and serve as a contrast to proposals for liberation that are set in utopian other places (Mühleisen 2002:186-188).

It is exactly this combination of masculine associated genre features with lowbrow connotations and porn movies and non-conventional female subject positions in addition to *Baise-moi*'s persistent focus on the relation between gender, sexuality, marginalization, and power that makes the film relevant in a postfeminist perspective.

How Is the Pornographic Aesthetics Interesting in a Feminist Perspective?

The philosopher Michel Foucault describes how the focus on and the scientific approach to sexuality as part of modern discourse on the subject led to an identification strategy and classification of many different specialized sexual practices. Even though this is part of a disciplining of bodies and subjects and a tool for and an effect of power, the outcome of this process is a confusing number of passions and perversions. The very *diversity* of these practices will according to Foucault involuntarily work against the former conception of an unambiguous norm against which everything is measured (Foucault 1978:48 in Williams 1999:114). I will therefore claim that the multifaceted expressions of pornography are interesting in a critical feminist perspective, as this perspective has a specific interest in deconstructing and criticizing norms connected to gender and sexuality.

The main issue here is to determine that a constant element in the history of sexuality has been the lack of conceptions and expressions of women's sexuality outside the domain of the dominating masculine pleasure economy. We may therefore ask whether the disciplining practices that Foucault describes so well have had larger ramifications for women's bodies than for men's bodies (Williams 1999:4)? And in this context, the modern pornography can be the key to such an approach, at least if we follow the reasoning of porn film historian Linda Williams. Williams provides several definitions of the pornographic movie. What she calls a minimal and neutral definition is as follows: "(…) the visual (and sometimes aural) representation of living, moving bodies engaged in explicit, usually unfaked, sexual acts with a primary intent of arousing viewers" (Williams 1999:30). And film researcher Anette Kuhn (1985:24) has suggested another constant element, namely that pornography in general produces meaning focused on gender differences.

However, feminist research and criticism have generally had problems with genres made by and for men – and in particular in relation to pornography. Until fairly recently it has almost been an anti-pornographic feminist reflex to employ the distinction between so-called hardcore and softcore porn to describe male sexuality as pornographic and female sexuality as erotic (Mühleisen 1999). This image has however changed as the romantic fiction of the mass market has become more and more sexually explicit and as hard-core porn films and movies no longer necessarily have men as their sole target group. Currently porn movies are targeted toward for example couples, women, lesbians, and others. Lars von Trier's production company in Denmark has experimented with woman-targeted expressions in the porn genre, and female porn producers like Candida Royalle in the US and the recent French art film movement make it increasingly difficult to maintain such an opposition. *Baise-moi* makes extremely relevant the question whether the distinction between a soft, tender, and not very explicit female eroticism and a hard, cruel, brutal, and explicit phallic pornography is about to break down (Williams 1999:6).

This question emphasizes the Foucault-inspired point of view that makes it problematic to construct ideas about utopian other places where power is irrelevant and where sexuality is part of idylls where difference does not exist and where agents are exempt from the contamination of power.

Is *Baise-moi* a Pornographic Film?

Baise-moi surely *seems* like a porn movie: it contains scenes which could have been taken directly from mainstream hetero porn movies, and it includes realistic sex involving two actors from the porn industry. The well-known American anti-porn and censorship advocates Catherine MacKinnon (1993) and Andrea Dworkin (1979) have defined pornography in relation to a selection of criteria which boils down to the assumption that women are consistently presented as sexual *objects*, as non-humans, by being exploited, raped, tied up, cut, and abused. According to these criteria, it is only the introductory, motivating rape scene in *Baise-moi* that can be defined as pornographic. However, in contrast to earlier porn movies, and in accordance with *Baise-moi*, the rape scenes in porn movies from the 1980s rarely show women who actually *enjoy* the abuse. Instead the focus is on the rape as violence against bodies and wills (Williams 1999:166).

Against this background, the motivating rape scene in *Baise-moi* is typical for a narrative porn movie from the 1980s onwards. Manu and her addict friend are the victims of an extremely brutal gang rape, as they are caught off guard in a park, about to share a couple of beers. They are taken to an abandoned garage. During the first part of the rape sequence we are shown how Manu's friend is abused and raped as she fights for her life. Thus the rape scene starts with the conventional binary relation – the woman as victim versus the man as molester. However, this scenario is reversed in the rape scenes of *Baise-moi* as Manu refuses to give the responses that usually serve to contrast and increase the molester's gratification: signs of pain, despair, and total humiliation. Halfway through the scene the rapists swap victims. When the camera focuses on Manu, who is now exposed to the same rapist as her friend was, there is an interesting change in the responses of the victim. She suppresses her anxiety and pain sensations and does not express any feelings whatsoever. When the assailant becomes frustrated over her lack of response while he is raping her from behind, he commands her: "Shit, it's like fucking a zombie! Move your ass a bit." Manu turns toward him and answers: "What's that between your legs, asshole?" This contemptuous response makes the rapist unable to continue the sexual assault as he loses his 'desire' and erection. And thereby the entire logic of the assault collapses, as the goal of the assault is the victim's self-hatred, desperation, and inability to act.

Although the rape scene functions as the motivation and catalyst for the subsequent act of revenge, Manu reassures, in contrast to her crushed friend, that rape is not the worst thing that can happen to a woman. The rape is both the narrative device which motivates the subsequent violent incidents and the underlying trauma which makes up the basis for rape revenge movies (Williams 2001:16).

In mainstream cinema, the rape scene often has the function of setting up a psychological profile of a character, for example an evil male or traumatized female character. In *Baise-moi* the rape scene is completely devoid of symbolism. Into the apparently realistic scene, in which punching, kicking, and abuse are central components, hardcore pornographic close-ups are incorporated which here appear to reverse the conventional pleasure effect of pornographic films and which insist on abjection, contempt, and pain: hardcore porn as repulsion effect. Something is presented here that cannot be named. This is a form of effect of realism which the American art historian Hal Foster calls 'the return of the real'. These are precisely images of the abject – catastrophic images in which the boundaries of the body are penetrated and maimed (Foster 1996:147). A trauma thus becomes transgressions whereby boundaries are broken and a characteristic response to such traumas is the urgent need to restore or establish these boundaries, as when the protagonists of *Baise-moi* transpose the violence and turn it against the others; the paradoxical restoration of violence.

Compared with the definitions given by the anti-pornographers, however, we may claim that the movie is "not" pornographic, as it is problematic to define the main characters as abused sexual objects – if we ignore the rape scene that motivates the women's reaction. Rather it is women who objectivize men and use them solely for their own pleasure, satisfaction, and abuse. It is not nice, it is not ethical or aesthetical, but it breaks the most important rule: the woman as victim. What has received most attention is the excessive female sexual and violent behaviour. The notion of excess may be related to both the ethical and aesthetical level: within the frame of what is considered culturally legitimate resides what is allowed socially and culturally, what is defined as order, as norm, as 'straight', as the ethically good and as the aesthetically beautiful. What lies beyond this space is not proper, not normal 'queer', distasteful, and despicable (Gentikow 1998:34). Excess in cinematic terms is related to scenes devoid of narrative contexts, where the main function lies in the appeal to the senses. Excess as a device traditionally belongs to the music halls and later to the genre of pornography. This effect has a determining function for the reception strategies related to pornography, involving distraction and diversion, far from the reception mode of bourgeois art (Hansen 1991:29). Departure from the set of reception expectations related to this art form may lead to scepticism and rejection, as was seen in the critics' response to *Baise-moi*.

Although the film departs from the female role of the victim, there is little doubt that *Baise-moi* deploys of the aesthetics of pornography and therefore does share *some* features with conventional porn movies. The sex scenes in *Baise-moi* are strikingly similar to the sex scenes of the conventional hetero porn movie. The poses, positions, and close-ups are far from being experimental, but follow the catalogue of expected sex scenes from the archives of the porn movie. Nevertheless, Manu and Nadine are extremely self-confident and competent in this conventional representation. However, the conventions and over-sexualization typical of the porn scenes also point to gender and sexuality as performativity (Butler 1990) and theatrical cultural repertoire, rather than the persistent coupling of sexuality, gender and *the natural*. The imitation and citation of the sexual scenes of mainstream hetero porn movies stand in contrast to the violent scenes. These are, as mentioned above, characterized by amateurism and make an unrealistic impression (an unrealistic form). However, in the apex of excess violence in the movie – the butchery of the guests of a sex club – the women strike the same self-confident, professional, and stylized conventional cinematic poses in their handling of their guns as their male filmic counterparts. Just like the staging of gender and sexuality is a *habit* staged via the materiality of the body and the signifying system of the cultural script, the stereotypically masculine exertion of violence is a habit that can be cited and internalized independent of gender.

The Deceitful Female Orgasm

There is an interesting concurrence between the invention of the movie as a representational system and psychoanalysis as a knowledge system. These are mutually confirming discourses of sexuality that produce specific forms of knowledge and pleasure (Williams 1999:46). And as the porn genre must keep close to the documented evidences of the assumed sexual truth, it has resisted complex narrative development, insisted on an episodic structure, resisted complex plots, character development, etc. These are features that we recognize in *Baise-moi*. Unlike the fetishization of the female body in classical movies, fetishization becomes a hindrance for the goal of porn movies to visualize women's desires. Women's possibilities for faking orgasms, which is rather difficult for men (at least if we follow certain standards for proof) seem, according to Williams, to make up the foundation for the genre's attempt to establish what it can never prove: the non-controlled orgasmic confession, or the hard-core 'frenzy of the visible' as she calls it.

The famous film *Deep Throat* (1972) is regarded as the first narrative porn movie with the length of a fiction film. This is the first porn movie that was accepted for the cinema in the US. In contrast to earlier porn movies, modern porn movies for cinema and video distribution often involve a drama consisting of an initiating phase, an excitement phase, a climax, and (usually) satisfaction for both male actors as well as the usually male audience. This is rather important, as the point is not only to show that penetration has taken place, but also satisfaction – orgasm. This narrative conclusion is achieved in the modern porn movie through the convention of external ejaculation, that is, outside the female body, what is referred to in production jargon as 'the money shot'. Sexual positions without this convention are referred to as 'meat shots' (Williams 1999:72). The significance of the moneyshot is of course in the documentation of the invisible, the proof of the orgasm, be it only through a masculine narcissistic self-reflection (Williams 1999:94). And this of course brings us to the problem of gender difference, as the female orgasm – again according to conventional standards – cannot be documented.

However, in the 1980s the porn movie showed an increased interest in heterosexual female, lesbian, and homosexual sexuality. Problematic aspects of female sexuality that appeared already in the 1970s, did not find their pornographic filmic response and expression until well into the 1980s. This is very much connected to the discourses introduced by feminism and the homosexual political movement of this time, which made current the con-flicts within the heterosexual paradigm. During the 1980s the porn movie came to represent a large variety of expressions, and female desire is no longer regarded as exclusively comic, grotesque, or threatening (Williams 1999:183), although critical reception of *Baise-moi* seems to have triggered these conventional responses related to the reception of female sexuality (e.g. Ebert 2001, Thomas 2002, Freeman 2002).

The Queer Utopian Element of *Baise-moi*

Interestingly, the pornographic scenes of *Baise-moi* depart from the narra-tive conclusion of the conventional porn movie. The money shot as docu-mentation of satisfaction is completely absent in this film. The sex scenes are exclusively meat shots, a showcase of different sexual positions typical of the heterosexual porn film. I think this is related to the focus on the fe-male protagonists' gratification and escapism in this movie. Thus the tradi-tional porn movie's focus on women's *loss of control* as a prerequisite of female sexuality does not dominate, as *Baise-moi* depicts women's *control* over the sexual universe. Desire, rather than the absence or loss of mascu-line control, is documented – in stark contrast to the introductory, motivat-ing rape scene. Besides, *Baise-moi* shows that the solutions to the 'problems' *cannot* be found in the bedroom, as is usually suggested in porn movies. In my opinion, the solution to the problems in this film takes place at two *uto-pian* levels: in the excess of violence and the relationship between the main characters. Regarding the excess of violence, I will limit myself to pointing to the fact that the social and gender-political problems connected to the marginalization of lower classes and women's exposure to violence and sexual abuse, find their response in the 'return of the repressed' in the violent scenes: violence's literal response to the trauma. It is also possible to see parallels between the female protagonists' violent excesses in *Baise-moi* and the male protagonists in films such as *Psycho* (1999) or *Fight Club* (1999). In these films violence in a confusing manner opens certain rooms for opportunities, either for the existential effects of violence or masochism, or for pointing to emotionally crippled individuals' literal needs of depth and pain through the physical touch and psychological effect of violence.

Williams emphasises that the genre of pornography generally operates with a utopian mode of problem solving. Hard-core pornography is in principle escapist and distracts the audience from the social and political sources of conflict between the genders and instead the problems are solved within the confines of the bedroom metaphor (Williams 1999:154-155). The British film theorist Richard Dyer also points to the fact that power is not politically addressed, and that the pornographic solution is sought through a utopian energy: excitement, intensity, and transparency related to the sexual act. He further claims that the problems that mass entertainment generally tends to avoid usually are fundamental conflicts related to class, gender, sexuality, and race (Dyer 1981:177). *Baise-moi*, on the other hand, addresses these issues explicitly– even though the solution is far from realistic.

While the conventional porn film has an escapist, utopian sensibility and presents the usually male spectator with solutions framed within the dominating heteronormative logic, it is difficult to identify such solutions in *Baise-moi*. In spite of this, *Baise-moi* preserves the escapist and utopian element of the conventional porn film in the presumably lustful, voluntary sex scenes where men are treated well. In this context sex functions as a bonus or gift that is given without any special occasion, as when the anti-heroines spontaneously invite random men to sex or when Manu in a hotel room gives her partner as a gift of love to Nadine: Manu and Nadine have invited two young men to a hotel room. They have sex in various sexual positions with the usual pornographic close-ups of genitalia, mouths, breasts, etc. During a break, Nadine's lover suggests that it would have been fun if the two girls licked each other. Manu smiles scornfully and throws him out. In other words, Manu refuses to gratify the male lover's desire to see the two women practice so-called lesbian sex adapted to and used as foreplay for the male heterosexual gaze. She throws him out. This prohibition against depicting lesbian sex is repeated later on in the film. When Manu later initiates sexual activities with her lover, her eyes meet with Nadine's; she whispers something to her lover, whereby he obediently and friendly offers his services to Nadine.

As mentioned above, it is my view that the film suggests a queer – or a queer utopian element related to the relationship between the two female protagonists. In my opinion, this relation has – in sexual terms – a specific utopian function, as it is barely suggested and the sexual relation is not explicitly staged or realized beyond this suggestion. This is an interesting point as the utopia loses its 'outsider' position – as what does not yet exist within the language of normativity if made concrete and explicit. If the queer-utopian relational element between the main characters had been sexually realized in the film, this could potentially have created a number of problems. My point here is that lesbian porn films – in spite of their differentness through focus on same-sex practice – also are placed within the frames of the heteronormative logic. Especially considering the fact that femininity and masculinity, despite obvious displacements, are cited with regard to the cultural construction of active masculine desire in contrast to passive feminine devotion. Within lesbian sexual iconography, same-sex queer imitation is connected to the staging of so-called 'butches' and 'femmes'. *Baise-moi* solves this by a self-imposed image prohibition: the suggestive 'lesbian' scene apparently works as a prelude and teaser to the expected hard-core heterosexual scenes. The 'lesbian' scene of the film also takes place in a hotel room. Nadine and Manu dance to disco music. Energetically and playfully they enter into poses that invite a 'lesbian' gaze. Dressed in sexy underwear they touch each other's bodies during the dance, Nadine embraces Manu from behind, they suggest sexual positions, cast glances at each other, and look at each other in the mirror. But the scene only mimics a foreplay, which is abruptly interrupted, almost censored as it cheats the voyeuristic gaze. Thus the scene does not satisfy our scopophilic desire.

Baise-moi can be viewed as a form of *queering* of the heteronormative porn movie and cinematic depictions of sex. The American literary critic Eve Kosofsky Sedgwick (1991), a notable author in the development of queer theory, urges us to ask whether texts involve a destabilization of heteronormative desire, that is, a form of *perverse aesthetic*. This is what *Baise moi* appears to do. First, the perverse aesthetic is apparent in the blending of genres and of incorporating lowbrow porn aesthetics into an art film project. Secondly, it is apparent in the break with the conventional female subject positions and response patterns related to marginalization, violence, and heterosexuality. Finally, the perverse aesthetic is apparent in the suggested queer, utopian relation between the female protagonists. However, *Baise-moi* does *not* represent a 'counter' movie which is an exemplary or didactic alternative to mainstream pornography. The problem with the exemplary, the alternative, that which apparently *is* queer, is that it is in danger of gaining a normative function. What is differently related to same-sex love in *Baise-moi* is defined through the *absence* and the sexual image prohibition in a film that in all other respects shows 'everything'. The relation remains in the imaginary realm and thereby achieves a utopian function serving as a phantasmatic backdrop for the revenge, which hardly constitutes liberation, but must be regarded as a perverted mimicry of the logic of power and violence.

Therefore, this film, which seems to mimic the violent film scenarios of heteronormativity, can be understood as a radical intervention into the cinematic aesthetics of pornography and heterosexuality. Sexuality and gender related to power, violence, and marginalization make up a pressing political thematic in the movie. It is part of the feminist project to unveil and deconstruct the norms that control the gendered social consequences and cultural significance of sexuality. In *Baise-moi* the suggested queer relation between the female protagonists functions as a not explicitly named backdrop and thereby also as a utopian possibility which tries to escape the excessive violent consequences of heteronormativity depicted in this film. The utopian dimension of the road movie has ultimately been given a conservative interpretation, as it offers a freedom that is impossible to realize (cf. Bjurstrøm and Rudberg1997:24). The brutal reality that the anti-heroines are escaping from also catches up with *Baise-moi*. However, instead of reading the queer utopian aspect into such a conservative message, I choose to view the unrealized potential as a suggested possibility condition. Love and humanity are reserved for this relation, which suggests an energy that might be able to break the traumatic logic of reaction and counter-reaction inherent in the film's realized scenarios of violence.

Notes

1. The typical plot of a rape revenge film often revolves around a young, attractive heterosexual woman who is established as independent and single. She is raped, and this is often brutally and explicitly depicted. This serves as motivation for the rest of the plot. The female main character seeks revenge in gruesome and inventive ways. The rape revenge film can be characterized as a subgenre of the horror movie.
2. Thanks to Rikke Christina Schubart for drawing my attention to this parallel.
3. 'Queer' has become a new term for what is not heteronormative, what in some way or another relates 'queerly' to the norm. This critical perspective is of particular significance for feminist research on gender, since the significance of *sexuality* is here fundamentally thematized. (e.g. Kosofsky Sedgwick 1991 and Petersen 1998).
4. Krewani also mentions Helen Zahavis' (1991) novel *Dirty Weekend* as an example of postfeminist writing.
5. For example Janowitz, Tama (1986) *Slaves of New York*.

References

Alderfer, H. N.D. Hunter & P. Califia (Eds.) (1986). *Caught looking: Feminism, pornography, and censorship*. New York: Caught Looking Inc.

Bjurström, E. & M. Rudberg (1997). Hungry heart – moderne mannlighet og kvinnelighet på vei. In M. Rudberg (Ed.) *Kjærlighetsartikler, kjønn og kjærlighet i forandring*. Oslo: Tano Aschehoug.

Brunsdon, C. (2000). *The feminist, the housewife, and the soap opera*. Oxford University Press.

Carter, A. (1978). *The Sadeian woman and the ideology of pornography*. New York: Pantheon Books.

Dworkin, A. (1979). *Pornography: Men powering women*. New York: Putman.

Ebert, R. (July 7, 2001). *Chicago Sun-Times*.

Foster, H. (1996). *The return of the real: The avantgarde at the end of the century*. Cambridge: MIT Press.

Foucault, M. (1978). *The history of sexuality. Vol. 1: An introduction*. New York: Pantheon Books.

Freeman, M. (2002). *Critical eye*. Retrieved from Internet Movie Database, http://www.imdb.com/.

Gade, R. (2000). "I want to feel real": Tracy Emin og det biografiskes realitet. Arbejdspapirer nr. 4. Nordisk institut, Aarhus Universitet.

Gentikow, B. (1998). Eksesser – et kulturkritisk blikk på sex- og voldstekster. *Norsk medietidsskrift*, 2, 98.

Griffin, S. (1981). *Pornography and silence: Culture's revenge against nature*. New York: Harper & Row.

Hansen, M. (1991). *Babel and Babylon. Spectatorship in American silent film*. Cambridge: Harvard University Press.

Hollows, J. (2000). *Feminism, feminity and popular culture*. Manchester: Manchester University Press.

Kappeler, S. (1986). *The pornography of representation*. Minneapolis: University of Minnesota Press.

Krewani, A. (1995). 'Harte Mädchen weinen nicht': Narrative Strategien des Post-Feminist-Writing. *Zeitschrift für Literaturwissenschaft und Linguistik*, Heft 98, 162-170.

Kuhn, A. (1982). *Women's pictures: Feminism and cinema*. London: Routledge & Kegan Paul.

Kuhn, A. (1985). *The power of the image: Essays on representation and sexuality*. London: Routledge & Kegan Paul.

Lotz, A. D. (2001). Postfeminist television criticism: Rehabilitating critical terms and identifying postfeminist attributes. *Feminist Media Studies*, 1 (1), 105-21.

McKinnon, C. (1993). *Only words*. Cambridge: Harvard University Press.

McRobbie, A. (1997). Pecs and penises: The meaning of girlie culture. *Soundings* 5: 157-66.

Mühleisen, W. (1999). Umulig begjær. Da seksualitet ble politikk. In C. Sandnes, B. Nossum & C. Smith Erksen (Eds.), *Matriark: Nesten sanne historier om å være kvinne*. Oslo: Gyldendal.

Mühleisen, W. (2002). *Kjønn i uorden. Iscenesettelse av kjønn og seksualitet i eksperimentell talkshowunderholdning på NRK fjernsynet*. Institutt for medier og kommunikasjon, University of Oslo.

Mühleisen, W. (2003). Spenninger i postmoderne feminisme: Kjønnet som estetisk iscenesettelse i dagens medieverden, *Kvinneforskning* Vol. 1, 2003.

Petersen, A. (1998). *Unmasking the masculine: 'Men' and 'identity' in a sceptical age*. London: Sage.

Sedgwick, K. E. (1991). *Epistemolology of the closet*. New York: Harvester Weatsheaf.

Sobchac, V. (2000). *Carnal thoughts: Bodies, texts, scenes and screenes*. Berkely: University of California Press.

Sontag, S. (1991). *Pornografien som forestillingsverden*. Oslo: Cappelen forlag.

Straayer, C. (1996). *Deviant eyes, deviant bodies: Sexual re-orientation in film and video*. New York: Columbia University Press.

Thomas, K. (2001, June 6). *Los Angeles Times*.

Thompson, K. (1986). The concept of cinematic eksess. In P. Rosen (Ed.), *Narrative, apparatus, ideology. A film theory reader*. New York: Columbia University Press.

Vik, S. (2002). Hvorfor *Baise-moi* gjør oss flaue. *Norsk Medietidsskrift*, Vol. 1, 2002.

Walters, S. D. (1995). *Material girls: Making sense of feminist cultural theory*. Berkely: University of California Press.

Williams, L. (1999). *Hard core: Power, pleasure, and the "frenzy of the visible"*. Berkely: University of California Press.

Williams, R. (2001). Sick sisters, *Sight & Sound*, July, 2001.

Over and Over Again

The Representation of Women in Contemporary Cinema

Ingrid Lindell

The method of investigating the politics of representation seems on the one hand necessary and on the other hand problematic. Part of my argument here is to set an agenda concerning the need for a method to study gender representation, as well as investigating the repetitious structures in cinema. From a cultural point of view it deals with how the analysed macrostructures could be seen as part of a historically long-lived reiteration of a power structure. Over and over again, we as film viewers are repeatedly presented with a specific kind of stereotypes, by a specific male dominance in the subject positions, and this is a matter of the cultural power of reiteration.

Focus will be put on the importance of considering the *social* side of gender representation as a basis for analyses of film as a signifying practice, and how cinema is a central symbolic order in a predominantly *visual* culture.[1] The film repertoire and its general representation is part of a cinematic flow of films. This flow constitutes a basic structure of certain repeated presentations. In short, whenever we consider exceptions it is as always central to remember the rule and our experiences as human beings matter when we make meaning of films. There is little contention about the fact that cinema is first and foremost a male space of negotiation and presence. But to what extent is this true today and is there any change to be seen? Does this matter when it comes to "reading" and appreciating films?[2] In what way could the interpretation of the 'strong' woman of a single film become affected by this gender representation in the film repertoire? Could it change its meaning?

This article draws on modern cultural theory to bring in the social means studying the cultural field of cinema as signifying practice on a macro structural level, and in this case from a gender perspective, at a specific moment in time (Hall 1997). This means that the life experiences of spectators become valid and that it is problematic to separate 'art' and 'life'. There are such things as conventions within film studies and not to mention the critical community, which claims certain interpretative procedures to be the only valid. By setting an agenda for what is to be negotiated in films and who sets the agenda for how we talk about cinema, the various agents in the field constitute a cultural power structure. This will be illustrated here through the description of a critical debate.

As many researchers lately have argued there is a need to incorporate the social into interpretative practise and film studies (Branston 2000:155-156, Perkins 2000:76-95). Gill Branston talks about how the study of the politics of representation has been considered more or less irrelevant since the 1970s and there has been a focus on pleasure and the audience's power over the text. This has created a problem for contemporary media studies in general with "a huge hesitation and anxiety about making *any* social interpretations of texts, settling instead for the pleasures of play, bricolage and the assertions that audiences are free to interpret and appropriate anyway." Tessa Perkins uses an even stronger artillery and says that the "almost total annihilation of a socially situated 'ideological' critique from contemporary academic discourse is counterproductive" (Perkins 2000:76). There is no doubt that this discussion will continue and I hope this article will be a contribution to it.

To emphasise the centrality of what the spectacle of visual culture represents when it comes to politics and symbolic order, is also part of some statements made by the American film theorist Bill Nichols (Nichols 2000:34-52). Starting with Plato he marks the vital part the human senses play in the production of knowledge, and his article focuses on the visual culture and the spectacle and how it is said to be an important feature of modernity. What Nichols brings forward is the need for this visual culture to recognise that the human senses are a type of knowledge production of the self, others, history and culture (Nichols 2000:41-42).

By selecting the three key concepts – visual culture, representation, rhetoric – Nichols argues that it is possible for us to connect film with social, political and identificatory concerns. Thereby he takes a different route from that of the cognitive psychology (Bordwell for instance), using a cultural studies framework. The road for future film studies, according to Nichols, is to join forces with other new disciplines as gender studies, where cultural visibility plays an important part. This entails studying cultural difference and the appeal to the human senses as a crucial, but often unacknowledged, form of knowledge production.

Obviously, there is a point in separating the representation of sexual violence and actual sexual violence, where what we see in the film could be said to carry a narrative function. However, what is left out and remains is the emotional and social, and, as Nichols says in his article, "film is not so much mind as body." In text-centered interpretations of films where the visual is sometimes seen as less important, there is also a tendency not to include the social, emotional and ethical aspects of film: "[T]he denigration of vision in a world where the power to make visible is a very great power indeed" (Nichols 2000:38). Another basic hypothesis here is therefore that there might be strength in the visual perception, which overpowers the intention of the auteur, since the images are part of a prevalent regime of representation in the surrounding flow of films. Consequently, I will not consider narrative functions as much as visual presence.

Most of us have a life long experience of different kinds of film stories in our mental library. We go to the movies, watch films on television and if you are a film buff in my home town Gothenburg you look forward to the annual film festival to see an alternative repertoire from around the world.[3] At a time when voices are heard that an increasing number of women tend to appear as agents in cinema as directors, producers and on screen in less stereotypical roles, my intention was to investigate to what degree their presence was noticeable during one year. In addition, I was interested in determining what gender stereotypes in fact were in evidence. Further, I wanted to connect this study with an example of how gender issues were negotiated in film criticism concerning one art film from that year. Finally, what conclusions could be drawn if the surrounding film repertoire and its gender representation were viewed as a primary interpretative background to this film? This could possibly explain the reactions in cultural criticism when the interpretative context is broadened and we bring in the social context.

The interpretative convention is that a film originates from a director, has one or two main characters and is valued and discussed in a reception situation. Therefore, the intention was to study film as a signifying practice from three communicative positions, those of the auteur, the main subject position of the film text, and the reception by film critics. *Who* are telling film stories, about *whom* and, to a limited extent, *how*? And how is this dealt with in critical practice?

Whenever we are discussing exceptions in the cinematic representation of women there need to be awareness about what these are an exception to. We need methods to illustrate the cultural basis in relation to which the exceptions occur. There is a tendency in film studies to focus on exceptions and this may have the media effect that there exists a general shift towards ever increasing female presence on all sides of the camera: script writers, producers, directors, leads, etc. However, as earlier research has shown and witnesses have been born from women in the business both in Hollywood and elsewhere, little change has been noted and there seems to be a continuing struggle for women to be part of the world of cinema on their own terms.[4] It could be that this conquest of male territory is not as evolutionary as one might think. There is a heavy and powerful flow composing most of the river, while there are certain currents more to be described as trickles.

Gender Representation in the Flow of Films

If we consider the life-world[5] experience of film flow it would be rewarding to reverse the conventional focus, i.e. making the context primary and the single film secondary. The hypothesis is that the single film, *Breaking the*

Waves by the Danish director Lars von Trier in this case, could be seen as a *minor* 'cinematic event', whereas the flow of contemporary films is the *major* cinematic event from a cultural point of view.[6]

The basis for my analysis of this major cinematic event then, will be the statistics found on gender representation in the film repertoire 1996 in Sweden. This study comprises all films on offer on television, cinema and film festival, concerning the subject positions 'director' and 'main character'.[7] Since my interest here is the general flow of films, I don't make a distinction between avant-garde films/high art and more popular ones. The sources employed offer a wide selection of films from different historic times and genres (including TV), recent films (cinema) and independent/art films from various parts of the world (festival). To gather this material I made use of film presentations in newspapers and film catalogues, and by now I have managed to double-check a majority of the cinema films and many from the film festival. After having studied the presentations of over two thousand films the results show a conspicuous male dominance in both positions, not surprisingly.

The concept 'representation' in this analysis is dual and embodies the representation of a specific sex together with the way female characters are grouped into stereotypes. The statistics will illustrate the presence of both men and women. However, since women in cinema could be regarded as the minority group represented, it is 'she' who is focused as a stereotype. This female focus is motivated by the extreme marginalisation of women in subject positions in film, that they are marked by a specific kind of 'difference' from a power perspective. They are the marginal Other.

To give you a summary of the investigation, it showed that the vast majority of films presented stories by men about men, in which 94% of the total had male directors and 72% had male leads. Correspondingly, films by and about a woman amounted to 3% of the total. Films with female leads (17%) were directed by men in four times as many cases as by women. In addition it was possible to deduce a selection of female stereotypes from this material, primarily involving sexual performance, voyeuristic functions, and (sexual) psychic threat. The overlapping groups were witches and psychopaths, victims and rapes, prostitutes and sexual performers, voyeuristic and scopophilistic objects, and lastly mothers, caretakers and take-care-of objects. Overall it could be noted that in more recent films there was a conspicuous and recurrent amount of prostitutes and rapes.

In this study I paid special interest to the alternative scene independent films offer. It then turned out that, although to a larger extent inscribed with art connotations, the *festival films* didn't constitute an alternative with regard to male/female representation neither as director/lead nor in terms of stereotyping. The majority of these films are brought in from countries all over the world and represent a less commercial repertoire. Nevertheless, these films depicted a large number of strippers, prostitutes, models, beautiful ladies, rape victims, avenging women, etc.[8]

To include an even larger amount of festival films I have made average statistics from 1995-2001. It turns out that there are normally 62% male leads and the combination male director/male lead amounts to 54%. The female equivalent is 7% female director/female lead. The average number of female directors in total appeared to be 17%. During this period there was no obvious change over time when it comes to gender representation. The fact remains, then, that in alternative cinema most stories are about men and are directed by men.

While scrutinising the film catalogues I again noticed that female roles were attributed specific types of descriptions.[9] Among the principal female characters in the 143 films of 1996 I only found one prostitute and one stripper, together with various other stereotypes mentioned above. On the other hand, there were as many as five prostitutes and two rape victims if we look at secondary female characters. Since the amount of films is fairly low, running the risk of the stereotypes found being accidental, I decided to examine the films of 1995 as well. Again, it turned out that it is among secondary female characters we find these examples. In films by male directors there were six prostitutes and seven rapes mentioned in the film summaries, and in yet another one a rape is impending. Many of these women roles were signified by traditionally 'easy women' in visual occupations as tightrope dancer, barmaid, waitress, ballet girl/stripper, young model with criminal background, etc. Examples of the stereotypes mentioned in the film presentations were: an under age prostitute; a mass murderer killing prostitutes; prostitutes; a raped waitress; a raped barmaid; a male protagonist protecting young girls at a school for juvenile delinquents from a rapist; an inflatable woman doll; a "tasty Dazzle Dent"; a "belle which has arrived in town"; and, in one film, a male protagonist who is tought about love and sex by four girls. In was clear from this material that it was mostly in films produced in the West we could see women as prostitutes, rape victims and murder victims.

The conclusion drawn from these stereotypical tendencies is that women presented in the alternative films align with the described features concerning popular films. Men direct the majority of films and when we see a woman in the principle part she is mostly directed by a man. When she occurs on the screen there is a fair chance that she is young, beautiful, mystical, victim of rape and involved in prostitution. This opens up for an interesting discussion on the difference between high art cinema versus popular cinema. One is that we tend to expect more differentiated representations on the alternative scene. On this level of gender analysis it could either be stated that there is no major difference or that the traffic of popular culture into high art has brought on these characteristics. In my mind, however, this is an example of a cultural gender structure that prevails, regardless of which position in the cultural hierarchy the film is aspiring for.

British film theorist Yvonne Tasker has claimed there has been a certain focus on the femme fatale in feminist film theory, but the prostitute has not had the same analytic interest (Tasker 1998). One reason for this is that it is more difficult to claim this stereotype as counterculture. Interestingly enough, then, I found a conspicuous amount of prostitutes, or other sexually related profession, and rapes recurring in my festival material, i.e. art films. To conclude, the prostitute is a remarkable stereotype in art film today and rapes are a common occurrence. One could argue that both the 'prostitute' and the 'rape' probably carry slightly different meanings in different films: in art films versus popular ones, for instance. However, my emphasis here is on the actual visual appearance of both these as categories. The stereotype is the prostitute and the presence of rape, not various inflections.

In agreement with earlier investigations from the 1970s and 1980s of gender representation in cinema, this study confirms that cinema still is a predominantly male space where few women are present as directors and seldom seen as main characters. However, there is a tendency of describing the situation of the 1990s in terms of an increase in the presence of female agents in cinema, mainly as producers or screenwriters but also as directors. Drawing on works concerning gender representation in large amounts of film by Molly Haskell (1987), Susan Faludi (1991) and primarily Yvonne Tasker (1998), I have found that there is little change to be seen. All three mention an increase, of female presence in cinema with certain reservations. Although from slightly different angles, they focus on Hollywood production. I have investigated a broader range and from a Swedish horizon, including the alternative scene and some films from the rest of the world. With their work as a rewarding background, I have been able to draw more detailed conclusions concerning my material. My study gives a description of a basic gender structure that I claim influences both textual analysis and the construction of cultural discourse over all.

In the feministic tradition of representation study in cinema there has recently been a search for more positive descriptions of alternative female subjectivities and counter discourses, which I support. However, my emphasis is on the overall gendered macrostructures in the vast majority of films and how they repeatedly are presented to us in the life-world flow of films. Apart from the obvious male dominance this study in addition puts a finger on the presence of female prostitutes and rapes, *both* in mainstream as well as avantgarde films in modern cinema. The main development in the representation area seems to be a slight shift in stereotyping nuances. As Yvonne Tasker (1998) has shown there is a constant connotation of sexual performance and work when women appear in mainstream films. During the 1990s we can observe an increasing degree of sexual violence towards women in films as well. Both of these tendencies are supported by my findings and proved to be central to the critical discussions on *Breaking the Waves* (1996). This brings us back to the social side of film studies and its relation to the audience and the symbolic order of cinema.

Are Gender Issues Breaking Waves in Film Criticism?

Few films manage to launch a cultural debate. But in 1996, after the opening of Lars von Trier's *Breaking the Waves* in Denmark and later in Sweden critical voices were raised against its allegedly degrading portrayal of the heroine. The 'proper' interpretation of the film and its presumed themes was at the centre of the lengthy and heated debates that followed. On a macro-level they basically circled around the following: interpretative practices and context, and the appraisal and evaluation of works of art. The debates exemplify how gender issues are negotiated in critical practice.

In 1996 the Danish director Lars von Trier introduced his film *Breaking the Waves*. In interaction with the media he was presented as an eccentric genius and the film positioned as innovative high art. If you on the other hand consider the film on its own, without any previous knowledge, it turns out to be a conscious interplay with high art cinema aesthetics and popular culture melodrama.[10] From an aesthetical point of view there is a specific visual style, for instance, which is conspicuous and marks a separation from popular culture. On the other hand there are obvious traits and characteristics from popular culture. However, I will not go into a detailed textual analysis here on the play between high and low, only mark its presence in the film. Whether you are familiar with this particular film or not, is of less importance here. My focus is, as said, the visual representation of certain stereotypes and their interplay with the ones in the overall film flow.

Breaking the Waves is a story about a young innocent and naive girl, Bess (Emily Watson), brought up in a remote coastal village shaped by its strict religious zeal. She has just found and married the love of her life, Jan (Stellan Skarsgård), an oil rig worker and an outsider. They have a short and passionate time together after the wedding, but to Bess's disappointment he has to leave for work. Jan is her only focus in life, and when she fervently prays to God to bring him home, he has an accident and is hospitalised and ends up paralysed. Jan wants Bess to be happy and, since he has lost his ability to make love, he commands her to take a lover or perform sexual acts and tell him about it. The story escalates into Bess forcing herself to more and more violating acts in an attempt to please her husband and her God at the same time. There are scenes where she is seen performing masturbation on a man on a bus, and she offers sexual intercourse to a man behind the local pub. She starts dressing and acting as a prostitute, offering her services and is violently abused by two sailors on a ship from which she escapes the first time, but later returns to fulfill her 'mission'. At the end, she is brutally molested and dies from her injuries. Miraculously, Jan gets well again and church bells chime from the sky. The portrayal of Bess gives the impression of an extremely innocent, naive girl, "clown like" (according to the instruction of the director), almost bordering on mentally retarded (this is hinted at several times in the film by the mother, a sister in law) (Bjørkman & von Trier 1999).

Before we consider the positions in the debates it could be stated from a theoretical point of view, that there are, on the one hand, *explicatory* practices or, on the other hand, *symptomatic* practices, when it comes to interpretation. These are concepts used by David Bordwell in *Making meaning. Inference and rhetoric in the interpretation of cinema* (1991) to illustrate positions taken when making meaning in cinema.

An explicatory position takes referential or explicit meaning as the point of departure for inference about implicit meanings. The focus is on the 'interior meaning' of the film and this position is commonly auteur-centred. The proper interpretative context is the director's other work; in addition there might be other film classics along with interviews with the director and/or actors. The inference tends to take the shape of "atomistic theme-spotting" with avant-garde critics concerning art film, where there is no coherence between the interpreted parts and just a casual game of finding themes (Bordwell 1991:69).[11] Part of this tradition is to cultivate the idea of the artistic genius; that we are dealing with a unified piece of art mainly referring to it self.

A symptomatic position, on the other hand, assumes that the sources of meaning are intrapsychic or broadly cultural, they lie outside the conscious control of the auteur. The sources are involuntary, concealed by referential meaning. This activity could then be referred to as a 'reading against the grain'. The filmic text is looked upon as *a symptom of its culture*, and an example of how a specific culture structures cultural power. The analysis wants to show how repressed meanings have social sources and consequences. Film as a signifying practise, then, carries a symbolic dimension of culture. Concerning genre criticism critics tend to play down visual style in favour of recurrent themes. And critics find that seeking the thematic base of a genre inevitably leads to broader social meanings. You could also look at how the film treats inherited conventions. Instead of putting together the imagined coherence of a unified work of art, you look for cracks, ambiguities, contradictions, and the ambivalences in this film. In academic film criticism the symptomatic interpretation is the most influential, Bordwell says, and especially when popular films are analysed. However, as Bordwell points out, in practical criticism, there is a tendency that the symptomatic critic switches into the explicatory mode when approaching an interpretation of avant-garde cinema. That here we wouldn't find cracks, ambiguities, repressed meanings. Much 'old' criticism and journalistic criticism is said to be blind to the ways its tacit theory governs its practice. This brings us to the example of critical practice and the reception of *Breaking the Waves*.

The Debates

These debates as a cultural phenomenon again spotlights an event where the explicatory and symptomatic readers of a text go in 'clinch' and accuse each other of reducing or misreading a work of art for different reasons. Consequently and since symptomatic readings demand a wider social context, this discussion also exemplifies a strong cultural anxiety concerning gender issues, and an ambivalence concerning the relationship ar and text on the one hand, and the social and ethics on the other. This is expressed and found in various ways as an undertext in the texts I have analysed. There tends to be a resistance among certain contributors of the cultural debate to discuss and accept gender issues, unless the auteurs themselves put it on the agenda. Gender issues are set on isolated, or perhaps parallel, agendas, and should not be brought up unasked for, it seems.[12]

Breaking the Waves (1996) was critically acclaimed at the Cannes festival in the spring earlier that year, and also in the reviews following the official opening in June (Denmark) and August (Sweden). However, immediately after there were other voices heard in the press reacting against the way the main character Bess was portrayed and the way the film was reviewed. In general, most critics seem to find the intention of the auteur central to their arguments, regardless of their attitudes toward that intention.[13] The participants in the debates strove to correct 'misreadings' in their need to reach a consensus concerning a 'proper' interpretation. From a more explicatory standpoint, it was either stated that a critical gender perspective was irrelevant since it was not part of the film's intention, *or* that it was meant to thematise feministic values in a positive way. There were some who in an opposing position read the film against the grain and questioned its intentions concerning religious and feministic issues and/or its value as a work of art. One of the other central issues following the critique was a protest against the unanimous praise of the film by the reviewers at the premiere.

To stick to a chronological order I will start with the Danish reaction. In the newspaper *Information* there was a lengthy debate, where statements were made from laymen as well as professional critics and there were articles as well as short letters to the editor. According to Morten Kyndrup, in an article on the debate six months later, there was a division of those *for* the film and those *against*, where the reactions primarily were emotionally based (Kyndrup 1997). He found it conspicuous the way the basic phenomenological conception of the film shifted. There was not only a difference in emphasis on the same elements, but also on totally different elements, as if the contributors hadn't seen the same film. Even if it was a matter of differences in taste, Kyndrup asked himself whether it possibly was a quality within the film itself? There were in fact a few debaters who hinted at the possibility, that it was part of von Trier's intention to provoke several optional interpretations.

Furthermore, Rolf Gerd Heitman, in an article in the literary magazine *Standart* called "Lars fun Trier", comments on this (Heitman 1996). As said, the reviewers in Denmark were full of admiration and in Cannes the global press was positive. Heitman argues that something went wrong in the cultural machinery, round about here, as he puts it. The audience was not as

exuberantly positive. Many were angry and meant that the film had a mi-
sogynous view of women. The other comment he makes is that the contributions in the debate tended to be surprisingly competent in their analyses
and contained many well-founded reflections. One of his major critical points
is on the community of film criticism and its reluctance to explain their basis
for declaring this a masterpiece. It ought to be the critics' duty to fill the gap
between audience and criticism, he says. He even goes as far as stating that
the film never was properly analysed, never reviewed. They declared the
film was Trier's first masterpiece and a classic without explaining on what
grounds. Heitman does not comment on the gender issue, apart from that
fact that he found the feminist comments to be the most profound. However, he also accuses some of them of not being able to decode a modern
work of art.

The Swedish reviewers were as positive as the Danish, and their texts
suffered from the same lack of analysis, in my opinion. The reviews themselves could be said to follow a formalized pattern of description. The content is presented as unproblematic and there is a focus on the description of
esthetical elements (the use of a moving camera, etc). On one rare occasion
the review is ended by the exclamation: " But what the hell is he trying to
say?" (Lindblom 1996).

What is interesting about the debate, then, is that it occurred at all. And
the take-off in Sweden actually was that the American Professor of Art, Abigail
Solomon-Godeau, complained that there was no reaction in Sweden concerning the film, referring to the discussion in Denmark. Her contribution
was from a feministic standpoint as well as academic where she criticised
the silence and the film critics for giving the film full acclamation as an eminent
work of art. From her point of view we were just presented with yet another
example of a degrading female portrait in a long tradition of "torture the
woman".[14]

The reaction to this signal was Maria Bergom-Larsson, a well-know literary critic, arguing that the professor totally had misinterpreted and reduced
this work of art along conventional feministic lines. According to Bergom-
Larsson it dealt with religion and to appreciate the film you need to let yourself go. To her you need to stay inside the film and not read against the grain.
The contributions that followed gave a range of views, and here I would
like to argue that the main dividing line runs between the two different types
of interpretative practices – explicatory and symptomatic – clashing against
each other. Both accusing the other of reducing the film's meaning and being narrow-minded. On the one hand there are those who refer to the world
outside the film, and those who demand the opposite: stay inside and refer
to other classic stories and references.

The fact that there exist different sources of interpretative practises is of
course never expressed or discussed as such. My interest here, then, is the
accusation from the explicators that those who bring in certain aspects of
the social and ethics are in the wrong. One important argument why was

the familiar mistake to take the film as a representation of the real world and not a story. And this is naturally an important aspect, but at the same time and by the same debater the same kind of argument is used: "The film shows what Life is like, deal with it!"

Once in each debate the symptomatic position is accused of not being able to interpret a modern work of art. In one case it seems to be a matter of viewers being uneducated! If they can't stay inside the work of art *and* go outside it to find *certain* intertextual allusions (from the Bible for instance) due to lack of education, they ought to rest their case. This is the most interesting focal point, I think. Apparently some in the audience have found other points of reference and allusions than the critics. From other intertextual libraries and a wider cultural frame in their life-worlds. This would, traditionally, be a sign of an inability to interpret more complicated work of art, since such an activity demands a distanced position. However, this position turns out to be problematic concerning this film. *Breaking the Waves* draws heavily on melodramatic excess and empathy, and some explicators even declare that it is the only position possible; to empathetically follow Bess' emotions and stay inside the film. *Not* to distance yourself.

From a symptomatic position they argue that 'staying inside' the text and not question the intentions of the director is narrow-minded. That is being gullible and part of an old fashioned tradition. From this stance we could even read long since discarded arguments in politically correct feministic theory, as one contributor demands 'proper images of women'. One Danish debater showed ambivalence concerning this (Plenge 1996). She wanted to be devoured by the film, let herself go, as she was supposed to. But she couldn't, she said. The reasons she gave were its content from an ethical point of view and that she found it lacking in classic artistic quality. *Breaking the Waves* got stuck in her throat. The aesthetics were marvellous, the actors brilliant – but still. On the other hand, one Swedish critic, hesitant about the film's message, landed on the conclusion that the aesthetics is just the reason why it is a great film (Tunbäck-Hanson 1996).

The debate in Aftonbladet was ended by a concluding comment by Solomon-Godeau who stuck to her first impression. She was sad to see that the discussion had a religious slant in Sweden and that there is an evident gap between the common academic practices and some of the contributors who couldn't accept arguments from an ethical and gender perspective.

Trier has made films since then. You could say that there for some remains a question mark on him as an artist and whether he is a genius or not. One fact still stands though. *Breaking the Waves* is proclaimed to be the best Danish film ever in *Gyldendal's Dictionary of Film*.[15] In this there is no mentioning of a cultural debate. The film critics set the historical agenda. There was in fact general confusion and ambivalence concerning the film, but on the part of the film critics in these two countries there was a general acclaim. Naturally, an explicatory or symptomatic position is a matter of interpretative choice. In the *messy reality*, which I in short have tried to describe here, these two are only displayed to a certain extent. Many critics mix the two. But one point could clearly be made and that is that there are those who refuse to accept a symptomatic position when interpreting art movies and it is in this aspect the concepts are useful. By categorising the critics according to their use of symptomatic or explicatory reading practices, a significant dividing line could be established. There are a large number of common interpretative conventions in the critical community, but also main grounds of contention regarding attitudes towards contextuality and interpretation. It is also evident that bringing up gender issues and criticising an art film/text from an ideological point of view is tricky and problematic in 1996. It raises a lot of anger still, even though it is more accepted of course concerning popular products, and this debate exemplifies a space where the problems with and negotiating of gender issues surfaced in print. So, are gender issues breaking new waves in film criticism? No, not really, but the field of art cinema and its critics are questioned and critical voices are raised. Obviously, there is a fierce negotiation taking place concerning this, since it can display a cultural debate of this kind, where old conventions are challenged and alternative interpretations and demands are claimed as valid.

These debates raise several questions: Is there no place for criticising the ethics of modern art film? For criticising its gender representation and its part in the repetition of stereotypes? Why is there a resistance to bring in the social when discussing art films?

Gender Structures and *Breaking the Waves*

In comparing *Breaking the Waves* (1996)[16] to the macrostructures of the contemporary flow of films and observable stereotypical patterns, the film takes on additional meaning. Regardless of its auteur's and/or its textual intentions, and of the fact that we are dealing with an artefact inscribed as a work of art with a potentially intended ironic distance, it is possible to state that on a macro structural level this film could be regarded as fairly conventional in its use of stereotypes and in its depiction of a woman victimised through sexual violence in accordance with the context: the films of 1996. This art film also finds itself in the category of a male director /female lead, a woman depicted by a man. Apart from statistics as a basis for comparison emphasis could also be placed on the fact that representatives of the actual reception of the film showed great ambivalence in their interpretations, even on a phenomenological level, as to what the film was about. Depending on where the contextual lines were drawn, by convention and/or intellectual decision, the results of the interpretations differed.

To focus on the *debaters* rather than *reviewers* is to move into a world where the social evidently matters. What we can trace among the reviewers is yet another phenomenon which leads up to specific conventions in finding 'meaning'. Bill Nichols touches on what kind of cultural construction the film critics seem to be creating with von Trier's film (Nichols 2000:34-52). What they excel in is turning both director and film into a fetish, which they desire, drawing on Marxist thought. Fetishism would here mean that the creative work is presented as a mystery of creativity or genius. This turns into a romantic denial of its existence as commodity as well as its connection to the life world of representation, it seems.

> Addressing this dynamic of desire and denial, awareness and forgetting gives representation an acute complexity lacking from approaches restricted to formal, textcentered interpretations (Nichols 2000:43).

Here again we see the conventions of criticism revealed as dependent on tacit theories and desires. Part of this is to deny the relevance of certain aspects of the film. From an explicatory position you could bring up several arguments against gender aspects of this film. It could be that the entire film is an ambiguity game of sorts which von Trier is playing to provoke the viewers, but there were quite a few who apparently were not up to it. One reason for this might be that they have seen it all before, if we remember the film repertoire and that it concerns their lives and life-worlds. Another argument could be that this film is showing a specific inflection of the 'prostitute' and 'sexual violence'. Could not the stereotyping be contradicted by linguistic, aesthetical and other enunciations? To the audience there was an apparent reaction against various elements of the film. This might be a fragmentation of something, which is supposed to be perceived as a unified work of art. And so be it. Their experiences remain, however, and carry cultural meaning as well.

In sketching some striking features of *Breaking the Waves* we could say that it turned out to be difficult to interpret or that there didn't seem to be any unambiguous or obvious 'message' to be found. Secondly, that it thematised in one way or the other a woman's victimisation, and her exposure to sexual violence.[17] The main character Bess is masquerading as a prostitute and she is raped of 'her own free will', perhaps. At the level of visual representation we actually *see* woman afflicted by sexual violence, prostituting herself and constituting a victim, in accordance with the above-presented analysis of the film repertoire. Here I wish to make a point of not elaborating on a textual analysis of the film. Of interest for my argument is to rest on the notion of visual representation. What do we see? As a consequence, the stress is put on the fragmentisation and ambivalence in the reception as well, and that there were negative reactions to the way the woman was portrayed. I will now move on to further explore the audience and make a connection again between the above and the importance visual culture plays in contemporary society.

Turn to the Audience and Visual Culture

There has been many 'turns' in critical theory during the last century, where one is the turn to the audience (Perkins 2000:90). In accordance with this there are other questions to be answered apart from the 'preferred reading' of the text. Are rapes and the representations of prostitutes really what they seem to be at the face of it? Can a rape on screen ever carry 'only', say, a narrative function? And, if so, what about the social effect? Mustn't we consider what 'rape', 'prostitute' and 'sexual violence' stand for emotionally in the life-world, and perhaps for women specifically? Another problematic question is whether the aesthetics and pleasure aspects in any way could out-rule the social for the viewer.

In the reception of this film there were many contradictory thoughts around the way the principle character Bess was to be comprehended, as well as what the film 'was about'. Some critics looked upon Bess as strong, others as weak. The question is not so much whether she *is* one thing or the other, as how she was perceived by the audience. For anyone expecting me to decide which way to go concerning her representation as 'strong' or 'weak', they will be left disappointed. It is not for me to figure out or say in this context. A textual analysis would definitely end up showing that she could be interpreted as both, depending on point of view. However, in comparison to the gender representation of cinema in general she would in my view be regarded as a victim, i.e. conventionally weak, but with streaks of a particular kind of strength in pursuing her aims.

Is that which we on the face of it perceive as a 'strong woman' really just that? If cinema is a predominantly male space, shouldn't this come into play when we analyse single films? American professor Carol J. Clover has discussed the possible connections between main characters and audience from a gender perspective (Clover 1992). Several of the issues I have brought up here could be connected to her work. To what extent is the sex of the viewer, or of the director, of importance? In Clover's study of the way in which extreme genres as the slasher and the rape revenge movie recurrently have a woman/teenage girl as last survivor and conqueror of the 'monster', she initially puts a question mark to the same-sex identification and talks more about cross-gender identification. In addition she argues that it is more important to consider the gender function of the so-called 'final girl'.

In her focus on the female victim-hero, the final girl turns out to be exceptional in several ways. She is unusual exactly because she is a 'girl' and this in a genre, which foremost is appreciated by a young male audience. In Cover's analysis 'she' becomes the only object of identification possible for these men when the emotional centre of the film is to horrify. Concerning identification this would then be a proof that men may identify with a female character, and that there is such a thing as cross-gender identification. However, she also points out that the purpose and function of the female character is still "a totally male affair," as she calls it (Clover 1992:52). The final girl is put there to function as a vicarious male; she is an instrument to release the fear of the male psyche. The presumed audience is male and she represents the 'female weak', the frightened side of the male psyche, which can only be culturally allowed in a female. The identification with the pursuit, which haunts this final girl and her final victory over the monster, is a representation of the 'female male psyche' (Clover 1992:5). Thus, the final girl is foremost a vicarious man/boy and in so a process of what modernity represses: the woman, the Other. Naturally, this doesn't stop her from being appreciated by female viewers, despite the fact that she is put there for the benefit of the young male audience. She could be perceived as a 'strong woman' on the face of it and 'she' is a female main character. In line with Clover and in reference to my position here, 'she' ought to be read in connection with film as a culturally signifying practice and the gender representation in general and the fact that the lion part of the film repertoire in itself is a male affair in excess. Conclusively, there is a risk in making simple analytical conclusions concerning the 'strength' of female characters embedded in a powerful male discourse. In the end, cinema is first and foremost a male space of negotiation and presence.

In one sense this could contradict the visual appearance of gendered bodies as being just that, when looking for cultural meaning in representations. However, in my view it is an elaboration of the visual gender representation, and needs further investigation into the importance of the visual, emotional and social.

One basic statement is that what we *see* and what we *feel* about what we see is of importance in the production of meaning. Even if we turn to the audience not many interviews have been made of how women actually respond to the kind of stereotyping I have described here. It is more a common knowledge that some of the more violent female stereotypes are disliked based on emotion and for being degrading. Therefore it could be of interest as well to consider the reactions from audiences by looking at how young girls in Sweden answered questions concerning violence and film (Stigbrand & Stolpe 2000). One of the questions asked was: which parts of films do you regret having seen? It seems that one of the worst events to watch is a 'rape', according to this research. Not so much people being killed. Another effect noted in this series of interviews was that young girls generally believe there to be twice as many murders or beatings to death of women as there have been reported (Stigbrand & Stolpe 2000:36-37). As many as 15 % thought there to be more than 1000 killings of this kind annually instead of the actual 40. So, their impression is that this is a much more common occurrence than it in reality is.

Conclusion

In this article there has been an emphasis on the way a cultural artefact is read against a certain cultural context when looking for cultural meaning. To delimit the boundaries of such a context is always difficult, but one central idea here is that it is problematic to single out one film and read it against only a specific set of other films. It is as problematic to exclude social and ethical issues, as well as the politics of representation, when discussing both popular and art film. Here I have shown the value of using a broader social perspective when reading a single film and what is revealed when the entire film repertoire is considered as a background. The overall importance here has been on visual representation and its general structure in contemporary cinema and how this is connected with the surrounding predominantly visual culture.

By turning to an audience conditioned by the dominant cinematic apparatus it was furthermore evident that these aspects of the art film *Breaking the Waves* caused a debate. Reactions tended to be concerned with the repetition of a woman as victim, exposed to sexual violence including rape, and portrayed as prostitute.

In contrast to discussions stating the importance of how viewers pragmatically use films for their own purposes, this article wishes to emphasise viewers' relation to existing macrostructures in the films and stereotypes on offer at a given period of time. By focusing on the macrostructures in the contemporary flow of films and on the media landscape as part of a cultural context in the life-world, the interpretation and impact of a film take on additional meanings. As this study contends, a single film is played off against other films in a stereo visual room, where the enunciation may even contradict the enounced, the spoken words and arranged order of frames. There might be a strength in the visual perception, which overpowers the intention of the auteur, since the images are part of a prevalent regime of representation in the surrounding flow of films. The ambivalence shown in the reception study also supports the idea that the emotional and intellectual impressions of a film are fragmented in spite of a striving for the creation of a unified interpretation both on the part of the creator and the viewer.

Notes

1. 'Signifying practice' as used in Hall 1997.
2. A broader textual concept is commonly used in cultural theory, which means that all sorts of cultural texts can be read: images, music, film as well as literature.
3. Ninety per cent of the films here will never be screened at ordinary theatres.
4. For example *Women Film Producers of Hollywood* (1998), producer Marc Rousseau, Bertrand Deveaud, Copywright Film Concept Associes. The situation in Sweden: Vinterheden, Marianne (1991). *Om kvinnor i svensk filmproduktion.* Svenska Kvinnors Filmförbund and Hermela, Vanja (Ed.) (2002). *Män, män, män och en och annan kvinna.* Stockholm: Arena, Svenska Filminstitutet.

5. The life-world is a concept used in social theory referring to 'stocks of knowledge', or skills and expectations that allow us to give meaning to and construct the social world within which we live.

6. For 'cinematic event' see Bordwell (1996:12). Within film theory Rick Altman has used this concept, see Altman (1992:4).

7. This paper is based partly on findings from my study *Over and over again: Gender representation and discourse in films 1996 in Sweden and Breaking the Waves* (2000) Gothenburg University, Sweden: Department of Literature.

8. One cultural difference appeared in that festival films from the West tended to present graphic violence, extensive nudity and sexual situations to a larger extent than examples from other areas.

9. The presentations are found in the Göteborg Film Festival catalogue 1995 and 1996.

10. At this time Lars von Trier had a lot of attention drawn to his filmmaking after the media presentation of the manifesto *Dogma 95*. This is a set of rules for film making where, among other things, shooting should be as 'natural' as possible. See Björkman & von Trier, 1999.

11. 'Atomistic' = from 'atom', split into pieces with no coherence and unity (Bordwell 1991:69).

12. In comparison one can note that class issues are not as controversial to comment on as gender.

13. For a symptomatic reader this is no prerequisite.

14. "Torture the women!" is said to be coined by the playwright Sardou and is also one of Hitchcock's motto in effective film making.

15. The most renowned and important compilation about film in Denmark.

16. *Breaking the Waves* (1996) script and direction: Lars von Trier. Denmark, Holland, Sweden, France: Zentropa.

17. For the record: the actual beating and abuse was not shown explicitly.

References

Altman, R. (1992). General introduction: cinema as event. In Altman, R.(Ed.), *Sound theory sound practice*. New York: Routledge.

Björkman, S. & L. von Trier (1999). *Trier om von Trier*. Stockholm: Alfabeta.

Bordwell, D. (1996). Contemporary film studies and the vicissitudes of grand theory. In Bordwell, D. & N. Carroll (Eds.), *Post-theory. Reconstructing film studies*. Madison, WI and London: The University of Wisconsin Press.

Bordwell, D. (1989). *Making meaning. Inference and rhetoric in the interpretation of cinema*. Cambridge: Harvard University Press.

Bordwell, D. & N. Carroll (Eds.) (1996). *Post-theory. Reconstructing film studies*. The University of Wisconsin Press.

Branston, G. (2000). *Cinema and cultural modernity*. Buckingham: Open University Press.

Clover, C. (1992). *Men, women and chainsaws. Gender in the modern horror film*. Princeton: Princeton University Press.

Faludi, S. (1991). *Backlash. The undeclared war against American women*. New York: Crown.

Göteborg Film Festival catalogue, 1995, 1996.

Hall, S. (1997). The spectacle of the Other. In S. Hall (Ed.), *Representation. Cultural representations and signifying practices* (*Culture, media, and identities, vol. 2*). London: Sage Publications.

Haskell, M. (1987, 1973). *From reverence to rape. The treatment of women in the movies*. Chicago: Chicago Press.

Heitman, R. G. (1996). Lars fun Trier. *Standart, 3*, Aug-Oct.

Hermela, V. (Ed.) (2002). *Män, män, män och en och annan kvinna*. Stockholm: Arena, Svenska Filminstitutet.

Kyndrup, M. (1997). Betydning som rum som betydning. En refleksion med Lars von Triers *Breaking the Waves*. Arbejdspapir, Center for Kulturforskning, Aarhus Universitet.

Lindblom, S. (1996, November 17). Jag trodde jag skulle bli förbannad, men... *Aftonbladet*.

Lindell, I. (2000). *Over and over again: Gender representation and discourse in films 1996 in Sweden and Breaking the Waves*. Gothenburg University, Sweden: Department of Literature.

Nichols, B. (2000). Film Theory and the revolt against master narratives. In C. Gledhill & L. Williams (Eds.), *Reinventing Film Studies*. London: Arnold.

Perkins, T. (2000). Who (and what) is it for? In C. Gledhill & L. Williams (Eds.), *Reinventing film studies*. London: Arnold.

Plenge, D. (1996, July 24). Jan og Bess' kærlighed. *Information*.

Stigbrand, K. & S. Stolpe (Eds.) (2000). *Tusen flickor om film och våld*. Våldsskildringsrådets skriftserie nr. 23, Stockholm.

Tasker, Y. (1998). *Working girls. Gender and sexuality in popular cinema*. London: Routledge.

Tunbäck-Hanson, M. (1996, September 9). "Filmdikt som får känslorna att svalla". *Göteborgsposten*.

Vinterheden, M. (1991). *Om kvinnor i svensk filmproduktion*. Svenska Kvinnors Filmförbund.

Women film producers of Hollywood (1998). Producer Marc Rousseau, Bertrand Deveaud. Copywright Film Concept Associes.

Lara Croft, Between a Feminist Icon and Male Fantasy

Maja Mikula

The Face: Is Lara a feminist icon or a sexist fantasy?
Toby Gard: Neither and a bit of both. Lara was designed to be a tough, self-reliant, intelligent woman. She confounds all the sexist clichés apart from the fact that she's got an unbelievable figure. Strong, independent women are the perfect fantasy girls – the untouchable is always the most desirable.
Interview with Lara's creator Toby Gard, *The Face* magazine, June 1997

Lara Croft, a widely popular videogame[1] superwoman and recently also the protagonist of the blockbuster film *Lara Croft: Tomb Raider* (2001), is a character open to feminist readings. She is the heroine of a series of action/adventure games titled Tomb Raider, which – like other products belonging to this genre – incorporate scenarios of quest, survival and combat and are set in exotic, often fantasy locations. Lara is rich, intelligent and physically fit. Her hyper-feminine body, accentuated by scanty clothing, has provoked criticism by anti-pornography campaigners. Feminists, concerned with sexual objectification of women, generally have little sympathy for excessively sexualized female icons of popular culture, whether real or virtual. Germaine Greer, for example, has called Lara a "sergeant-major with balloons stuffed up his shirt [...] She's a distorted, sexually ambiguous, male fantasy. Whatever these characters are, they're not real women" (Jones 2001). In fact, in her latest book, *The Whole Woman*, Greer has unequivocally condemned the enforcement of artificial and oppressive ideals of femininity through pop icons such as Barbie Doll (Greer 1999). Lara Croft, whose "femaleness" is clearly shaped by a desire to embody male sexual fantasies, can indeed be read as an antithesis of Greer's ideal of the "whole woman". On the other hand, Lara – an independent, strong, intelligent, no-nonsense character – has all the potential for becoming a desirable feminist role model. Lara Croft thus raises a number of questions related to the current predicament of feminist identity politics, epitomizing the range of contemporary feminist stances in relation to the body and the consumer culture of late capitalism.

Feminists associated with postmodern theory have endeavored to deconstruct an essentialized feminist "we" and any politics emphasizing "common bonds". Over the last decade or so, a number of feminists have sought to "reclaim" feminine appearance as a source of empowerment, rather than oppression (Wolf 1993, Roiphe 1993, Denfeld 1995). They set out to "appropriate and reinvent female stereotypes to their own advantage" (Lumby 1997:8), employing multivocality and parody as modes of positive self-reference. The feminist readings which acknowledge Lara Croft's subversive potential thus resonate with queer theory's strategic use of a parodic exposure of sex-gender-desire continuity in order to destabilize its perceived normativity and allow all "cultural configurations of sex and gender [to] proliferate" (Butler 1990:190).

Gaming in a Mans World

Up until recently, the only female characters who gained entry into the macho world of videogames, were "damsels in distress" – vulnerable victims of violence, to be rescued by muscular male heroes. Conversely, Lara Croft is never the "object" of rescue, but rather the protagonist and the driving force of the game plot. Since Lara's groundbreaking entry into this traditionally male world, the number of female characters in action videogames has been on a steady increase (suffice it to mention Elexis Sinclaire from Sin, Grace Nakimura from Gabriel Knight series, Annah from Planescape: Torment; Elaine Marley from Monkey Island games; or Tifa Lockhart and Aeris Gainsborough from Final Fantasy). Nevertheless, the number of heroines in this videogame genre is still considerably lower than the number of males (Mayfield 2000).

Following the established videogame-industry marketing trends, developers of Tomb Raider, Derby-based company Core Design, identified the target audience for the first Tomb Raider game as "males between 15 and 26 years of age" (Pretzsch 2000). In the early stages of development, two alternative protagonists were considered – one male and one female. The female character, initially called Laura Cruise, finally prevailed, despite fears in the marketing department that such an unheard-of choice would undermine the sales of the product.

Women gamers are often discouraged by a market catering specifically for "male" interests and offering the potential female consumers mostly products reflecting unrealistic and stereotypical visions of their supposed needs. The "girl games", which multiplied on the market since the mid-1990s almost exclusively, focused on shopping, fashion, dating and appearance. A study undertaken two years ago by the American Association of University Women Educational Foundation (AAUW) indicates that girls "often dislike violent video games and prefer personalized, interactive, role-playing games" (Mayfield 2000). Lara's violence, embedded in a narrative of good versus evil, fulfils the perceived expectations of the male segment of the market

(Kafai 1996), respecting the narrative codes of the action-adventure genre. It is never violence for its own sake, but rather a necessary self-defence in the course of exploration.

Another difference between male and female gamers seems to be the desired level of identification with the main character: according to one study, the identification element is more important for female gamers, who tend to become "irritated" when they cannot identify with their female character (Wright 2000). Despite the first-person format of the gameplay, Tomb Raider undermines any possibility of smooth identification between the gamer and the highly complex and contradictory protagonist of the game. The possibility of identification is further forestalled by the cinematic concept, which enables the gamer to "impersonate" Lara while having her body in full view. This particular cinematic model defies the gamer`s learned perception of "self" and "other", "subject" and "object". In contrast to the fragmented experience of the self in the first-person action-adventure games which employ the more accommodating cinematic concept of allowing the gamer to see only a part of her/his virtual body – usually the hands – on the screen, the Tomb Raider model empowers the gamer with an orthopedic, illusory vision of integration and totality. Through agency and control, the gamer assumes her/his virtual "identity". The first-person voice of the game play, combined with a third-person cinematic angle, offers the gamer an ambivalent experience of "self", which becomes simultaneously the subject and the object of the game. The illusion of empowerment emanates from the gamers experience of being Lara, while simultaneously seeing and controlling her.

An enthusiastic male reviewer of the first Tomb Raider game has declared that "having a *person* in the game" [emphasis is mine] made him "more cautious and protective". Ironically, he found himself not "just controlling Lara", but "looking after her as well" (Olafson 1997:100). His experience of the game thus encapsulates the patriarchal rhetoric of "control" and "care", by a male subject of a female object. Ironically, even when offered empowerment through a possibility of conflating the subject-object distinction, male players seem to view themselves in the position of the subject and see Lara as the object of their "control" and "care", with her exaggerated sexuality subjected to their disciplining gaze.

The fact that no Tomb Raider game envisages multi-player or Internet play options contributes to a closer relationship between the player and the videogame protagonist, with resemblances to real-life "romantic" liaisons. The feeling of "closeness" is reinforced through the narrative structure of Tomb Raider games: at the beginning of each game, the player is invited for a game-play training session to Lara's family mansion, where s/he has access to the heroine's most private space – a privilege usually granted in real life only to close family members, lovers and intimate friends.

Contributions by female participants to an Internet forum on Tomb Raider[2] indicate that women's experiences of the game are quite different from men's and that the empowerment activated by game-play is strongly influenced by different gamers experience and enactment of gender codes. It involves experimentation with and testing of these codes reminiscent of the widespread gender swapping practices in the virtual worlds of Multi-User Dungeons (MUDs).[3] By and large, women enjoy "being" Lara, rather than controlling her. According to one female gamer, Lara is "everything a bloke wants and everything a girl wants to be"; for others, she is a role model, symbolizing "adventure, independence, possibility and strength". One enthusiastic woman gamer admits: "Heck, I imagine I AM [sic] Lara when I'm playing, I know some might say "come on, it's only pixels" but what Lara and her environment is made of is irrelevant in my eyes."

Lara was originally conceived by Englishman Toby Gard: another female "creation" by a male "creator" in a long series of patriarchal representations of women, epitomized in the western tradition by the story of Pygmalion in Ovid's Metamorphoses (X 243-298). Grad's original description of his creation included elements of an intentionally ironic masculinist imaginary, such as "Lara likes to work with underprivileged children and the mentally disabled. She has a degree in needlework [...]" (Pretzsch 2000) A twenty-something year old familiar with products of a globalized popular culture, Gard went on to imbue his vision with elements of such iconic creations as Indiana Jones and James Bond. According to media reports, Gard had consciously resisted fitting his heroine out with "spangly thongs and metal bras so popular with digital women", because he felt that she "had more dignity" (Jones 2001).

Soon after the release of Tomb Raider I, Toby Gard left Core to found his own company, Confounding Factor, purportedly because he wanted to "have greater control over the new characters and games [he] wanted to design" (Gibbon 2001). He described his distancing from his mind-child as "similar to losing a love", since "you're not really allowed to go near her"(Snider2001). Since then, Core and Eidos have avoided naming a single person as Lara`s creator and have consistently emphasized a collective authorship of the game, reinforced by Eidos/Core franchise ownership.

After Gards departure from Core, i.e. in the sequels to the original game, both Lara's aggression and sex appeal were on the steady increase, effectively blending a death wish with the pleasure principle and thus digging deeply into the essence of the Freudian Id. In an editorial review at WomenGamers.Com, we read that [in] Tomb Raider II and III, Lara became an obnoxious sex object, more intent on stealing the hearts of men than relating to her female following. Her physique became more and more unrealistic as the series progressed. Her attitude became more deliberately sexual as well (Lara Croft Tomb Raider Series 2001).

Lara's transformation is emblematic of the impossibility of "ownership" of products of popular culture in our media-saturated world. Her estrangement from her original creator(s)/owner(s) can be observed at two levels: at one level, the embryonic Lara "betrays" Toby Gard by developing into a consumer product "owned" by Core and Eidos; at the other, Lara is reconceptualized through media manipulations which by nature cannot be

Tomb Raider (Simon West, 2001), Paramount.

controlled by either of her creator(s)/owner(s). The first "betrayal" involves moulding of the character by the Core design team, to simultaneously anticipate and reproduce the demands of the market.

This type of "betrayal" has been common in cultural production for centuries, but with the advent of new technologies it has assumed a new dimension. In the past, products of the so-called "high culture" were likely to be consciously shaped by their authors with reference to the tastes and desires of influential patrons instrumental in supporting the production stage and/or facilitating the circulation of the final product. By contrast, works pertaining to popular culture often cannot be attributed to a single author and their ever-changing individual re-enactments reflect the artist/performer"s expectations of her/his temporary audience (Lord, 1960). The new technologies of computer-mediated communication have refashioned the circulation of popular culture mainly by undermining the possibility of "fixing" the audience and thus anticipating their likes and dislikes, as well as their cultural knowledge, experience or skills which would equip them to fully appreciate a given product.

Lara as an Empty Sign

To appeal to an essentially unpredictable global market, Lara had to be conceived as an "empty sign", which would allow diverse, often contradictory inscriptions and interpretations. To quote Lara's cinematic avatar Angelina Jolie, Lara is "a bit of everything. She's like every kind of sexy Italian actress I've ever watched, and yet she's also that guy in Crocodile Hunter in Australia – completely in love with danger" (Kolmos 2001:105). In fact, the only "inscription" undertaken and proliferated by Core Design and Eidos Interactive is the one understood unmistakably to signify power. The heroine's constructed identity is no more than an amalgam of values representing all the different faces of empowerment in advanced capitalist societies: class, wealth, appearance, physical fitness, strong will, independence and intelligence.

Lara is confident, self-reliant and, most importantly, she is a loner. Loneliness penetrates the ever-changing layers of Lara's virtual and fluid biography, which for example states that the heroine "prefers non-team sports, such as rock climbing, extreme skiing and marksmanship" and emphasizes her single marital status (Pretzsch 2000). Relating more specifically to gender, this loneliness can be interpreted as female independence. A (female) participant in the WomenGamers Discussion Forum emphasizes this aspect of Lara's character: "I like the fact that she's a loner. She doesn't rely upon any male character to lead her around, or to rescue her if she were to break a nail." In the game, Lara acts alone and all the other human characters are her opponents.[4] In the film, she has allies, from the ethereal presence of her father Lord Henshingly Croft (played by Jon Voight) to her butler Hillary (Chris Barrie) and a resident computer whiz, Bryce (Noah Taylor). There is also her former boyfriend and now rival in the quest, Alex Cross (Daniel Craig) and a treacherous scholarly colleague of Lord Henshingly's. Reviewers have noted that ironically, Lara's personality "had more depth when she was computer-generated and on her own" (Banshee 2001). Lara's "loneliness" is forsaken in the comic-strip medium as well, where her allies are often women as independent and intelligent as she is.[5] In fact, there were great expectations of the latest Tomb Raider game title, *The Angel of Darkness*, which introduced a new male character, Kurtis Trent, who is controlled by players just like Lara. Anticipating the new game, Lara's aficionados expressed hostility to (jealousy of?) the new male character: "he better not take over too much of the game, cause I need to spend some quality time with Lara, as I haven't talked with her in ages"; or "I hate to control a male in Tomb Raider. Tomb Raider is the world of Lara!"[6]

Lara is comfortable with ambiguities and contradictions – they are in fact the very "material" she is made of.[7] The values of an idealized world of security and tradition are brought in by means of Lara's constructed biography, well known to the faithful, which was conspicuously created in response to public demand only after the first game was finished. Lara Croft is a member of British aristocracy, a graduate of Gordonstoun, Prince Charles "alma mater, with a mission to "[prepare] students for a full and active role as international citizens in a changing world"[8]. Following a plane crash in the Himalayas, where she is the only survivor and struggles for two weeks to stay alive in the wilderness, Lara renounces the safety of her former *modus vivendi* in favour of a life of uncertainty and adventure. Despite this rupture, she remains branded by the world she originates from, through her polished British accent, tea-drinking habit and – when considered appropriate – through her complete mastery of what may be considered a "refined" social behaviour.

Lara thus brings together the aspirations of modernism – the imperialist pursuit of power and global prestige – and their postmodern problematization and fragmentation. Paradoxically, she critiques neo-imperialism by enacting her own complicity with it. The element of "critique", however, may be promoted or indeed entirely overlooked in individual readings. Lara's appeal, as well as that of other virtual characters created for a global market, rests on this multivocality, parodic potential and a capacity for endless contextualization. In fact, each contextualization by definition reduces the multivocality and jeopardizes the characters universal, i.e. globally marketable appeal. This is particularly evident when the characters are contextualized in environments and the media other than the virtual environment of the videogame medium they originated from. Lara's appearance in advertising[9] and film[10] has by necessity "betrayed" some of the heroine's virtual possibilities by fixing her according to the imperatives of the medium and the genre. The same is true for her trans-contextualizations in comic strip,[11] music[12] and narrative fiction.[13]

In the mythology surrounding Lara Croft, there is hardly a hint of the notion of moral responsibility, but while the earlier game titles focused on violence in the service of adventure and self-defence, the latest release, *The Angel of Darkness*, aims at bringing forth Lara's true "dark side". The rejection of moral responsibility goes hand in hand with the overall abandonment of faith in a "universal truth" motivating moral choices, characteristic of postmodernism.

Laras Body-Image

The principle of multivocality also underlies the visual/graphic representation of Lara Croft. Her facial features and skin colour are fairly non-descript and invite diverse readings; her exaggerated body ironically "compensates" for her non-corporeality. Overstated muscles for males and Barbie-like proportions for females are a commonplace in the videogame genre. With Lara's extravagant curves in full view, gamers can indulge in sexual fantasies, manipulating camera angles to focus on the most prominent bodily parts.

Lara's physique is objectionable to some feminists as yet another bid to impose impossible demands on women's bodies. Within this line of argument, images of women of Barbie-like proportions are intolerable, as they cause men to objectify women, and contribute to the lack of female self-esteem that leads to depression, eating disorders, and the operating table (Fazzone 2001). For other feminists, however, Lara is a model to emulate, her body symbolizing power and self-control. Like Barbie, she may be interpreted as signifying "a rebellious manifestation of willpower, a visual denial of the maternal ideal symbolized by pendulous breasts", with her impenetrable body of "hard edges [and] distinct borders" (Urla and Swedlund, 1998: 420). Moreover, while Barbie is conceived to use her body mainly to please her male admirers (as evidenced by her interest in make-up, clothes, shopping and dating), Lara uses hers to explore and fight.

More importantly, claims that Lara's sexuality is submitted exclusively to the male gaze may be read as heteronormative and rooted in victim rhetoric. It is indeed just as possible to interpret Lara as a vehicle for the queer female gaze – a theme explored in some of the game patches described in the following section of the paper. It is also unlikely that anyone would expect women to emulate Lara Croft's body-image, with her wombless torso and huge breasts, "just as we never expected anyone to climb walls like Spider-Man or have supersonic hearing like the Bionic Woman" (Fazzone 2001). Thus Lara Croft could help us admit that real-life models, emulated by women at irreparable cost are as unreal as she herself is. According to Fazzone`s optimistic vision, "with that admission might come a more natural definition of what's sexy, by which the genuine confluence of health and DNA is deemed preferable to the handiwork of a Photoshop virtuoso" (Fazzone 2001).

As noted earlier, Lara Croft's separation from her original creator(s) occurs at two levels: one, described above, is conservative, normative and market-driven; the other, more provocative and subversive, happens in the indomitable sphere of cyberspace, driven by online game hacking culture. Patch distribution is a widespread activity in the gaming community, which offers alternative versions of game plots and characters, engendering transformations at the borders of official game genres. Hackers alter the original source code from a game engine to modify game structure, characters appearance and game play itself. By far the most popular unofficial interventions in the Tomb Raider source code are related to the heroine's sexuality and enactment of gender. The fact that this aspect of Lara's virtual identity is also left ambiguous – i.e., there have been no clear "hints" in the games pointing to the heroine's hetero- or homosexuality – has intrigued the participants in Tomb Raider fan forums, who speculate on her "gayness", "straightness", relationships, attitudes to marriage, maternal instincts: "She's a good girl who wants a husband and babies"; or, "there is much about her that is consistent with a sapphic orientation, and nothing that rules it out"; or, "when Lara retires, I think she'll be an incredible wife, sitting near a fireplace telling her children about her adventures – while her husband is washing the dishes".[14] Similar speculations often inform Tomb Raider fan fiction and artworks, where fans reproduce their own ideas on sexuality and gender.

The most widespread patches exploiting Lara's ambiguous sexuality are the so-called "Nude Raider" patches, which replace Lara's already scanty clothes with nude skin textures.[15] The more straitlaced among Lara's aficionados oppose this disrobing trend and display "Nude Raider Free" banners on their Internet sites. Other interventions, such as Robert Nideffer`s Duchampian[16] manipulations of the original Nude Raider patches, represent Lara as transsexual or butch lesbian. As an empty sign, Lara is the ideal gender-bender for the hacking community and cyberspace critics interpret this as her primary subversive potential:

Virtually Anything

From Lara as female automaton, Lara as drag queen, Lara as dominatrix, Lara as girl power role model, to Lara as queer babe with a shotgun, and from the gaps in between, a new range of subject positions will emerge in online game hacking culture that challenge given gender categories and adapt them to the diverse gender sensibilities of men, women and others (Schleiner 2001).

A subversive manipulation of Lara Croft with a specifically feminist bent was staged by a group of participants in the International Women's University (ifu) in Hannover in August 2000, within the project entitled "Reconstructing Gender". They chose Lara for their performance, because they were attracted by her virtuality and multivocality.

Since she is virtual she could be anything – but she is limited to heroine and sex-symbol; she could be fluid and challenge existing borders – instead she reinforces them; she could subvert traditional meanings and meaning-making – instead she is represented to us in the most traditional contexts; she could be used to explore the implications of postmodernism, of new technologies, of changes in society – both the chances and the threats – instead she is used to try and convince us that in spite of all the changes thing will essentially remain the same.[17]

The group involved in this project kidnapped a cardboard Lara Croft figure out of a MacShop in Hamburg. The women then dressed the cardboard Lara in traditional costumes from different cultures and staged her in contexts she is not normally associated with – for example, as pregnant, or, in the toilet. Finally, they decorated the effigy with 250 URLs related to feminism and returned her to her original "abode", the MacShop.

We have seen how Lara Croft – initially an "empty sign" – has been inscribed with meaning in numerous trans/contextualizations. Her formidable body is itself a parody, simultaneously enacting and denying female oppression and thus offering the possibility of "exorcizing personal ghosts – or, rather, enlisting them in their own cause" (Hutcheon 1985:. 35). It can be "kidnapped" and used for political purposes, feminist and otherwise. But, the relevance – and especially the political relevance – of Lara's parodic potential will always be controversial, since her circulation in cyberspace is impossible to control and the user's capacity for "decoding", which fully depends on her/his cultural knowledge, cannot be assumed.

Notes

1. Since Tomb Raider is both a 'computer game' and a 'videogame' (PlayStation, Sega Saturn and Game Boy), the two terms will be used interchangeably in this paper.
2. Eidos' official web site, http://www.eidosgames.com/ubb/Forum22/HTML/034058.html.
3. According to Turkle, people use gender swapping as a 'first-hand experience through which to form ideas about the role of gender in human interactions' (Turkle 1996:362). Players become conscious of social practices related to gender that they tend not to notice in real life: as female characters, male MUDers are sometimes surprised to find themselves 'besieged with attention, sexual advances, and unrequested offers of assistance which imply that women can't do things by themselves' (Turkle 1996:362-3).
4. In the first Tomb Raider game, Lara's opponents were mostly animals; the number of human adversaries has been gradually increasing in the sequels.
5. For example, archaeologist Vanessa Fenway (Jurgens, 1999-2000).
6. http://www.eidosgames.com/ubb/Forum22/HTML/034613.html (May 2002).
7. Even her date of birth – 14th February 1968 – brings together the numbers commonly associated with such mutually 'irreconcilable' concepts as 'love' (14th February – Valentine's Day) and 'dissent' (1968, the year of revolts).
8. Gordonstoun Mission Statement from http://www.gordonstoun.org.uk.
9. In an aggressive marketing campaign, Lara's debut on the computer screen was soon followed by mass production of a wide variety of merchandise for the ever-growing hordes of her aficionados: from action figures to paint-it-yourself resin statues, from screen savers to clothing. It has been noted that the images of Lara featuring on a majority of these products depict the heroine as a sex object and that the products themselves – for example T shirts, which are only available in sizes XL and XXL – are obviously aimed at a male consumer: 'There is no imagery inviting a woman's gaze or trying to establish a bond between Lara and a female viewer. Most representations seem to completely ignore women

as potential viewers.' (Pretzsch 2000). The same study also identifies this bias towards male viewers in advertisements for Tomb Raider games, as well as some other unrelated products – such as Seat cars and Lucozade soft drinks – where Lara is used in the advertising campaign. Moreover, the tensions between seemingly contradictory aspects of Lara's personality – aggression, sex appeal, speed, loneliness, intelligence etc. – tend to be resolved in favour of the features considered compatible with the advertised product. Advertisements for Seat cars thus capitalize on the concept of speed. We are also reminded that the car industry has in the past extensively used images of sexy women to promote the concept of success 'promised' to potential buyers.

10. Tomb Raider is not the first videogame to cross the boundary from the computer to the cinematic screen – suffice it to mention Super Mario Bros. with Bob Hoskins and Dennis Hopper, and it becomes clear that the crossing is not an easy one. Reviews of *Lara Croft: Tomb Raider* (2001) have been largely negative, mainly focusing on the unconvincing and contrived plot, as well as a rather superficial portrayal of main characters. The film's shortcomings can also be interpreted in terms of the argument outlined above: for the film version, the unresolved tensions and contradictions cohabiting in the virtual medium had to be resolved in favour of 'privileged' interpretations. As a consequence, Lara's exploratory spirit, her intelligence, panache and a certain humour are hardly noticeable in the film.

11. Lara's entry into the comic medium dates back to 1997, when Michael Turner included her for the first time in an episode of his widely popular *Witchblade* series. Rather than as a mere subordinate to the heroine, New York policewoman and Sandra Bullock lookalike Sara Pezzini, Lara featured as her equal partner in stopping a bloody vendetta. Other episodes followed, with the two sexy women joining forces to exhibit their formidable bodies and fighting power. Since late 1999, Eidos has published a series of comics, written by Dan Jurgens, in which Lara appears as the main character. The comic genre abounds in strong self-reliant females – from Modesty Blaise, Superwoman, Wonderwoman and Darkchylde, to Catwoman, Elektra, Glory and Tank Girl.

12. Lara's ironic and ultimately subversive aspects have up to date only been discerned and put to good use in the music scene, by the German punk rock band Die Ärzte and the Irish pop band U2. The former use Lara in a video-clip for a song satirizing the macho stereotype, entitled *Ein Schwein namens Männer*. Lara is shown in a gunfight with the three members of the band – a fight she herself initiated and which she leaves victorious. The three men seem unimpressed by Lara's body and engage in a serious fight with her, but they cannot match her wits and dexterity. The latter, U2, featured Lara on a large video screen during their PopMart tour in 1997-98, to accompany the song 'Hold Me, Kill Me, Kiss Me, Thrill Me' from the soundtrack of the film Batman Forever. Lara's screen appearance reinforces the theme of the song: shown in the beginning as loving and shy, she then quickly disappears on her motorbike, only to return with a gun and aim it at Bono, the lead singer.

13. David Stern's novel *Lara Croft: Tomb Raider* (2001), based on the screenplay for the film, suffers from very much the same maladies as the film itself: the ambiguities of the heroine are resolved in an unconvincing, dull way; the potential for ironic critique is left unexplored and even the action itself is paralyzed through uninspired narration.

14. http://www.eidosgames.com/ubb/Forum22/HTML/032935.html. (May 2001)

15. There have been rumours that these patches were originally launched by Eidos itself, in an attempt to boost the publicity of Tomb Raider Games. Whatever the origin of the patches, it is true that – despite a clear increase in sexual overtones with each new title in the Tomb Raider series and a decidedly suggestive marketing campaign – Core and Eidos have characteristically avoided nudity and pornographic innuendoes, and thus managed to keep the game's rating at PG-13.

16. Nideffer's patches are reminiscent of Marcel Duchamp's well known parodic addition of a moustache and a goatee on a reproduction of Leonardo's Mona Lisa, entitled L.H.O.O.Q. ('Elle a chaud au cul', or 'She has a hot ass').

17. http://www.vifu.de/students/ (May 2002).

References

Bailey, C. (1997). Making waves and drawing lines: the politics of defining the vicissitudes of feminism. *Hypatia*, 12.3, 17-28.

Banshee (2001). Tomb Raider: the movie review. Retrieved June 15, 2002, from http://www.womengamers.com/articles/trmovie.html.

Butler, J. (1990). *Gender Trouble: Feminism and the subversion of identity*. New York: Routledge.

Denfeld, R. (1995). *The new Victorians: A young woman's challenge to the old feminist order*. New York: Warner Books.

Fazzone, A. (2001). Washington Diarist: game over. *The New Republic*, July 2, 42.

Gard, T. (1997). Interview for *The Face* magazine. Retrieved June 1, 2002, from http://www.cubeit.com/ctimes/ news0007a.html.

Gibbon, D. (2001). "The Man Who Made Lara". *BBC News Online*, June 28, 2001. Retrieved June 1, 2002, from http://news.bbc.co.uk/hi/english/entertainment/new_media/newsid_1410000/1410480.stm.

Greer, G. (1999). *The whole woman*. New York: Doubleday.

Hawthorne, S. (1999). Cyborgs, virtual bodies and organic bodies: theoretical feminist responses. In S. Hawthorne & R. Klein (Eds.), *Cyberfeminism: Connectivity, critique and creativity* (pp. 213-49). Melbourne: Spinifex.

Hutcheon, L. (1985). *A theory of parody: The teachings of twentieth-century art forms*. New York and London: Methuen.

Jones, C. (2001). Lara Croft: fantasy games mistress. *BBC News Online*, July 6, 2001). Retrieved June 2, 2002, from http://news.bbc.co.uk/hi/english/uk/newsid_1425000/1425762.stm.

Jurgens, D. (1999-2000). *Tomb Raider the series*. Santa Monica, CA: Top Cow Comics and Eidos Interactive.

Kafai, Y. (1996). Gender differences in children's construction of video games. In P.M. Greenfield & R.R. Cocking (Eds.), *Interacting with video* (pp. 39-66). Norwood, N.J.: Ablex Publishing.

Kolmos, K.M. (2001). *Tomb Raider the book: Prima's official strategy guide*. Roseville: Prima Games.

Lara Croft Tomb Raider Series (2001). *WomenGamers.Com*. Retrieved June 14, 2002, from http://www.women gamers.com/dw/lara.html.

Lord, A.B. (1960). *The singer of tales*. Cambridge: Harvard University Press.

Lumby, C. (1997). *Bad girls: the media, sex and feminism in the '90s*. Sydney: Allen & Unwin.

Mayfield, K. (2000). A pretty face is not enough. *Wired News*, December 18, 2000. Retrieved June 6, 2002, from http://wired.com/news/print/0,1294,40478,00.html.

Olafson, P. (1997). Dance to this tomb: Tomb Raider is novel and gorgeous, March 15, 1997. *Computer Gaming World*, 100-101.

Ovid (1980). *Metamorphoses,* trans. A. E. Watts. San Francisco: North Point Press.

Pretzsch, B. (2000). A postmodern analysis of Lara Croft: body, identity, reality. Retrieved May 10, 2002, from http://www.frauenuni.de/students/gendering/lara/LaraCompleteText WOPics.html.

Roiphe, K. (1993). *The morning after: Sex, fear, and feminism*. Boston: Little, Brown.

Schleiner, A. (2001). Does Lara Croft wear fake polygons? *Leonardo* 34, 3, 221-226.

Snider, M. (2001). Tomb creator saw no profits, but has new game. *USA Today*, June 18, 2001. Retrieved May 10, 2002, from http://www.usatoday.com/life/enter/movies/2001-06-18-tomb-raider-creator.htm.

Stern, D. (2001). *Lara Croft: Tomb Raider*. New York and London: Simon & Schuster.

Turkle, S. (1996). Constructions and reconstructions of the self in virtual reality. In T. Druckrey (Ed.) *Electronic Culture: Technology and Visual Representation* (pp. 354-65). New York: Aperture.

Turner, M. (1997/8). *Witchblade/Tomb Raider Special 1*. Santa Monica: Top Cow Comics and Eidos Interactive.

Turner, M. (1999). *Witchblade/Tomb Raider 1-2*. Santa Monica: Top Cow Comics and Eidos Interactive.

Urla, J. & Swedlund, A.C. (2000). The anthropometry of Barbie: Unsettling ideals of the feminine body in popular culture. In L. Schiebinger (Ed.), *Feminism and the Body* (pp. 397-428). Oxford: Oxford UP.

Watch out, Indiana, here comes Lara Croft (2001, March 26). *Time*. 157.12: 66-67.

Wolf, N. (1993). *Fire with fire: The new female power and how it will change the twenty-first century*. New York: Random House.

WomenGamers.Com Discussion Forum (1999). Retrieved May 2, 2002, from http://forums.womengamers.com.

Wright, K. (2000). GDC 2000: Race and gender in games. *WomenGamers.Com*. Retrieved May 2, 2002, from http://www.womengamers.com/articles/racegender.html.

Run, Lara, Run!

The Impact of Computer Games on Cinema's Action Heroine

Kim Walden

It has been asserted that when new media technologies emerge established ones look for ways to compete and maintain their position within the media landscape. One of the ways they do this is by appropriating features of the new media and thereby renewing themselves – this has been termed 'remediation' (Bolter and Grusin 1999). So today we see radio programmes with on-line discussion boards enabling audiences to 'join in', and on-line VCR-style 'replay' facilities as part of their programme service. Similarly TV News programmes incorporate textual by-lines, graphics, Computer Generated Images (CGI) animations as well as stills and 'live' feeds in on-screen windows giving the programme both the look and feel of a web page (Bolter and Grusin 1999).

To gain a clearer picture of the relationship between old and new media, it is necessary to look at the degree of remediation in operation between them at a given time. There is a currently a burgeoning dialogue between video games and films. The acquisition of film licenses by video games companies has become standard practice with movie tie-in games such as Activision's *Spiderman* and Game Boy's *Star Wars Episode II: Attack of the Clones* forming a major plank in the brand's merchandising portfolio. From the early days games designers freely adopted styles and language from popular cinema such as the set piece car chases and spaceship dog fights, to the extent that games became known as "interactive films". Nowadays games are routinely designed in conjunction with film production. Electronic Arts' game version of Peter Jackson's second film in *The Lord of the Rings*-trilogy, *The Two Towers*, promotes itself as adding "authenticity" to the cinematic experience, integrating cinema and game play with level environments appropriated from the big screen as well as sound effects, actor voice-overs and the original academy award winning film score. Clearly remediation works both ways.

Remediation underlines the material nature of the media as each emerging form has to find its economic feet in the market place by supplementing or replacing what is already available. Certainly the competition for film by video games is real enough. Sales indicate that computer and video gaming is the fastest growing entertainment sector worth £1.6 billion in the UK alone (*Game On*, 2002) With games consoles retailing at a fraction of the price of multimedia computers and games providing excellent entertainment hours value-for-money, it is of no surprise that Britons now spend more on games than on videos and cinema visits (Entertainment and Leisure Software Publishers Association, 2002).

So what are the aesthetic consequences of this? What exactly is the nature of the aesthetic dialogue between video games and film? In order to address these questions this article will consider two films whose heroines share a common relationship with videogames. The first, *Lola Rennt* (1999) (English title *Run Lola Run*) directed by the young Berlin-based film director Tom Tykwer, has a narrative framework constructed in the shape of a video game, while the other, *Lara Croft: Tomb Raider* (2001) directed by Simon West, is a feature film based on the eponymous video game franchise with Angelina Jolie in the title role. Through an examination of these two heroines we can start to consider what the cinematic heroine has learnt from her game sister and what the game sister has borrowed from her cinematic counterpart.

Remediations between games and cinema are not a new phenomenon. Twenty years ago Disney's *Tron* (1982) directed by Steven Lisberger told the story of Flynn, a computer programmer who enters the company computer system in order to prove that his boss is a crook. He soon finds himself at the mercy of a malevolent mainframe called the Master Control Programme and is forced to play games on the grid to survive. The film's highlight were the 'light cycle' races in which game-style episodes were created with a combination of early CGI and back lit animation to provide the look and feel of an arcade game. The film was not a box office success, but it was subsequently turned into an arcade game. Since then arcade games have moved into the living room with the advent of small but powerful games console technologies and their popularity is reflected in a steady stream of 'video game' films including *Super Mario Brothers* (1993), *Mortal Kombat* (1995), *Wing Commander* (1999), and most recently *Lara Croft: Tomb Raider* (2001), *Final Fantasy: The Spirits Within* (2001) and *Resident Evil* (2002).

Tron is something of a period piece now reflecting the gendered nature of gaming in the early 1980s with all the main 'gamer' characters being male (Skirrow 1986). The first generation of female game characters were narratively marginal to game play functioning primarily as 'window dressing' or as prizes in games. However in the last ten years the changing location of gaming has been accompanied by a changing demography of players. Growing enthusiasm for games amongst girls has been mirrored in the increasingly prominent roles of female characters in games: Tina in *Dead or Alive*, SCEE, Xiaoyu in *Tekken 3*, Aki Ross in *Final Fantasy* and, most popular of all, Lara Croft star of the *Tomb Raider* providing new manifestations of the action heroine.

The Narrative Structure of *Lara Croft: Tomb Raider*

As a subgenre video game films have been critically ignored – dismissed as brand spin offs only interesting to computer game fans. However on closer scrutiny it becomes clear that films like *Lara Croft: Tomb Raider* do not simply appropriate videogame characters and storylines but have absorbed some aspects of game narrative structuring and modes of address as well.

One of the most distinctive features of videogame narrative is its temporal organisation. In his analysis of video games, Steven Poole adopts the cinematic concept of the "back story" known as the *diachronic* story which tells what happens in the past and crucially sets up the conditions for the present. Whilst the *synchronic* story takes place in the present and constitutes the action which we watch unfold (Poole 2000). Computer games are heavily weighted towards the synchronic story but as they reward repeat viewing, the synchronic action doesn't tell a compelling story.

Lara Croft: Tomb Raider is structured as a race against time recalling the media's arcade game origins. The film's 'Kubrick's *2001*-style' shots of the planets in space moving inexorably towards their alignment punctuate the story at regular intervals like some kind of galactic time piece to remind us of the story's timeframe. Whilst the back story of *Lara Croft: Tomb Raider* consists of an elaborate scenario about a secret society called the "Illuminati" whose ambition is to locate the two halves of an ancient icon forged from meteorite material which fell to earth at the exact moment of the last planetary alignment. This ancient icon bestows power over time itself on the owner and it is this power which the Illuminati seek. It is the task of the archaeologists to locate it in time for the next planetary alignment. The story's rationale is loose and the logic of this scenario is never tied down but it provides the back story to what will take place in the present tense of the film, narrated in a letter from her father and dispatched in an elaborate but brief CGI episode at the beginning of the film.

By contrast with the epic proportions of the diachronic story, the synchronic story which forms the film's present tense is narratively slight. The pleasure of games narratives is essentially experiential and lies in the present tense and this is a quality which cinema seeks to mimic in its own way. Basically the synchronic story consists of a race and puzzle game formula clearly motivated by simple objectives – Lara is presented with a series of challenges which she must solve to move the story on towards its ultimate goal.

New media theorist, Lev Manovich, argues that games are one cultural form which require algorithmic-like behaviours. Videogames are experienced by their players as narratives principally through the fact that the player is set a clearly defined task whether it is to achieve the highest score possible, complete all levels or win the match. From mad dogs to secret doors, all narrative elements encountered by the player take her closer or further away from reaching these objectives. The reason why the narrative appears rather slight is that it is little more than a disguise overlaying the fundamental structuring of the game which is a simple algorithm. The narrative is driven by the logic of the algorithm, which has to be executed into complete it.

However the film does not simply mimic the narrative syntax of the video game, it strives explicitly to rival the new media through what cinema has always done best – the big screen spectacle. Film competes with games by generating huge action episodes designed to be played out on the big screen. Game levels are transformed into genuine locations for spectacular stunts, special effects performed by screen stars to the accompaniment of a compilation of contemporary musical hits on the soundtrack. These episodes are extended disproportionately to their narrative function for the sake of spectacular pleasures they afford their audience. Much like the choreographed song and dance interludes in Hollywood musicals and they draw attention to the difference in scale between small screen and big screen.

Conventionally the film's realist aesthetic draws the audience into the story and its construction is thus effaced; Bolter and Grusin characterise this as *immediacy*. However, when the film breaks into a spectacular episode our attention is drawn to cinema's capacity to generate its own unique audience pleasure. These spectacular episodes are excessive to the sparse needs of the algorithmic narrative and constitute a *hypermediacy* which breaks with the realist mode of story telling. The oscillation between these two cinematic modes of immediacy and hypermediacy is a dynamic which characterises the video game film's narrative as it seeks to rival its original.

The film's mode of address acknowledges its gaming origins and the viewers' familiarity with the *Tomb Raider* game series. From the outset the cinematic Lara is closely aligned with her pixellated sister. The audience's view of Lara is frequently mediated by screens to simulate game play. During the invasion of Croft Manor Lara fights off the intruders by instructing her techie side kick Bryce to be her 'eyes'. Using a CCTV monitor and mobile telephone she appears on his monitor like a game avatar and he becomes the game player. Bryce coordinates her actions via the screen and when she hits her target, he shouts "Bingo!" mimicking game player reactions. The fast tempo of musical soundtrack generates dramatic tension with surround sound audio technology immersing the film viewer in the action – to engender the sense of 'being there' – to rival the video game.

In keeping with the gaming origins of the film, this heroine's objective is not determined by free will but by her dead father played by Angelina Jolie's real life father Jon Voight. Like the game player, Lara's father serves largely as an off-screen presence guiding Lara's adventures. The only times he appears in person is in dream sequences and once at the end of the film when the dimension of time opens up at the moment of alignment. His controlling hand is nevertheless manifest in the story in two ways – through flash backs and through the spirit-like small girls who appear to Lara at various points in the quest to remind Lara (and us) that she is not alone. In the end despite all the trappings of a strong heroine, Lara's purpose here is to enact her father's will, completing his work by finding and destroying both halves of the triangle and so thwarting the ambitions of the Illuminati. In other words her father is the 'game player' directing her actions and she is the 'played'.

Clearly, Hollywood has appropriated more than just the video game storyline here. A closer look reveals that the narrative strategies – a kind of video game 'vernacular' has infused the medium of film as cinema acknowledges the power of the videogame to engage audiences in new ways, but at the same time the oscillation between immediacy and hypermediacy indicates a rivalry and revision of the medium as film asserts its ability to thrill audiences too.

The Narrative Structure of *Lola Rennt*

When we view a film in the theatrical setting of the cinema, the narrative is played in a fixed sequence over which the viewer has no control whereas in a video game the player has more freedom to determine the path of events as she goes. So games have no predetermined story in the conventional sense, there are only readings or versions played out by the viewer/player (Bolter 1991). Given this distinction it is interesting to consider the German film *Lola Rennt* (1999, English title *Run Lola Run*) which has a narrative form more in common with a video game than the linearity of a feature film. In the space of eighty odd minutes three versions of the same story are told with three different outcomes. The film's tripartite plot is best characterised as what Janet Murray calls a "multiform narrative" – that is to say a narrative that presents "a single situation of a plotline in multiple versions that would be mutually exclusive in our ordinary experience" (Murray 1999).

This structure draws attention to one of the most recognisable qualities of video game narratives – the replay facility. Narrative cinema has tended to avoid repetition which has been relegated to the marginal realms of the animated cartoon, instructional films and peep shows (Manovich 2001). This repetition or looping reveals the traces of early video games technology which experienced storage limitations. Since it was not practical to animate every character in real time, designers tended to rely heavily on stored loops of character' motions that could be recalled at times in the game (Manovich 2001). This technical constraint has played a part in shaping the development of the video game narrative and can still be seen in today's game formats. In *Lola Rennt* German director Tom Tykwer appropriates this format to tell the story in a full-length feature film.

The three versions of the story are repeated as if each telling is a replay in a videogame. The main character encounters a series of people and obstacles in slightly different configurations each time. At the end of each version Lola game-overs and by the last story she has learnt from her experiences in preceding versions and deals with the obstacles she encounters. As in game play the possible outcomes depend entirely on the performance of the player. So for example in story one Lola runs down the apartment stairwell past a menacing lad with a snarling dog. In story two the lad extends his foot and trips her up causing her to tumble down the stairs hurting herself. It's only by story three that Lola anticipates this obstacle and takes avoiding action by leaping over the dog and growling back at the hound.

As in other Tykwer films where spatiality plays an important determinant in shaping the relationships between characters in the film, in *Lola Rennt* game play provides the structuring presence[1].The two dimensional space of the film (videogame) screen is experienced as text rather than context. The space in which this narrative is played out is an urban locality but not a specific city locale. A familiar eye will recognise Berlin but Lola's Berlin does not correspond with the real city. The route Lola takes does not correspond with any real route you can follow through the city. The story does not seek to localise the space but rather to configure the space in game terms as knowable – comprehensible. In each of the three versions of the story we see Lola run across a square in three ways from three different perspectives. Only in the last version does the camera reveal the place showing recognisable landmark buildings. What is crucial here is not the specificity of the locality but that the space is comprehensible at speed – entrances and exists can be recognised – that the gamer can traverse the space.

Instead of the classic filmic linear narrative model in which the course of the story is said to reflect the chronology of human life, here the narrative experience of video game play is represented in the metaphor of a spiral, which is inscribed into the composition of the film. The spiral narrative model illustrates how the (game) characters go round the loop gaining knowledge and expertise, as they get closer to their quest. Just like a spiral the plot of *Lola Rennt* appears to loop back on itself through the repetition of the story but in actual fact it never forms a perfect loop but starts a new one and linear progression is achieved in the end. The spiral trope permeates the film in many ways – the motorised white whirling spiral above the pharmacy on the cross roads behind the phone booth where Lola's boyfriend Manni spends much of his time in the stories, on the lover's pillow and in the spiralling camera work in the animated credit sequence.

Like *Lara Croft: Tomb Raider*, the temporal organisation of the story reflects the prevailing narrative structure of the video game with the diachronic story set out at the start of the film and the synchronic story serving simply to resolve the dilemmas of the back story. The diachronic section of the narrative opens with the phone call from Manni to tell Lola of his predicament. In black and white flashback Manni's voice over relays the events leading up to his phone call to Lola. Manni works for a black market car dealer and was supposed to have collected a large amount of cash and couriered it to his boss, Ronnie. However Lola was late picking Manni up on her scooter and so he takes the subway and forgets the money on the train. He has twenty minutes before he is to meet Ronnie and if he can't replace the 100.000 marks his boss will kill him. The black and white film's diachronic section is clearly distinguished from the rest of the story denoting the past whilst the synchronic story of what happens next denotes the present and is told in colour. Within the film the story's structure is gendered too in that the diachronic story belongs to the male character and the synchronic story belongs to our action heroine, Lola, who must act to solve the narrative's central dilemma: How to find 100.000 marks in twenty minutes?

In another parallel with video games, characterisation is slight and the emphasis is on plot. In this sense, as Poole notes, video game stories are more like folktales than novels. A point underlined by the choice of Hans Paetsch voiceing over the film's prologue , an actor whose voice is well known to a German audience and is synonymous with fairly tale narration. In his study of folktales Russian theorist Vladimir Propp discovered that stories are made up of a series of simple narrative functions and stock character types (Propp 1968). A Proppian analysis of the film's characterisation reveals a palette of stock character types. No time for realistic, psychologically rounded characters here. Lola's boyfriend Manni is ostensibly the hero – a point rein-forced by the casting of well known German heart throb Moritz Bliebtreu in the role , while Lola is clearly the princess figure as Manni's girlfriend whose quest is to save her love. Indeed, the script alludes to Lola as the princess.[2] But it is only when the synchronic story commences that the film inverts these character types. The hero is paralysed with fear by his predicament. He must remain by the phone booth waiting for Lola to save him so he becomes the princess-hero while it is Lola the princess who must act so she becomes the hero-princess. She is the driving force in the synchronic story and does all the running. Lola bears some similarity to game figure Lara Croft whose natural action is to run rather than walk in the *Tomb Raider* games.

The three versions of the story explicitly 'play' with the narrative's stock character types. In the first film the princess-hero (Lola) dies; in the second story the princess-hero survives and the hero-princess (Manni) dies and in the third story both characters survive and walk off together in an arche-typal happy-ever-after ending. The gaming format of the narrative has shown how the outcome of the story can change as a result of minute actions which liberate characters from their stock plot functions.

The final aspect I want to consider here is one of the films most striking – its multimedia narrative spaces. The film's credits and each of the three stories commences in hand-drawn animation with Lola running down the apartment stairs shown on the TV. As the camera approaches, it seemingly enters the TV screen providing a visual metaphor for immersion into the realm of game play. Thereafter the film is shot on 35mm in both black and white and colour but there are sequences shot on videotape too. Tykwer uses the 35mm sequences to define the world of Lola and Manni and the videotape depicts the world of other characters she comes into contact with but does not see first hand. The consequent drop in image quality and the introduc-tion of scan lines in the video image gives a sense of unreality to scenes beyond the main character's subjectivity. Photographic style stills are used to represent the film's flash forwards. As Lola runs through the streets she literally bumps into people precipitating a flash forward in which the character's future is imagined in photo shot series overlaid with the click and whirr of the camera shutter on the soundtrack. In each of the story's versions the flash forward plays out a different future for the character. The action heroine Lola becomes a cross between a game avatar and a hyperlink with powers to open up different dimensions in the film.

So what are we to make of this? To gain some understanding of this intriguing filmic strategy Lev Manovich's theories about new media are illuminating here too. He argues that cinema has always provided an interface to narrative taking place in a 3-D space but now cinema language is becoming an interface to all types of media (Manovich 2001). He describes how we inhabit a culture made up of high-density information surfaces epitomised in the web news site and the multi-levelled video game which he goes on to suggest has created an "aesthetic of density" – a new cultural logic (Manovich 2001). This constitutes an aesthetic challenge to cinema which it has to meet if it is survive in the new media order.

In many ways Tykwer meets this challenge in *Lola Rennt*. In the figure of the action heroine, the film has an interface to all kinds of media spaces creating a new depth to the cinematic screen. It is in this sense, more than any other, that the film fulfilled cinema's need to once again assert the power of film as a medium for storytelling in the age of digital media.

Body Spectacle: Lara Croft

In Britain, *Tomb Raider* is probably the best-known video game title of them all. Launched in 1996 it now includes five game titles and has sold more than 28 million games worldwide (Eidos Interactive 2002). The figure of game avatar Lara Croft is at the heart of this franchise. She has become a lucrative brand in her own right with recognition sufficient to advertise other products including the soft drink Lucozade renamed Larazade last year "in her honour" to mark the release of the *Tomb Raider* filmatization.

Critics talk about the game figure as an icon that has captured the popular imagination and to underline this the high profile style magazine *The Face* gave her the star treatment in an extensive feature which propelled her to celebrity status in Britain (Cubeit 2002). Even the British Government, wanting to cash in on the zeitgeist, adopted Lara Croft as the UK's ambassador for science and technology. So what is it about Lara Croft that warrants this level of interest?

Jeremy Smith, managing director of Eidos (developer of the Lara Croft games series) maintains that part of the attraction here is that "glossy blankness – the computer look" which makes her not too realistic or individuated (Poole 2000). In a similar vein commentators have suggested that the reason for Lara Croft's impact is that she is "an abstraction, an animated conglomeration of sexual and attitudinal signs – breasts, hot pants, shades, thigh holsters whose very blankness encourages the (male or female) player's psychological projection" (Poole 2000).

Psychological projection? Maybe. But this action heroine did not materialise out of nowhere and it is not the first time audiences have encountered a figure like Lara. She may be made of polygons but Lara clearly draws on familiar media templates. Game-Lara conforms precisely with the visual codes of the Hollywood archetype – the pin-up – intended to personify perfection of a particular body shape prevailing during the 1930s and 1940s – long legs, perfect teeth, large breasts. In other words: a sexual spectacle (Dyer 1986).

As a caricature of this cinematic template Lara conforms to the visual codes of the pin up. The body form is closely defined under hot pants and T-shirt which both serve to reveal the contours but conceal the facts. Disproportionately huge breasts but definitely no nipples. Leg displayed but not splayed. The key to this image is revelation of the body by suggestion rather than deed. The figure is adorned with fetishised accoutrements. Lara Croft sports a low-slung belt drawing attention to the hips and the crotch while the gun holsters place visual emphasis on the top of the legs in a manner reminiscent of the clichéd stockings and suspender belts.

The other template discernable behind the Lara Croft figure emanates from the videogames culture to the east. In Japan videogames took their aesthetic cue, not from film, but from the graphic forms which preceded it such as *manga* (comic books) and *anime* (animated cartoon films). Lara is drawn in a combination of kawaii girlish cuteness with her swinging ponytail and somewhat deformed anime-style sexuality spectacle with her massively enhanced breasts. She has all the classic characteristics of the 'virtual girlfriend', a phenomenon which though common in Japanese gaming culture, has not really crossed over to the west.

The Japanese entertainment market has sporned a vast array of virtual girlfriend fantasies across a range of media such as *Video girl Ai* (Hamilton 1997). Whilst video games such as *Toki-Meki* enable the player to improve himself in order to win the prize fantasy girlfriend figure of *Shiori Fujusaki* (Hamilton 1997). There are also software generated virtual girls known as *kisekae dolls* which are a variation on the old children's game paper doll dressing, whereby the gamer is able to drag items of clothing from the figure one by one for their sexual gratification (Hamilton 1997).

This Japanese videogame genre provides us with an insight into understanding the popularity of the figure of Lara. On the one hand the filmic pin-up provides her audience with a sexual spectacle; on the other hand the attraction of Lara Croft lies precisely in the fact that her image is not driven by realist aesthetics, in fact quite the opposite. Here it is the distance from reality which is key to Lara's attraction. The highly stylised and artificial quality of this *anime*-style character is part of what makes Lara Croft appealing to her audience. In Japan this type of figure is known as a *nijikon fetchi* or "two dimensional fetish" and whilst the term is generally used to describe fan devotion to any manga, anime or video game character, it provides a clue to understanding the popularity of Lara Croft. In essence what makes her so attractive to her audience is that she provides risk free engagement with the concept of "sex".[3]

These two modes of address – the pin up and the *nijikon fetchii* are built into the Lara persona and carefully 'quoted' in the cinematic version of the game. Lara Croft is an action heroine designed to appeal to the core audience who go to see action-adventure films – young males. From the outset Lara Croft is drawn as a girl rather than a woman from her schoolgirl plait to her nonchalant teenage gait. Moreover within the film's diegesis she has no current love interest other than a daughterly devotion to her father. From the earliest scenes in the film, the cinematic look may be described as a through-the-keyhole-teenage-peep rather than leer. We are introduced to the cinematic Lara played by Angelina Jolie in the shower. Yet the camera keeps a discreet distance from the naked Lara peeking through round a muslin curtain.

This scene culminates in the theatrical presentation of the real life Lara framed by a stone arch and muslin drapes overlaid with seductive rhythmic music on the soundtrack. The whole scene is carefully designed to illustrate that cinema can go one better than its rival and turn the pixellated video game character into flesh. As the polygon figure is made flesh on the cinema screen, the Lara body becomes a spectacle designed to be looked *at*.

Lara Croft is the latest manifestation in a long tradition of cinematic action heroines which has seen discernable shifts in body shape since the heyday of the pin-up. Gone too are the bodybuilt muscles of her predecessors Ripley (played by Sigourney Weaver in the *Alien* series) or Sarah Connor (played by Linda Hamilton in the *Terminator* film of the 1980s and early 90s). Replaced here by prosthetic technology of her weaponry carried holstered to her legs and not-so-subtly augmented breasts. The new action heroine is a cyborg – a combination of human and technology

The film's opening scene clearly establishes the cinematic action heroine's connection to the game figure as actress Angelina Jolie adopts stock poses reminiscent of the game avatar. The cyborg heroine has enhanced physical capabilities – she can flip through 180 degrees, swing on ropes single-handed and is apparently not subject to the laws of gravity. The heroine's movements mimic the menu of console driven actions available in the game; Croft runs at her adversary shooting both guns at the same time which looks distinctly incongruous in a live action heroine but remains true to the capabilities of the game figure.

The film's action sequences are choreographed to produce a vicarious sense of kinetic involvement for the audience in simulated game play. This is underpinned with fast tempo music on the soundtrack which generates a sense of tension combined with computer screen framed point of view shots of Lara and first person perspective shots. Gaming playfulness is dynamised in the film's action sequences so the viewer may enjoy the spectacle by looking *through* her perspective as well as *at* her. The viewer can 'be' her as well as 'look' at her at the same time.

The popularity of Lara is based on the fact that she is a veritable compendium of media conventions – pin-up, *nijikon fetchi* and action heroine with a tacit adoption of the modes of address to their audiences which underlie them. In the film Lara Croft is represented by a range of contradictory images of femininity from the dominatrix to the dutiful and doting daughter all dressed up in frock and flowery straw hat grieving at her father's memorial. Lara Croft is not a three-dimensional character. There is no fixed feminine identity within the film which relates to femininity in the real world. We are looking at a representation of a videogame character or, if you like, a representation of a representation. Lara Croft may the first videogames character to have live models aping her image but she is not real. In the film Angelina Jolie's Lara Croft can only refer to representations of her digital self.

Gender operates as a form of masquerade. An action heroine who can assume whatever persona she requires but is not confined or defined by any one position. The film's heroine plays with the construction of femininity and by so doing demonstrates the construction of masculinity too. She adopts conventional notions of masculine behaviour just as readily in the closing scene's fight to the death between her and the film's arch villain Manfred Powell in which she pulls her punches and presses her fingers into his wounds to inflict pain proving herself to be more than a match for her adversary.

One reason why Lara's appeal is so broad is that the pleasures in watching Lara can not be accounted for solely in psychological terms of the game player identification with the avatar (being Lara) or the cinematic male gaze (watching Lara) alone – a dualism characteristic of digital media. The cross-media heroine offers a further layer of pleasure to the audience conversant with the figure of Lara Croft operating across a range of media platforms. For the audience who are viewers as well as the players there is the pleasure of recognition; the pleasure is recognising versions of the same story as different media borrow, quote, and appropriate from one another in a play of mutual remediations.

Body Spectacle: *Lola Rennt*

Although not quite on the scale of her gaming sister, Lola has enjoyed success too. The film garnered a clutch of awards at international film festivals and became Germany's highest grossing film in the year of its release as well as gaining the accolades of best director, best film and best soundtrack at the German MTV awards.

Lola has generated cultural resonances in feature films, TV series, commercials and even featuring in an episode of The Simpsons (Tykwer-online 2003). The film's heroine was recruited into the service of party politics when Berlin's Mayor Eberhard Diepgen (CDU) appropriated the design of the *Lola*

Rennt film posters to kick-start his campaign for re-election. Riding on the back of Lola's celebrity, the poster depicted Diepgen's head photoshopped onto the shoulders of Lola in an attempt to promote the politician as being a dynamic leader – running to ensure the advantages of his city ahead of the elections with the words "Diepgen Rennt" printed in the familiar font from the film's title sequence. Hundreds of posters were plastered all over the city the winter of 1998 much to the chagrin of Tom Tykwer who threatened to bring the case to law. As a result the posters were hastily removed but Diepgen's subsequent success in getting re-elected is attributed in part to this publicity coup (Sinka 2002).

Remediations like this illustrate how the Lola-look became a visual short-hand for a hip, fresh contemporary Germany. The idea caught on. Lola was syndicated for the political purposes again, transformed this time into the Germany's Minister for Culture, Michael Naumann (SDP). Here Naumann's head is pasted onto Lola's running figure and this image appeared in the Berlin press trumpeting the successes of the German film industry.

So how can we explain this film character's resonance beyond the screen? What is it about Lola that has captured the imagination of her audience elevating her to iconic status in Germany which seems to even cross gender boundaries?

Not only the narrative structure of *Lola Rennt* but the central character herself bears some of the hall marks of the video game. From the film's credits we encounter our heroine as an animated figure tracked from a third person player perspective like a videogame avatar. At the start of each 'run' she transforms from her live action self into a cartoon version running down the apartment block stairs which we watch on her mother's TV screen. Lola oscillates from one representational mode to another, shifting from live action sequences to animation and back again. This generates the same hypermediation we saw in *Lara Croft: Tomb Raider* whereby the viewer is not allowed to settle into the classic Hollywood cinematic mode of immediacy but is constantly reminded of the filmic interface through which the story is experienced. The message is clear. Cinema can subsume other media languages and here is a film which promotes itself as *the* format of convergence.

Like the game avatar Lola features in most scenes which follow. She is the film's driver and like Lara she has a predilection to run. Her pace is the film's pace.When Lola pauses for breath so does the camera and soundtrack. When Lola sets off so does the camera and the music.

Aside from her on-screen presence Lola is a gaming style action heroine in other ways too. She operates through action rather than words. The object of the (story) game is spelt out in the phone call from Manni – Lola must find 100.000 marks in twenty minutes. There is no time for speculation. Words are redundant – timed out – a point underlined by the phone card running out of units and ejected onto the floor of the booth. It's time to act, not to talk as Lola throws the telephone receiver in the air as she runs from the room and ignores her mother's request to run an errand.

Lola Rennt (Tom Tykwer, 1998) Angel Films.

And as if to underline this new media heroine, the cinematography defines her by what she is not. The juxtaposition is made between conventional female roles and this new screen heroine. Before Lola sets off the camera silently tracks around Lola's room survey's the conventional trappings of a young woman's room. We see her pictured in a Polaroid as a typical fun-loving gal with her boyfriend and a collection of Barbie dolls in various states of undress but neither of these role models will do now. If she is to save the day, she will have to do more than be a girlfriend in a Polaroid snapshot or look good like a Barbie-doll. She will have to run!

Like Lara, she's dressed for action. Lola's attire is pared right down. However, whereas Lara's appearance had a militaristic flavour with combat boots, monochrome action gear and gun holsters worn echoing video gaming origins in defence industry combat simulations, Lola is dressed for action on the street in urban styles characterised in the army surplus Doc Martens-style heavy boots, purse belt, cropped trousers and vest top. Lola's image draws on the sartorial styles of the city which have their origins in punk. The cantilevered Hollywood pin up of Lara Croft is replaced here to Lola's layered look. A vest-top revealing bra straps – "underwear as outerwear" Vivian Westwood-inspired style. The army surplus store may have provided the starting point for life on the street but here it is transformed by the do-it-yourself ethic. This is clearly signalled in the home cut flame red dye of Lola's hair, tattoos and ear piercings.

Numerous reviews described *Lola Rennt* as an extended music video in essence taking their cue from the fact that all but two of the sixteen tracks on the film's soundtrack album were composed by Tom Tykwer for the film. The three versions of the story are accompanied by the pounding techno beat and the conventional codes of narrative film are superseded by those we more familiarly associate with music video. During the running sequences visual edits are determined by the tempo of the soundtrack which has been dubbed the "MTV aesthetic" (Dickinson 2002). Characteristically combining fast paced shots, split screen montages, slow-motion, jump cuts focused on the figure of Lola throughout the duration of the tracks from different angles her running legs, her face, in profile, in bird's eye view. Indeed, the close syncopation of the camera work with Lola transforms her running into a kind of high-energy dance performance.

It is the voice of the actress Franka Potente on the soundtrack accompanying the on-screen running Lola which clearly signals that the film's subjectivity is hers. The song is seen. The monotone delivery of three main themes "Running One, Two and Three", "Believe" and "Wish" ("Komm Zu Mir") serve the same function of the film score providing emotional contact with Lola expressing her inner thoughts directly to the film viewer whilst the ambient sound of contemporary Berlin are completely muted. There is a parallel between the first person address of the soundtrack and the third person view of the character running though Berlin. Potente is both a musical performer and a character at the same time. As with Lara, we look 'at' her and 'through' her eyes at her on-screen self.

Lola Rennt (Tom Tykwer, 1998) Angel Films.

By the end of the film, the soundtrack switches genre from the first person address of the Potente songs to the conventions of the music compilation soundtrack with Dinah Washington's version of "What a difference a day makes" prompting a temporal shift from the rythms of techno music to the blues. The sequence takes its cue from the soundtrack playing in slow motion. Throughout the film Lola, like Lara, is drawn through a collage of visual and aural styles with the result that it makes us aware of the film medium as the interface. This excess of styles leads back to the experience of hypermediacy and seems to be an aesthetic response to the perceived competition of video games to cinema.

A New Kind of Action Heroine?

'Potente' means "strong" in Italian. However, Lola's brand of heroism differs from Lara's in one notable way. Within the film's diegesis Lara's actions are always determined by her father. He is the player, she the played. In contrast Lola is both the played and the player at the same time. In interviews Tom Tykwer has likened her to the Swedish children's book character Pippi Langstrumpf (Pippi Longstocking) whose motto "Ich mach emir die welt, wie sie mir gefallt" mirrors Lola's attitude to life. When events do not unfold to her liking, she recreates them until they do. At the end of the first version of the story where Lola dies, she asserts her will as the player. She says "I don't want to leave…" and so the second version of the story starts. Then at the end of the second version when Manni is hit by a truck, she determines that he will not die and starts again. Like a player who keeps whacking the reset button, she works on her 'game' until events turn out the way she wants them to. In the last version Lola and Manni are reunited, the money is found and they walk off together in a happy-ever-after ending.

Lola's will is asserted not through words but screams. Unlike the videogame avatar whose destiny is determined by the player, the filmic heroine can offer a different form of autonomy with which her audience can engage. Like her predecessor, Oscar Mazerath in Volker Schloendorff's filmatization of Günter Grass' novel *The Tin Drum* (1959), Lola's will is manifest most forcefully in a scream, which can shatter glass. At times Lola screams so loud she stops the film in its tracks .She silences both Manni and her father and by the time she gets to the roulette table in a last ditch attempt to win the money in the third version of the story, she has gained enough strength to change the path of fate. Lola is able to oscillate between the role of the player and the played and thus implicitly rivals the video game's new forms of audience engagement.

What does this all tell us? Well, clearly both Lara and Lola are fashioned out of media languages. For Lara, the traditions of the Hollywood pin-up together with the nijikon fetchii of Japanese manga and anime. For Lara – the media conventions of animation, the sartorial style of punk and music video. What these action heroines share, however, is the influence of the video game. Both action heroines are clearly fashioned in the style of their gaming sisters. Neither Lola nor Lara are conventional cinematic heroines. There are no fully formed psychologically rounded characters here. For their audience the first point of reference is not the real world but other media languages. They are both carved out of a mix of contemporary media 'vernaculars' which their media-savy audience recognise. Heroines for a media age of convergence.

Of all new media influences cinema is particularly challenged by video games and in different ways Lara and Lola bear witness to the growing cultural significance of this cultural form. What has become clear from this analysis is that both films not only pay homage to but explicitly rival videogames. To secure its future cinema needs to maintain its attraction for young audiences. Videogames have changed the narrative expectations of the youth market and in order to compete, cinema has done what it has always done: refashioning itself to meet the challenge. This article has traced the aesthetic consequences of this.

Notes

1. In Tykwer's *Heaven* (2002) the August institutions of Italian city life are represented in the arial panning shots across the grid of grandiose buildings around and through which human relationships are shaped and determined in the film.
2. Lola sings on the film's soundtrack: " I wish I was a princess /with armies at her hand/I wish I was a ruler/who'd make them understand". Also the guard at her father's bank calls her the "house princess" in story one, then in story two lectures her about the virtues of queens.
3. For a fuller discussion of sex, consumerism and the techno-digital culture in contemporary Japan, Fran Lloyd's *Consuming Bodies: Sex and Contemporary Japanese Art* (2002) is highly informative.

References

The bit girl (1997). *The Face* June 5. Retrieved May24[th] 2002 from http://www.cubeit.com/ctimes/images/facefc_0jpg.

Bolter, J.D. & Grusin, R (1999). *Remediation: Understanding new media* London: MIT.

Bolter, J.D (1991). *Writing space: the computer, hypertext and the history of writing*. New Jersey: Lawrence Erlbaum.

Dyer, R. (1979). *Stars*. London: British Film Institute.

Dickinson, K. (2002). Pop, Speed and the 'MTV aesthetic' in recent teen film. Retrieved December 5, 2002, from http://www.nottingham.ac.uk/fil/journal/articles/pop-speed and mtv.htm.

Eidos Interactive corporate. Retrieved May 24 2002, from http://www.eidosinteractive.co.uk/corporate/index.html.

The Entertainment and Leisure Software Publishers Association media pack. Retrieved May 24 2002, from http://www.elspa.com/mediapack/intro.html.

Game on: teacher's pack: the completed game. Retrieved May 24 2002, from http://www.gameonweb.co.uk/education/unit6mid.html.

Hamilton, R. (1997). "Virtual idols and digital girls: artifice and sexuality in anime, kisekae and Kyoko Date"(1997) *Bad Subjects*, 35. Retrieved February 18 2002, from http://eserver.org/bs/35/hamilton.html.

Lola references retrieved January 2 2003, from http://www.tykwer-online.de/lola/eng/lolareferences.htm.

Lloyd, F. (2002). *Consuming bodies: Sex and contemporary Japanese art*. London: Reaktion.

MacCabe, C. (Ed.) (1986). *High theory/ low culture: Analysing popular television and film*. Manchester: Manchester University Press.

Manovich, L. (2001). *The language of new media*. London: MIT.

Murray, J.H. (1997). *Hamlet on the holodeck*. Cambridge: MIT.

Poole, S. (2000). *Trigger happy*. London: Fourth Estate.

Propp, V. (1968). *Morphology of the folktale* (2 ed.). Austin: University of Texas.

Sci/tech: Licence to thrill. Retrieved May 24 2002, from http://www.news.bbc.co.uk/hi/english/sci/tec/newsid.

Schodt, F.L. (1996). *Dreamland Japan: Writings on modern manga*. Berkeley: Stonebridge Press.

Sinka, M. (2002). Tom Tykwer's *Lola Rennt*: A blueprint of millennial Berlin. Retrieved April 23 2002, from http://www.dickenson.edu/departments/germn/glossen/heft11/lola.html.

Tasker, Y. (1996). *Spectacular Bodies: Gender, genre and the action cinema*. London: Routledge.

II. Genre Fictions

Soldiers' Stories

Women and Military Masculinities in *Courage Under Fire*

Yvonne Tasker

> Masculinity... becomes legible as masculinity where
> and when it leaves the white male middle-class body
> Judith Halberstam, 1998, p. 2

> Sometimes masculinity has nothing to do with... men.
> Eve Sedgewick quoted in Modleski, 1997, p. 541

Both images and narratives focused on military women disrupt very directly assumptions that behaviors or qualities designated masculine are reserved only for men. Obviously they are also framed by ongoing, hard-fought arguments concerning the proper role of women in the US military, arguments that involve factors including combat and non-combat roles, new technologies and (in Hollywood films at least) shifting political ideas about the role of US intervention. I don't want to argue here that cinematic images of military women should be understood in any straightforward way as "transgressive." After all, a respect for rules and order as well as fantasies of inclusion and belonging are so central and so powerful in the films I'll be discussing. Indeed what strikes me most forcibly about the two most high profile American films of the 1990s to focus on military women in combat, *Courage Under Fire* (Edward Zwick, 1996) a melodramatic war movie which provides the main focus for this essay, and the Ridley Scott-directed *G.I. Jane* (1997) is that whilst the central female characters are tough and masculine-coded, they are also both normalized and revered. To the extent that such images are transgressive at all then, I would argue that this lies not only in the act of proposing a viable female masculinity, but in their construction of heroic female protagonists whose very desire to be part of a masculine conformity troubles both the cinematic world in which they operate and many assumptions that have come to be conventional within feminist film criticism.

I want to suggest here that masculinity is important for understanding contemporary cinematic representations of women, and not only when the female protagonist appears explicitly in male guise. As such this paper is part of an ongoing attempt to untangle gendered concepts, terms and images that are regularly used in both feminist-informed (typically psychoanalytic) film studies, and more sociological explorations of masculinities, not to mention popular discourses about gender. In effect I'm trying to think through a critical slippage that occurs between talking about gender as a set of qualities or characteristics culturally aligned with men or women, and the ways in which both images and identities regularly transgress these borders or boundaries. The paper argues for a more flexible model of gender in thinking about popular cinema (or indeed art cinema). Most importantly I'd like to suggest that contemporary cinema makes use of images of 'men' and 'women' that articulate a complex relationship between sex and gender: a complexity that, even in fantasy genres (I'm thinking of 1990s movies such as *Strange Days* or *The Long Kiss Goodnight*) may speak to lived experiences of gender in which, "post-feminism," women are constituted in terms of gendered discourses and not simply in terms of femininity.

Before moving to a broader discussion of the perspectives that film studies had developed on masculinity, it is worth saying a little more about *Courage Under Fire* and the generic context which helps to frame the film and my reading of it. A more or less explicit re-working of Kurosawa's *Rashomon* (1950), *Courage Under Fire* uses a complex series of flashbacks to explore themes of guilt, courage and heroism through the investigation of events leading to the death during the Gulf War of Capt. Karen Walden, a medevac pilot played by Meg Ryan. Although Ryan and Denzel Washington co-star they don't share a single scene (despite the suggestion of promotional images). Instead the film works to construct a fairly sophisticated set of parallels between them, interweaving their stories. Col. Nat Serling's (Washington) task is to establish whether or not Walden be posthumously awarded the Medal of Honor. He visits her family and her crew, building up a fragmented and contradictory picture of her character, and gradually piecing together the circumstances of her death. The investigation culminates in Serling's discovery of a mutiny. Worse, fearful of the court-martial that awaits him, Monfreiz (Lou Diamond Phillips) reports that the injured Walden is already dead, leaving her on the ground to be engulfed in the flames of an air strike. Running alongside this story of betrayal, we follow Serling's attempts to come to terms with his own failure in combat: in the opening scene his mistaken order results in the death of Lieut. Boylar, a close friend under his command. In its elaboration of bravery and cowardice, of judgement, authority and failure within the context of combat and its aftermath, the film thus maps masculinity across several soldiers' stories.

Military Masculinities

Military movies and war movies typically feature a carefully managed tension between conformity and individualism, the uniformity and sublimation of personal desires suggested by service against the award of medals for distinction. Thus Robert Ashley's *Sight and Sound* review of *G.I. Jane* suggested that the film was about the individual rather than the team, its insistent message, despite the recuperative ending, that women can never really be incorporated into the male group. *Courage Under Fire* can equally be read as a narrative that demonstrates the problem posed by women in combat. Walden's men fail to respect her authority at the crucial moment. At the same time however, these films both offer powerful fantasies of incorporation, fantasies central to the war movie at least since films of and about WWII, with their emphasis on the development of allegiances across differences of race, religion, ethnicity and class. The boot camp sub-genre within which *G.I. Jane* is situated, for example, emphasizes the need for exceptional individual strength on the one hand and self-effacement in the interests of the group (and by extension the nation) on the other.

The cynical, world-weary soldier is another stalwart of the genre. Though the Gulf War has shifted this somewhat, the prevailing stereotype of the veteran has long been that of an alienated, violent male soldier whose physical and mental scars nonetheless operates as marks of (masculine) character. Military women cannot be coded quite so easily in terms of dutiful but melancholy heroism, since whether or not they get to do the job at all remains such a contested issue. Can a privilege that has been fought for so hard be safely presented as a burden reluctantly shouldered? The terms in which male masculinity is constructed in the war film is in many ways quite at odds with the emerging stereotype of the determined, somewhat idealized military career woman showcased in television movies such as *Serving in Silence: The Margarethe Cammermeyer Story* and *She Stood Alone: The Tailhook Scandal* (both 1995). It is interesting in this context to look back to the TV series *M*A*S*H* (1972-83) in which major Margaret Houlihan (Loretta Swit) functioned as the sexualized butt ("Hotlips") of the show's oddly macho pacifism. As a career army nurse, Houlihan stands in for an extreme of military conformity in a particularly invidious way. She is ridiculed for being simultaneously too evidently female (read sexually demanding) and too masculine (read ambitious). Although a figure of fun, Houlihan's female masculinity nonetheless underlines the extent to which bodies and behaviors do not always conform to type, even as they are reinscribed within a stereotypical frame.

Although it inevitably frames the film, *Courage Under Fire* focuses resolutely on individual dramas, only implicitly acknowledging the wider questions around the combat role of military women. Similarly, Serling's self-searching and antagonistic yet respectful relationship to the military suggests that he also struggles with the normative masculinity that a white political establishment represents, without ever explicitly addressing the racial politics of the US military. A kick-ass woman's picture, *G.I. Jane* is much more direct on both counts: O'Neill's acceptance by her male colleagues is approvingly developed through the course of the narrative. The role of military women is explicitly discussed, with a black soldier comparing the bar on women in combat roles to the racial exclusions of the past. The script quite explicitly presents the case for (exceptional/masculine) women in combat, which is not to say that it simply endorses it. *Courage Under Fire* offers a rather different elaboration of these discourses around the body of a (dead) white female captain through the point of view of a vulnerable black male colonel, constructing a narrative in which masculinity is understood in both raced and gendered terms.

Media coverage of military actions has a double significance in relation to military women whose exploits, achievements and failures are subject to commentary by both journalists and politicians. Like the more recent *Three Kings* (David O. Russell, 1999), *Courage Under Fire* acknowledges the intensely mediated character of US military involvement in the Persian Gulf, insistently juxtaposing television images with the physical, material experience of war. Thus the film opens with a montage of familiar images, the US military defined starkly against the Iraqi people (military and civilian). Ghostly images of attacks at night, of George Bush and Saddam Hussein, and, briefly, of Colin Powell lead us from the discredited precision of the tactical air strikes to the messiness of the ground war which provides the setting to which the film will repeatedly return. Although here President Bush speaks of clear goals and defined objectives, elsewhere in the film the White House is treated with cynicism.

Courage Under Fire commences in the tension and confusion of battle at night, with Serling and his men about to move into combat at Al Bathra. Inadvertently ordering an attack on another US tank, he causes the death of his friend Boylar (of whom he later says "he was like a brother to me"). The following day Walden is killed at Al Kufan in the uncertain circumstances that Serling must investigate. Since caught up in controversy over *The Siege*, here Zwick casts the Iraqi forces as stereotypical movie villains – Ilario (Matt Damon) nervously recalls hearing enemy laughter as they dig in. Serling begins his investigation by interviewing the Black Hawk crew saved by Walden. Images and sounds from the incident itself and the conversation in the interview room overlay each other, blurring the distinction between remembrance and event. The bonding over shared memories of combat is reinforced by the following brief exchange:

> *Lieut. Chelli:* ... now the fuckers are letting... (silence, awkward pause). I'm sorry Sir, the Iraqis, are letting loose with everything they've got
> *Serling:* You were right the first time (group laughter).

Putting the men at their ease, this moment of bonding against the enemy recalls Serling's opening gung-ho attitude ("let's kill 'em all"), though moderated to some extent by Washington's trademark understated style and undercut by the subsequent death of Boylar. These shared memories of fear and exhilaration are only partly triumphal, their function being to emphasize the shared experiences of combat in a film that is concerned to test the integrity of US military masculinity.

Courage under fire (Edward Zwick, 1996), Fox.

Courage Under Fire juxtaposes Scott Glenn's earnest Washington Post reporter (a determined ex-military man), with the feminized political world of public relations. Crucially, Glenn/Gardner is involved in investigating Serling's war record and not the circumstances surrounding Walden's death or the broader issue of military women. In this way although an intense media scrutiny is acknowledged, this focuses on Serling whilst a military scrutiny – conducted via the figure of Serling – of Walden's performance is a more private in-house affair. Whether male or female, military masculinity is defined in *Courage Under Fire* not only, or even primarily, in relation to the enemy but against the insubstantial world of politicians and the domestic media. An opposition between male soldiers and female soldiers is thus framed by the wider generic discourses of the war movie, discourses in which soldiers' stories are valorized even when particular conflicts are questioned.

Mapping Masculinities

Over the past twenty years, feminist film criticism has worked and re-worked the analysis of those relatively few high-profile Hollywood movies in which female protagonists are more or less explicitly coded in terms of masculinity. Whilst this coding is most centrally to do with agency and self-determination these women are also variously decisive, self-possessed, tough, resourceful, capable with vehicles, weaponry and machinery: in short, it is a distinctly military masculinity (or at least one associated with war and action movies) that has entranced critics and audiences. The titles make familiar reading by now: dating more or less from Ridley Scott's original *Alien* (1979) through the reference points of *Terminator 2* and *Thelma and Louise* (both 1991) with recent entrants *Strange Days* (1995) and *The Long Kiss Goodnight* (1996) now receiving attention. For Ros Jennings, Weaver's Ripley represents the possibility of an autonomy "in desire and action" which *doesn't* involve "masculinization" (1995:204). For others Ripley is "tough," a "warrior," whilst Linda Hamilton's muscular Sarah Connor is described as "tough-minded, fearless and strong" (Jeffords 1993:240) or cast, along with Thelma and Louise as figurations of a "literally empowered womanhood" (Pfeil 1995:53). Neither the term "masculine" nor discourses of masculinity are regularly foregrounded in the discussion of these iconic figures; Connor and Ripley are more often understood in terms of a re-vision of *femininity*. Lesbian criticism has shown less reluctance to framing cinematic women in terms of masculinity: Paula Graham sees Weaver, Hamilton and Jodie Foster (in her role as Clarice Starling) as "masculinized" (Graham 1995:179), whilst Sonya Andermahr reads Weaver and Hamilton in terms of an invitation to identify with/desire "masculine beauty in female form" (Andermahr 1994:34). Although in her discussion of *Aliens*, Jennings sees discourses of masculinity as displaced onto the more evidently butch figure of Vasquez, the term is nonetheless introduced. More typically Sharon Willis situates her discussion of Ripley/Connor in terms of "a form of drag based on a masculinity that aggressively displays its difference from an anatomical base" within a chapter indicatively titled "Combative Femininity" (Willis 1997:113).

Perhaps a reluctance around terminology represents little more than a desire to keep hold of femininity, whilst appropriating for women many of the qualities conventionally associated with men and masculinity (purpose, independence, even aggression). Broadly speaking though, and despite the inadequacies of 'femininity' as a discourse within which to exclusively situate women in Hollywood movies, let alone the cinema's pattern of ambivalence towards male masculinities, it is striking that most feminist writers don't even come near putting into play masculinity as a term that has some relationship to women until confronted, say, by the spectacle of a female movie star engaged in some serious macho posturing. I'm thinking here of Demi Moore as Jordan O'Neil in *G.I. Jane,* single-handedly reviving the workout montage so beloved of 1980s cinema, although the cross-dressing protagonist of Greenwald's western *The Ballad of Little Jo,* hunched over her food, picking up the defensive-aggressive body language of a prospector, serves just as well. It might be argued that military women represent one such extreme – a sort of limit case for gendered representation. Perhaps. But I would argue that a discussion of such images of female masculinity does more than illuminate these few examples, posing larger questions for the analysis of other less obviously (i.e. less embodied) masculine images of women.

My own use of 'masculinity' in relation to action movies of the 1980s and early 90s both alludes to and to some extent sidelines biology, implying that a muscular physique can function as a signifier of strength for both male and female protagonists (Tasker 1993:146). Musculinity proposes a sense in which masculinity is both culturally constructed and physically embodied. In this way Moore's muscular physique and shaven head in *G.I. Jane* signal her commitment to a masculinized military identity. Yet it seems to me that masculinity is more complex, more nuanced, than this kind of reduction to an impersonation or physical performance might suggest. Whilst the suggestion that Meg Ryan's Walden was "butch" was reportedly one of the reasons the US military refused to co-operate with Zwick's production, her butchness is actually relatively understated within the film. (Just as significantly, officials apparently objected to the portrayal of Serling's drinking and the suggestion of a military cover-up). And although, as Clare Whatling has noted, a Hollywood butch is "virtually a femme anywhere else" (Whatling 1997:77), it is precisely the understated mobilization of discourses of masculinity, indeed the insistence on the co-existence of her military *masculinity* and her status as a military *woman* that makes *Courage Under Fire* such an intriguing movie. If butchness is associated with masculine clothing and appearance it is thus once more linked if not to the physical then to the visual as much as to narrative agency. We should be aware then of the fact that Ryan/Walden's "butch" wears the uniform of a *military woman*, not a pass-

ing woman or even necessarily a physically masculine woman. Her clothes
are neither illicit nor borrowed. She has earned her uniform and its decora-
tions, even as the narrative revolves around the question of whether she
should really have the right to wear them.

Feminism's fundamental critique of essentialism notwithstanding, it is no
surprise that criticism finds it tricky to keep apart terms that western culture
so continually and consistently conflates (men/masculinity/activity) and can
end up replicating the very terms it wishes to redefine or to challenge. To
some extent the messy ways in which a term like "masculinity" or even
"masculinities" get used is to do with its position within (at least) two distinct, if mutually informing, intellectual traditions. Firstly, analyses which take
as their reference point a psychoanalytic terminology and the framing concept of the male gaze, a critical trajectory firmly rooted in the modernist
paradigm of psycho-semiotics. Secondly, perspectives which emerge from
the distinct context of cultural studies, exploring constructions of masculinity in relation to the diverse lived experiences of distinct groups of men. Both
trajectories might use similar terms and phrases but with very different objects in view. Thus, although the interaction between a psychoanalytic feminist film studies and an ethnographic cultural studies has undoubtedly produced a situation in which masculinities have been increasingly explored
within a social/political context, there nonetheless remains some confusion
as to what is actually being discussed when critics or theorists talk about
masculinities and movies. The value of psychoanalysis lies partly in its insistence on the instability of identities, on the permeability of categories as
they are experienced rather than in the abstract. And yet, as Dimitris
Eleftheriotis notes, all too often a normative model of heterosexual masculinity remains in place within psychoanalytic film theory, continuing to operate as a kind of structuring norm in relation to all the "other" masculinities
it defines, "the logical outcome of a methodology that theorizes dominant
masculinity as universal" (Eleftheriotis 1995:236).

The conflation of men and masculinity tends to obscure differences
between men, differences that are frequently foregrounded in the war movie
and have arguably preoccupied other action genres in recent years. Since
discourses of gender are quite evidently linked to economies of class, race
and sexuality in western political ideology, it is not only women, but "other"
kinds of men who are excluded from the masculinity which film theory typically analyses. As Robyn Wiegman suggests in her discussion of *Boyz N the
Hood*, it is in part the critical reduction of gender "to the specular embodiment of woman" that has so often erased both African-American men and
the complexities of gendered discourse from contemporary film theory
(Wiegman 1993:180). Leaving aside for one moment the importance of
masculinities for images of women, Weigman's comments underline the
importance of questioning both "which men" and "which movies" provide
film theory's object. There was good reason for the title of an early 1990s
anthology to suggest that film theory might "go to the movies" more often.

It is precisely by talking about non-canonical films that critics have argued for an historical and cultural specificity lacking in the homogenizing application of a "film theory" model to the subject of masculinities. Many of the contributors to Cohan and Hark's *Screening the Male* attempt to redefine monolithic assumptions about "dominant masculinity" through the analysis of genres (the epic, the musical) or stars (Valentino, Astaire) that underline the heterogeneity of popular representations. The diversity of gendered discourse in the popular cinema is too easily erased within a film theory that confines itself to the work of a few filmmakers and stars.

In relation to action genres the bi-racial buddy movie – within which race and gender are mapped onto but exceed each other – has been one site for a more detailed critical reflection on the intersection of these discourses. To some extent this sub-genre frames *Courage Under Fire* as well, although the construction of the narrative in terms of a thematic parallel between Walden and Serling is quite unusual. As I'll suggest in more detail below, it is the film's construction of masculinity across a range of characters (a staple of the military movie) that underlines the need to understand gender as experienced in relational rather than individual terms. Such a discursive construction of military masculinity across male and female protagonist contrasts with a marked critical tendency to emphasize an Oedipal model of narrative centered primarily on the hero's goals.

Since masculinity is commonly reserved as a term to describe men and their relationships to each other, female characters in the movies are often, by default, left with a femininity constructed in opposition, pieced together out of remnants and discarded values. Of course, to some extent the work that discourses of masculinity most obviously perform is to delimit ways of "being a man." There is even some agreement on what a normative or dominant masculinity might consist of – qualities such as strength, control, restraint (possibly heroism, possibly violence). So it seems to make perfect sense to understand masculinities in terms of different and distinct ways of "being a man," negotiations around the demands of a patriarchal culture and its divisions and hierarchies of class, race and sexuality. Within a cultural studies frame then, discussion of constructed masculinities leads to concerns of diverse male identities and, within film, to an analysis of images of men (whether as fantasy response, anxious negotiation or ideological reflection of wider gender relations). There is an obviousness and an inevitability to this chain of association. And yet neither paradigm seems to immediately offer a way to think about a small, but growing number of cinematic images of women which are codified as "masculine" but are not rendered as perverse. This isn't to say that there aren't plenty of images of masculine-codified women that are rendered perverse, implicitly or explicitly, through sexuality, violence or other signs of a transgression taken "too far." Yet as I've noted already, one of the most suggestive aspects of *Courage Under Fire*, and of the more recent *G.I. Jane* is that these images of military women are normalized precisely <u>through</u>, and not despite or against, discourses of masculinity. Is it too much to wish for a film criticism that is alive to such images, rather than discounting them as exceptions that once more proves the rules of gendered hierarchies?

Becoming Butch: The Mobility of Gendered Discourse

Gender can be best understood as a set of discourses that are contested, accepted and resisted within networks, rather than binaries. Instead of proposing an analysis of movies in which female characters tell us about femininity and male characters about masculinity, an analysis of gendered discourse opens up these qualities operating across characters, scenarios and narratives as well as interacting with other discourses. Thus I'm not suggesting that a movie like *Courage Under Fire* simply offers its central female protagonist as masculine, though the film raises a question as to whether a self-reliant woman inevitably becomes coded as butch in the Hollywood cinema. The film maps the acquisition of Walden's status through naming and questioning the plausibility of her heroism. Thus she is variously described as "a soldier," as "tough," as "afraid," a "wreck," a "fucking coward," a "real good mom": different versions to try on for size. And of course, ultimately a 'truthful' one, shaped by all the other renditions we have seen and heard. This is also, inevitably, a sort of testing of Meg Ryan as a star/performer – can she carry a dramatic role? – just as *G.I. Jane* was widely discussed in terms of Demi Moore's physical transformation and commitment to her performance as aspiring Navy SEAL (her shorn head, her muscles). As one review had it, *Courage Under Fire* asks both "Can a woman be a real soldier?" and "Can America's sweetheart, Meg Ryan yell 'motherfucker' with conviction?" (Brown 1996:57). It might seem that these questions pull the film in different directions. But it is their superimposition, whereby Ryan's 'ordinariness' secures the generic heroism she is called on to perform, that is ultimately crucial to the military masculinity the movie enacts around her.

There is an exchange early on in *Courage Under Fire*, which rehearses something of this complexity. Serling makes the first of his visits to the members of Walden's crew, asking each in turn what they remember of the incident at Al Kufan. Rady, her former co-pilot, injured during the crash (and unconscious through the key part of the action) is now a civilian. Serling and Rady sit outdoors with Rady's girlfriend Annie, a pretty blonde woman. Here the perspectives of the soldier and the former soldier, rooted in loyalty to the (implicitly masculine, if not, in this context, male) group, are juxtaposed with those of a (femme) female civilian:

> *Rady:* I remember the earth ... (shots of Al Kufan) ... I remember Ilario's face ... (distressed) ... I wish...
> *Annie:* If she hadn't needed to be a hero so bad...

Rady: That's not fair – we were just doing our job. It's not 'Ren's fault I got hit... she sure as hell saved the lives of those guys on that Black Hawk.
Annie: You always defend her...
Serling: (to Annie) Why didn't you like her?
Annie: She was so *butch*...
Rady: Honey – shut up. (to Serling, smiling) She *was*, you know...
Annie: Those women who want to be officers...
Rady: Annie, shut up! She gave her life for those men! (turning to Serling) She was a soldier.

Petite, serving coffee, relegated to the background and excluded from the soldiers' exchange of significant looks, Annie is the outsider here. The camerawork underlines her position, pulling away slightly as she speaks – just enough to bring Serling into the frame and to emphasize her marginality. It's perfectly acceptable for the *soldiers* – Rady and Serling – to talk about Walden as butch. The disagreement is not about being "butch" but the value attributed to Walden's toughness, an evaluation that mirrors the film's central narrative question (is she a hero?). A rejection of the butch/military woman as inappropriate comes here from a marginalized female character, defined primarily as a civilian, and then later from Monfreiz who defines himself as a good soldier, a combat veteran and Walden as a "cunt," a term of abuse that explicitly seeks to re-code her in terms of the (female) body. Whilst for Rady butch is an affectionate term, he recognizes that for Annie it means something different. He rejects the implicit de-valuing of masculinity by appealing to a shared understanding with Serling – masculine bonding we might say – simultaneously silencing her.

Later in the film, when Serling is falling apart (drinking too much, living in a motel, unable to speak to his wife) and is convinced that he is being lied to, flashback images of Walden graduating as an officer are introduced. These images of ritual and celebration are framed and overlaid by the taped words of Ilario (one of the crew who, we later learn, has betrayed her) speaking of her courage and decisiveness:

Karen – the Captain – she had this quality: the heavier the pressure, the calmer she got. She, y'know, she put up with a lot of shit to become an Officer. Y'know – had to work twice as hard as everybody else, be twice as good. She never let her guard down – show any sign of weakness. But she was tough. She could handle it.

In the original interview we hear only the first line of this speech – followed immediately by a discussion of the besieged crew's fearful anticipation of the attack that is to come at first light ("I don't know why people think only good things happen when the sun comes up"). Replayed on Serling's recorder over dreamlike images of Walden with her peers, the film presents us with an elegiac sense of her toughness, her capacity to "handle it" and, crucially, underlines the labor she has put into her military identity, to becoming an officer.

The insistence on Walden's struggle to become an officer underlines that, far from being a coward, Walden possesses the very qualities that Serling is loosing – he can't handle it, showing his weakness through his drinking. Later, when Serling is "out of the loop", pursuing the investigation unofficially with the help of sympathetic journalist Gardner, we see another such montage sequence. As he looks at a photo of Walden, Serling imagines her singing softly, with her daughter and with her crew. At a moment when Serling is waiting for events beyond his control to work themselves out, Walden's image functions as a moral anchor, signifying the good soldier whose toughness helps her overcome the odds in training, if not in combat. These imaginings prefigure the elaboration of a revised, heroic narrative around the "friendly fire" incident that opens the movie in which a tape of communications between US tanks reveals Serling's rapid response to and recovery from his mistake, his own courage under fire.

Tough, a soldier, a good mother: Walden's records describe her as an "Officer of exceptional moral courage." Of course many action movies cast strong female protagonists as iconic mothers, though this doesn't mean that the image somehow inevitably returns us simply to femininity. At a superficial level it might seem that *Courage Under Fire* operates a sort of separation of the martial and the maternal or familial. Accounts of Walden as a good mother are given by her parents (who now care for their granddaughter) whilst praise for her as a soldier comes from her male colleagues. And yet the two are hard to keep apart. Her father also speaks of the importance of duty to his daughter. And, crucially, Walden has a strongly paternalistic role in relation to her crew – her fear of letting them down is expressed when her final letter is read on the soundtrack at the close of the film: "These people depend on me. They put their lives in my hands. I just can't fail them." Moreover the film evokes maternal toughness in physical terms quite explicitly in Walden's contemptuous comment to the mutinous Monfriez (who has shot her), "I gave birth to a nine-pound baby, asshole – I think I can handle it." Whilst centrally concerned with power and status, then, becoming butch is insistently not about becoming male.

Masculinity and Medals

As the crisis in his personal life mounts, we see Serling absorbed in the details of appearance, carefully pressing the creases in his uniform, insisting on the decorative details as a way of holding together his faith in the military. We might recall here Marjorie Garber's astute comments on the different connotations of "making" men and women, together with the anxiety she pinpoints that it might not, after all, be that difficult to literally – surgically – make a man. Garber also, although briefly, turns her attention to medals, uniforms and the dressing-up involved in the military. Discussing the story of Dr. Mary Walker (who wore the Medal of Honor) she notes that:

> ...the wearing of military orders by women has been regarded as a curious reversion to "feminine" taste, a kind of jewelry. Does the sight of women wearing medals or "Orders" attached to their lapels suggest that such "orders" can be unpinned, detached, from men? The spectacle of women in men's clothes, or at least men's uniforms, both military and lay, seems to lead back to the question of male cross-dressing and its relationship to structures of hierarchy and power (Garber 1992:55).

It is interesting to note that for Garber this leads us back to cross-dressing and to men. But when women wear the medals and uniforms on their own account, a rather different articulation of female masculinity is foregrounded.

Both *Courage Under Fire* and *G.I. Jane* end with an indicative contrast between a public ceremony in which gallantry is rewarded and a private one in which a courageous man passes his own medal to a woman who has proved herself in combat. After confessing his mistake to Boylar's parents, Serling lays a medal on Walden's grave. Following her public admittance to the SEALS, Jordan finds in her locker a medal tucked into a volume of D.H. Lawrence poems (no less), a discovery followed by a silent exchange of looks between Moore and her erstwhile tormentor Urgayle. Crucially these ceremonies are moments of recognition and incorporation, testament that while official recognition has its place, it is just as, if not more important to be recognized by one's peers. Thus although Urgayle is Jordan's commanding officer, his gesture of approval is distinguished from the machinations of politicians that structure the film, inscribing her within a revised "us and them."

The ambivalent elaboration of discourses of masculinity in action movies is nowhere more evident than in the melodrama of the soldier, an heroic figure who is respected and decorated, yet simultaneously a commodified body (cannon fodder in the most extreme instance). Both heroism and decoration (medals, uniform) mask an awareness which permeates war movies of the disposability of soldiers bodies. Such an awareness is evident in quite distinct ways in the spectacular opening scenes of carnage on the beaches of Normandy and the death of the highly individuated Captain Miller (Tom Hanks) in Spielberg's *Saving Private Ryan*. Within war movies female bodies, defined primarily in terms of sexuality, have typically been disposable in rather different ways. Ironically it is in part an American anxiety about female bodies that, officially at least, so long kept women out of combat. In *G.I. Jane* both soldiers ("her presence makes us *all* vulnerable") and politicians ("no politician can afford to let women come home in body bags") argue the case in these terms. This anxiety is foregrounded in *Courage Under Fire* through the construction of a parallel between the two protagonists. Walden's status as modern military woman who strays into combat and is killed is evidently over-determined. She provides the locus for Serling's self-doubt and for his quest to have the truth made public, whilst her story is explicitly appropriated by a cynical political establishment, personified in the White House aide who is pushing for her to be awarded the medal of honor. Whilst the public recognition of her heroism is revealed to be a superficial public relations opportunity, for Serling Walden is primarily a soldier to whom he wishes to do justice. The fact that there is a political motivation in giving him the case – a "way back" as his mentor General Hershberg puts it – only serves to underline Serling's desire to know the real story, his refusal to rubber-stamp this, or any file.

Although the comparisons between *Courage Under Fire* and *Rashomon* were deemed rather superficial by some, they repay further attention. Zwick's movie doesn't end on quite the same ambiguous note; after all, Serling's desire for something to be clear, for "somebody to be a hero" is ultimately fulfilled. We might say, if so inclined, that the film offers an Oedipal story – the spectacle of a male soldier, Serling, growing up (accepting his limits, coming to terms with failure) through the investigation of a female soldier/body. Ultimately he is reconciled to his life, able to return to domesticity. Similarly *Rashomon* concludes with an image of the woodcutter quite literally holding the baby, accepting responsibility within an uncertain context (however cynical we might be by this stage). Writers have tended to regard the ending of both films as too pat, overly sentimental; yet in neither case is it particularly helpful to reduce the movie to that one narrative moment, collapsing the complex orchestration of images and moments to the supposed resolution found in the ending. It may be the case that Walden/Ryan (unlike *Rashomon*'s Machiko Kyo) offers no account of herself and her actions, other than via her final letter or the fantasized gesture of approval she bestows on Washington's Serling in the films final moments. Yet if finding the truth enables Serling to resolve his own personal turmoil, this doesn't mean automatically that her figure is somehow negated, subordinated to a narrative dynamic concerned with Serling's story alone.

Both *Courage Under Fire* and *Rashomon* explore the public face of bravery and heroism, terms central to discourses of masculinity. They underline the posturing at stake in narrating bravery – and the suspicion of imposture that accompanies such narration. The physical chaos of combat, as well as the intensity of shame, cowardice and fear, are set against the public performance made of military success, whether in the award of medals or simply in personal bragging, inordinate boasting of individual strength. In *Rashomon* both the murdered nobleman (speaking through a medium) and the bandit, Tajomaru, offer heroic accounts of their performance in battle. The woodcutter's recollections from a spectator's point of view, by contrast, emphasize the awkward physicality of the fight (sweating, breathless stumbles), and the evident fear of death displayed by both men. Despite their differences, a shared social code – of which the woman is a sign – compels them reluctantly into combat. Thus while *Courage Under Fire* is centered on

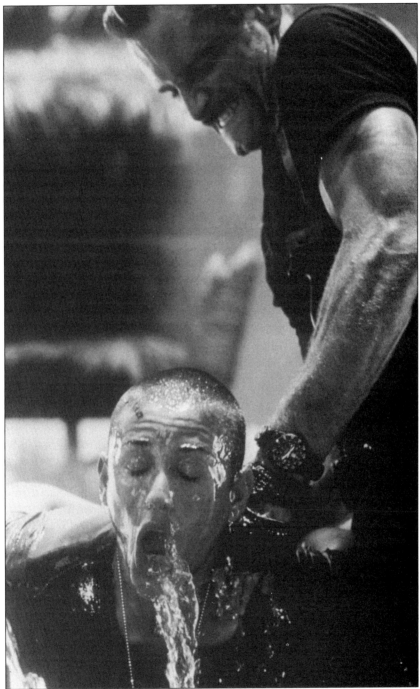

G.I. Jane (Ridley Scott, 1997), Caravan Pictures et al.

a crew's betrayal of their officer, *Rashomon* is concerned with a rape and murder, with a woman's body as the object of sexual exchange, with the physical expression of a rivalry between men of different classes, and not least with the stories men and women tell and the rather messier version of events that these stories aim to make intelligible. Crudely put the narrative question – which revolves around the impossibility of all these stories being true – is whether or not the woman "deserved it." Did she kill her husband when he rejected her following her rape, or did she incite the bandit to kill him? Either way she comes out pretty badly – as does everyone else of course. More importantly, across all of the versions that the film recounts, even when she is the most "spirited," she is constituted primarily in terms of an hysterical femininity.

In the martial setting of *Courage Under Fire*, the narrative question of arthouse rape-revenge is supplanted by a testing of moral courage and physical resilience: was she really butch or, perhaps, "was she butch enough." "She was a fucking coward" spits Monfriez in his first interview; "She was a soldier" (Rady); "She was tough" (Ilario); "If she hadn't needed to be a hero so bad... " (Annie). These questions revolve around the relative significance of Walden's tears ("just tension") and an M-16 (who was firing it during the rescue). Serling's investigation looks past the tears to focus on the action, the M-16. Of course war movies constitute one of the few genres in which men get to shed tears, typically over each other's corpses. Sure enough one of Serling's closing gestures is to don all his medals before finally shedding tears as he confesses to Boylar's parents that it was he who gave the order to fire.

If power was self-evident, medals wouldn't have the resonance that they do. Suggesting a tension between display and embodiment, the role of the medal in naming and constructing masculinity is nicely – and of course comically – acknowledged in *The Wizard of Oz* when Bert Lahr's camp cowardly lion is given a badge of courage as both the solution to his fears and a sign of having overcome them. Chris Holmlund has linked a notion of masculinity as display with Stephen Heath's contention that "male masquerade is more intimately tied to power structures than female masquerade" citing his observation that "the trappings of authority, hierarchy, order, position make the man" (Holmlund 1993:213). Here again we are back to male and female. However, within the current historical and cultural context, the significance of the military woman for the codes of Hollywood cinema is that her masculinity is tied to such power structures. By constructing its narrative around an exploration of whether a butch woman should be awarded the medal of honor, *Courage Under Fire* works to complexly repudiate the feminizing/superficial world of media and public relations, and to achieve the incorporation (albeit posthumously) of a female soldier into the community of military honor.

Courage Under Fire stages a careful balancing act in relation to the symbols around which its narrative revolves. To the extent that medals honor bravery in combat they are valuable tokens. Yet, their use as political symbols is understood with cynicism. Serling must decide whether Walden be awarded the medal of honor, having been awarded a medal himself in the military's cover-up of events at Al Bathra, events of which he is ashamed. Meanwhile the White House demands results, for the investigation to be completed so that the planned ceremony in the rose garden can take place (tears again: "There is not going to be a dry eye from Nashua to Sacramento"). Serling's disgust with all this is generic, rendered in terms of a soldier's suspicion of the superficiality of politicians. That the military codes Serling falls back on have been broken becomes, in the films terms, particularly shocking.

Women and Military Masculinity: A Longing for Belonging

The played for straight performance of masculinity articulated around the military women in both *G.I. Jane* and *Courage Under Fire* can be situated within the context of a wider discursive presentation of military women in terms of a threatening sexualization of a single-sex workplace. As war movie meets the woman's film, military women pose the issues raised by women's entry to supposedly male workplaces in a distinctive, polarized fashion. And it's not just the military who find this disturbing or who resort to a sexualized language in response: consider the following from the *Guardian*'s "Women" section on December 22, 1998:

> Equality rarely leaves a bad taste in a woman's mouth, but the missile raids [on Iraq] have done just that. American women pilots made military history by flying combat missions for the first time during Operation Desert Fox, according to a report in yesterday's Times. Now it's not just Monica who's reaching for the mouthwash.

The US/UK raids were widely referred to "Operation Monica," the attacks seen as an attempt to divert public attention from a sexual scandal surrounding a President who, we might recall, became so publicly embroiled over lesbians and gays in the military in the opening months of his first term of office.

Media discourses about military women express the "incursion" of women into western armies, navies and airforces in terms of a discursive disruption of masculinity. It is in this context that Amy Taubin praises *G.I. Jane* as an exhilarating gender-fuck, taking the opportunity to dismiss *Courage Under Fire* out of hand as "thoroughly reactionary" for using "its female hero to whitewash militarism and the stranglehold of the Pentagon on the post-Cold War economy" (Taubin 1997:73). I began by posing a question: how to make sense of images of women codified as masculine but not as perverse? Moore/Jordan's notorious challenge to Urgayle to "suck my dick" is richly redolent, yet if either of these films can be read as transgressive it is not in any particularly grand fashion. Jordan has the shit kicked out of her and appropriates it into a sign of equality. Her desire to be treated just as bad as everybody else (and thence to participate in the action movie's masculine narcissism) whilst she is still effectively marked as different – whether as an officer, a woman, as smart (her background in intelligence) – enacts a tension between individual and team that is central to the war movie. Demi Moore's star status, together with her involvement as co-producer, simply allows (or requires) a more spectacular packaging of Meg Ryan's (extra)ordinary butchness.

What Taubin seems to miss is that the pitch of both films is for women to be included in the sentimental brotherhood extolled in movies like *Saving Private Ryan*. Of course it doesn't work out quite like that: both films feature key scenes in which male soldiers disobey their female officers orders in combat situations (actual in *Courage Under Fire*, simulated in *G.I. Jane*). Monfriez's mutiny leads to Walden's death in *Courage Under Fire*, whilst in *G.I. Jane*, Sgt. Cortez (whose individualism marks him as a problem early on) gets the whole team captured during a training mission by ignoring Jordan's orders. Monfriez is shown screaming at a recruit: "you never leave a man behind." The film works to argue that, in effect, this is exactly what he has done. In this way of course the films both rehearse one of the standard arguments against involving women in combat situations (military women lack the right stuff; military men get disorientated around them). Indeed *Courage Under Fire*'s artful structure allows it to condemn Monfreiz's neurotic (and racially othered) masculinity whilst ultimately avoiding taking sides on a contentious issue. Instead, argument is rehearsed and resolved through a discursive masculinity that renders Walden tough enough just as Moore's Jordan proves herself by triumphing over and then rescuing her commanding officer. If these debates seem bound to the context of both contemporary fiction and warfare, we might consider Judith Halberstam's comments on how World War I provided "some masculine women" with:

> ... the opportunity to live out the kinds of active lives that in peacetime they could only fantasize about. Although [Toupie] Lowther's ambulance unit was constantly hampered by conventional notions of female activity, they also did see active combat, and many of these women were applauded for the first time in their lives for behaving more like men than women (Halberstam 1998:85).

It is important to note that fantasy and applause (public recognition) are as significant here as the notions of female activity, combat and masculinity that Halberstam brings together. That is, a militarized female masculinity here embodies both the transgression of gendered codes and a longing for belonging.

Accepted by some into the military group and rejected by others, there is no doubt that Karen Walden signifies disruption for a conservative institution in transition. To this extent she figures a problem of representation, of gendered discourse. But within this, her ordinariness (so central to Meg Ryan's star image) and her butchness are both central. It is not even the case, as we might expect, that her ordinariness (or her death) somehow mitigates her butchness and the perversity that this might suggest. Rather her status as a good soldier is constituted in terms of a discursive masculinity, which purports to value star performer *and* extras, officers *and* crew. That is, her butchness normalizes her at the same time as it renders her exceptional.

There is a thorough-going perversity within popular culture which provides images and narratives that disrupt the gendered and other binaries through which we seek to make sense of them (voyeurism/fetishism, sadistic/masochistic, active/passive). Such images suggest a need to extend to women the implications of Michael Uebel's comment that masculinity be understood not as "the defining quality of men, of their fantasies and real experiences of self and other, but one co-ordinate of their identity that exists in a constant dialectical relation with other co-ordinates" (Uebel 1997:4). Movies are sophisticated forms of representation, sets of images with the power to articulate complex sets of relations, investments (erotic, emotional) and ambivalent, even contradictory desires. The articulation of martial masculine prowess – courage under fire – around a female soldier/officer works both to underline qualities of self-sufficiency or leadership as learned, whilst simultaneously clinging to a romantically redemptive concept of honor. The co-existence of public and private award ceremonies recognize that symbols of success are both compromised and valued. In the search for grander transgressions, we run the risk of missing the significance of just what is being offered up as "mainstream" these days.

References

Andermahr, S. (1994). A queer love affair? Madonna and lesbian and gay culture. In D. Hamer & B. Budge (Eds.), *The good, the bad and the gorgeous: Popular culture's romance with lesbianism*. London: Pandora.

Brown, G. (1996, July 16). Battle cry. *Village Voice*, p. 57.

Collins, J., H. Radner & A. Preacher Collins (Eds.) (1993). *Film theory goes to the movies*. London: Routledge.

Eleftheriotis, D. (1995). Questioning totalities: Constructions of masculinity in the popular Greek cinema of the 1960s. *Screen, 36*, 3, 233-242.

Garber, M. (1992). *Vested interests: Cross-dressing and cultural anxiety*. London: Routledge.

Graham, P. (1995). Girl's camp? The politics of parody. In T. Wilton (Ed.), *Immortal, invisible: Lesbians and the moving image*. London: Routledge.

Halberstam, J. (1998). *Female masculinity*. Durham: Duke UP.

Holmlund, C. (1993). Masculinity as multiple masquerade. In S. Cohan & I.R. Hark (Eds.), *Screening the male: Exploring masculinities in Hollywood cinema*. London: Routledge.

Jeffords, S. (1993). Can masculinity be terminated?. In S. Cohan & I.R. Hark (Eds.), *Screening the male: Exploring masculinities in Hollywood cinema*. London: Routledge.

Jennings, R. (1995). Desire and design – Ripley undressed. In T. Wilton (Ed.), *Immortal, invisible: Lesbians and the moving image*. London: Routledge.

Modleski, T. (1997). A woman's gotta do... what a man's gotta do? Cross-dressing in the western. *Signs, 22*, 3.

Pfeil, F. (1995). *White guys: Studies in postmodern domination and difference*. London: Verso.

Stecopoulos, H. & M. Uebel (Eds.) (1997). *Race and the subject of masculinities*. Durham: Duke UP.

The article is published in *Quarterly Review of Film & Video Journal*, vol 19, 2002, and reprinted by permission of Taylor and Francis (© copyright by Taylor & Francis 2002).

Tasker, Y. (1993). *Spectacular bodies: Gender, genre and the action cinema*. London: Routledge.

Taubin, A. (1997). Dicks and Jane. *Village Voice,* September 261997, p.73.

Whatling, C. (1997). *Screen dreams: Fantasising lesbians in film*. Manchester: Manchester UP.

Wiegman, R. (1993). Feminism, 'The Boyz', and Other Matters Regarding the Male. In S. Cohan & I.R. Hark (Eds.), *Screening the male: Exploring masculinities in Hollywood cinema*. London: Routledge.

Willis, S. (1997). *High contrast: Race and gender in contemporary Hollywood*. Durham: Duke UP.

Iconic Eye Candy

Buffy the Vampire Slayer and Designer Peer Pressure for Teens

Deneka C. MacDonald

The world of television and film media has extended its boundaries in recent years. In conjunction with the fashion industry, on screen celebrities are increasingly portrayed and marketed in fashion magazines, strengthening the great myth of body and beauty and providing further boundaries between average women and the elite of Hollywood actresses. The very concept is aimed not at mainstream or mass population groups, but rather at younger and more specialized audiences within society, namely young white western females who have proven to continually buy into such myths. While (multi) media has both influenced and been influenced by social and cultural conventions of any given period, in the late twentieth century this became (and continues to be) a particularly complicated phenomenon. Continuous cultural differences and fast paced challenges to previously conceived social norms have meant that media platforms such as television, film and women's magazines must continually redraw and adjust their boundaries to reflect influences and shifts in cultural norms. One such influential shift in the twentieth century is, of course, feminism.

As feminist ideals merge with popular culture, there has been a surge of female heroines in texts who no longer portray the strong woman as mad (or even bad), but rather as chic and friendly.[1] Often sexualizing 'feminist' heroines, such texts problematically claim to interrogate a stereotype of Woman while upholding her as an object and offering her fetishized image to an audience hungry for this contemporary vision of strong feminist Woman; one such text is *Buffy the Vampire Slayer*. Using the first two seasons of *Buffy the Vampire Slayer* as a primary text, this paper addresses issues of interaction between pulp culture programs and popular media campaigns directed toward the teen viewing experience within western culture.[2] As female audiences are bombarded with visual peer pressure from various media experiences, I discuss the motif of body image and sexuality as they are represented to young women.

Overview of Program

In 1992 Twentieth Century Fox produced *Buffy the Vampire Slayer*, written by Joss Whedon and starring Kristy Swanson. While the film was not a box office success by Hollywood standards, it did spark a spin off television series which has generated incredible interest, not least because of its claim of *legitimate* 'girl power' with a rounded three dimensional female heroine. The series *Buffy the Vampire Slayer* has enjoyed extraordinary appeal to young audiences (as well as adult and indeed academic audiences) worldwide. In fact, in early 2001, Professor David Lavery at Middle Tennessee State University and Rhonda Wilcox at Gordon College started *Slayage: The Online International Journal of Buffy Studies*, dedicated to the scholarly analysis of the television program. The Journal celebrated its first international conference in October 2002 in East Anglia, England with plans to convene in North America in 2003.[3] Since, books and articles have abounded on the subject, making *Buffy the Vampire Slayer* a household name that has inspired phenomenal interest. Claims of new feminism abound.[4]

The television series *Buffy the Vampire Slayer* has enjoyed seven successful seasons and the core characters have, for the most part, remained the same. Because this paper deals almost exclusively with the first three seasons of the program, I will provide a brief synopsis of the characters and their individual significance to the series. *Buffy the Vampire Slayer* is set in Sunnydale (California), a small town in the United States of America and the center of the Hellmouth, which means that it is particularly beset with demons and vampires. Buffy Summers is the Slayer, a specially chosen girl, whose destiny centers on slaying evil from the world. She is assigned a Watcher, Rupert Giles, who is responsible for interpreting ancient vampire prophecy and scripture, and for training Buffy in her active role as Slayer; as Watcher, Giles is a protector of Buffy, but he has no supernatural abilities. In the first episode of the first season (1:1) we learn that Buffy has moved from Los Angeles with her mother, Joyce, recently separated from Buffy's father and completely unaware of Buffy's role as Slayer. Buffy is initially befriended by Cordelia, the most beautiful and popular girl in school, but she quickly rejects Cordelia and her clique (called the Cordette's). Instead, Buffy chooses to bond with Willow, a female science 'geek' and Xander, an equally unpopular 'loser', as Cordelia points out. Willow and Xander become Buffy's closest friends as they learn of her position as Slayer and the trio becomes known as the Scooby gang. Significantly, Willow and Xander are not part of the socially acceptable popular clique that is so common in the highly political social circles of any North American high school system. From the onset, Buffy meets Angel, her major love interest throughout the series, yet she is unaware until later ("Angel" 1:7) that he is a vampire (Angelus) who has been cursed by gypsies to be aware of his own humanity. Angel suffers, uniquely, from having a soul. Angel's possession of a soul makes him a sensitive and wounded character, haunted by his past murderous acts and unable to participate in 'acceptable' vampire behavior. Since he was cursed with a soul he has not killed a single human being and suffers daily from his guilty conscience. Buffy's romantic feelings for Angel complicate her position as Slayer on several occasions. The interest in Angel's character led to a spin off series in 1999.

Buffy as a Feminist Text?

Conventionally, images of powerful supernatural women in fantastic literature, film, television and multimedia have existed primarily in male 'authored' (and often male-centered) contexts. Such texts work to explore the 'story' of male characters and consequently their patriarchal 'kingdoms'. As a result, women in male-centered texts have been represented as having token power whilst waiting for a more powerful male character to sweep in and 'save the day', or women who are legitimately powerful have typically been characterized as mad, evil or ambitiously corrupt, accompanied by a token 'good' woman to complete the binary relationship.[5] These stories, varied throughout textual history, have a common theme; they invoke the notion of female power, only to defuse it by disallowing full investigation of the meaning of their power. As a result female characters are both one dimensional and uninteresting; while we are aware that major power lurks in the background in the form of one female character or another, they are denied any telling of their own story. They remain frozen images of 'badness' among a whole entourage of fuller masculine probed characterization. These women need only 'be there' – their presence is required for the plot to work, but they are essentially silent, best seen but not heard. Not surprising, such portrayals have been attacked with great force within feminist discourse.[6] Yet programs like *Buffy the Vampire Slayer* have challenged this traditional portrayal of the supernatural woman. Buffy is not bad and she is still powerful.

Because both the film *Buffy the Vampire Slayer*, and its television counterpart, rely on the female protagonist, the 'chosen one', to slay vampires while still maintaining her girlish femininity, the most asked question about the program is: Can *Buffy the Vampire Slayer* be read as a feminist text? Moreover, since the series itself claims to be a feminist vision of sorts, it invites appropriate analytical responses. In "Killing us Softly? A Feminist Search for the 'Real' Buffy," Sherryl Vint asks that precise question and finds that "Buffy strikes me as a positive role model for young women, one which feminism should celebrate [because] the show delivers this 'message' by working through the desires and concerns of teenage girls (for acceptance and love, about sexuality and partnerships) rather trying to "preach" to them about appropriate feminist behavior" (Vint 2002:1-2). Vint's work is intriguing because, like myself, she is interested in the interplay between Buffy the character in the series (or the primary text) and Sarah Michelle Gellar, the actress, and her subsequent fame in film and media (the secondary texts). Moreover, Vint finds that the program itself does sexualize Buffy, although she argues that "it always combines this sexualization with demonstration of her power" (Vint 2002:2). However, unlike my own work which focuses on the early series (1 and 2) of the program, Vint's work concentrates on the later, more daring, refined and 'seasoned' series of *Buffy the Vampire Slayer* (4 and 5). As such, Vint excuses the sexualization of Buffy stating that "Gellar, herself a young woman who has been formed by these cultural forces, has demonstrated the ability of young women to maintain an ironic distance from their exploitation" (Vint 2002:6). While this may be the case for later *Buffy the Vampire Slayer*, with its established mixed audience and solid footing, can we say the same about early *Buffy the Vampire Slayer*? I do not think we can.

In his analysis of cultural trends within fiction, Scott McCracken notes "often new oppositional trends, such as feminism, are absorbed and assimilated by the entertainment industry, changing its nature" (McCracken 1998:30). McCracken's point that movements such as feminism can be assimilated into popular culture is particularly interesting. While it is clear that major television companies (like 20th Century fox or WB Network), can hardly ignore the impact of the women's movement on the world at large, the degree to which they choose to participate in it, anticipate it, subvert it or *manipulate it* is intriguing for popular culture programs like *Buffy the Vampire Slayer, Xena: Warrior Princess, Charmed* or even (the non-supernaturally inclined) *Ally McBeal* and their media created characters. Moreover, as television companies and media representatives struggle with the notion of feminism in the twentieth and twenty first centuries, lines are continually drawn and redrawn in terms of who we accept as our masculine and feminine heroes. Presumably this is what Vint means when she states that *Buffy the Vampire Slayer*, "works through" teens' concerns instead of "preaching" to them. Vint argues:

> Young women often reject a feminist identity because they associate such an identity with the negative stereotype of a man-hater, or because they believe feminism is about a kind of "political correctness" that rejects the pleasure they find in culture and judges them for finding such pleasure. It is imperative that feminism find a way to connect with the cultural life of young women, and *Buffy the Vampire Slayer* strikes me as one productive avenue through which this work can be done. It is inevitable that young women will be exposed to what feminism would label negative stereotypes of women and that they may be attracted to such stereotypes. Rather than condemning these stereotypes – and hence the desire that women might find in them – feminism should help young women to critically interrogate the stereotype and its constructed appeal. A feminism that seeks only to judge and condemn will continue to convince young women that this is a postfeminist age (Vint 2002:2).

Vint clearly sees *Buffy the Vampire Slayer* as having a more 'refined' feminist agenda that I do. In the first place, while there is little doubt that feminism should seek to embrace North American teens more effectively, its discourse and goals can not be abandoned and compromised to cater to them either. In other words, 'dumbing down' feminist issues and excusing the objectification or sexualization of women is not the answer. Nor are such excuses a valid argument toward youth or otherwise for 'accessing' feminist ideas. While I do not accuse Vint of encouraging this, I would argue that iconic visions of Woman in texts like *Buffy* are only *capable* of offering a pseudo-feminist, or more accurately, a patriarchal constructed 'feminist', perspective to young women. Moreover, while Vint is certainly correct to acknowledge that feminism should help women to critically interrogate stereotypes and their constructed appeal, I hasten to acknowledge such effort in *Buffy the Vampire Slayer*. Can a program that purposefully sexualizes its female heroine be seen to interrogate the stereotype that it upholds?

Buffy as Icon

Young women like Buffy (the character), appeal to, and were originally created for, a specific target audience or demographic – young teenagers. Presumably, the draw lies in her iconic qualities of beauty and 'positive' role modeling. But she is also a sexual symbol, a visual focal point, for both girls and boys; indeed as John Berger has so influentially noted: "Men look at women. Women watch themselves being looked at. This determines not only the relations of men to women, but the relation of women to themselves" (Berger 1988:47). As well, as we will see, in the early series of *Buffy the Vampire Slayer*, characters like Buffy represent an appearance of power without actually possessing any. In fact, she seems stereotypically disempowered; she is superficially designed to cater to and persuade audiences to "buy into" preferred images of the body and beauty. Early *Buffy the Vampire Slayer* (the program and the character) create constructed sex symbols – visual focal points for those who followed the program. Buffy *is* iconic eye candy, a [C]osmopolitan[7] vampire killer.

In making Buffy a vampire slayer, *the chosen one* no less, she automatically assumes a position of power, but does she have any real power and is she a feminist? Or can one claim that the series has a feminist subtext? Granted, this is not our prototypical "ditzy blonde in horror flick" character. Buffy has both brain and brawn; she is three-dimensional. She takes an active role without always having to be saved, upstaged, or lectured to by a more powerful male character. Indeed this genre of popular culture has the ability to "create strong heroines who are as accomplished as any male in terms of physical competence and hard headed cunning [...]" as well as the capacity to "unsettle rather than maintain the status quo" (Moran 1999:42). And perhaps more recent *Buffy the Vampire Slayer* does this. However, in the early series of *Buffy the Vampire Slayer*, Giles takes the role of male authority figure and he possesses more political power than Buffy. In the first instance, Giles is an adult, while Buffy is a teenager, and this gives him immediate power over her. As well, Giles holds the position of both Watcher and father-figure, since it is clear that Buffy's biological father will have no presence in the text. Giles schedules Buffy's battles, instructs her on how to fight, pushes her to 'train', to hunt and indeed gives her little choice but to embrace this role. It is quite clear that in her role as 'chosen one', Buffy does not choose, rather, she *is* chosen. Let us not forget that initially Buffy emphatically states that she would rather 'go shopping' and it takes some heavy handed persuading (by the dominant male characters of the program) to convince her to agree to 'slay' instead. Thus, at least initially, Buffy is an instrument of patriarchy.

Traditionally, strong women on the screen have been represented as negative archetypes.[8] Anneke Smelik makes the point that powerful women in cinema are often portrayed as women of vengeance and asks, "has feminist work in cinema unleashed the Erinyes onto the silver screen?" (Smelik 1998:91), because powerful women in literary discourse or narrative text have also been evil or mad women.[9] Moreover, such women have been negatively portrayed for their ability to display or become angry, an emotion not traditionally validated for women. Indeed, women have been denied the expression of healthy 'anger' because it is not feminine: "it's unseemly, aesthetically displeasing, and against the sweet, pliant, feminine image to be angry" (Kaplow 1973: 37). However, in keeping with popular trends, the new female image of "girl power" is *not* the Medusa or Medea of the twenty first century – she is strong, she is powerful, but quite crucially, she is *not* bad. Additionally, she is still beautiful, sexy and feminine. Intriguingly, however, she is still not allowed to get angry.

Buffy never gets angry or loses her composure with the vampires she slays or the men who manipulate her to Slay. She calmly, professionally and 'femininely' hunts the villains of the program, thus combining aspects of a career woman with those of a sexualized (and fetishized) icon. Hardly the vision that Helen Cixous had in mind when she described the 'natural woman' bursting with repressed energy like a "force never let loose before" (Cixous 1989:113). Instead Buffy offers a calming presence; she is able to kill the 'bad guys' with composure, whilst maintaining a carefully constructed image. Producers and media representatives have worked hard to portray Buffy as the 'good guy' – Buffy fights evil, she does not embody it, and she still has time to apply her lipstick and do her hair.

The 'feminism' presented in *Buffy the Vampire Slayer* is dangerous because it promotes a patriarchal ideal of strong Woman that is reflected in various aspects of her character, notably in her attitude toward education. Buffy's character gives the appearance of intelligence with her witty and quick retorts in various episodes, yet it is clear that she loathes studying and is disinterested in education. For example, in "Never Kill a Boy on the First Date" (1.5), sporting a sleeveless dress, six inches above the knee and calf-high leather boots with heels, Buffy encounters Owen in the library. Owen is a one-episode love interest. When Owen openly insults her intelligence and states that he is surprised to find her in a library, Buffy dismisses the comment (literally) with a giggle and a head tilt. Immediately following Owen's departure, Buffy is love-sick and has difficulty resuming her concentration of Slaying matters with Giles. Giles confirms Buffy's reputation for non-scholarly pursuits by stating: "Buffy, while the very fact that you wanted to check out a book would be grounds for a national holiday, I think we should focus on the matter at hand." Buffy responds, "Right, I'm sorry, you're right . . . Vampires. . . Does this outfit make me look fat?" It is significant, moreover, that Buffy's character is contrasted in the program with Willow, who represents intelligence and educational dedication. Willow is repetitively seen with books in her arms or in front of a computer where she is doing research or studying. Willow also tutors Buffy in some episodes, highlighting the intellectual differences between them. This kind of character contrast is, importantly, also the case aesthetically. The characters in *Buffy the Vampire Slayer* balance the Buffy character, each illustrating what Buffy is or is not: Willow's plainness highlights Buffy's beauty, Xander's awkwardness with the opposite sex serves to illustrate Buffy's prowess and ease with men, and Giles' bookworm attitude to slaying highlights Buffy's hands-on approach to slaying. Buffy is superior to all of the characters on the program because she is 'average' smart (but not overly clever), more beautiful and popular, more comfortable with her own sex appeal and above all, she is still vulnerable and sweet: "the quintessential American teenager" (Daugherty 2001:152).

As an archetype of sexuality, Buffy embodies the patriarchal fear of female sexual power and she therefore, must (and does) lose in the game of love. As the program operates in the highly political system of television programming where the bottom line is ratings, Buffy must possess both power and sex appeal to be successful. But she must also be susceptible to weakness in the same areas, otherwise she is a threat to the masculine identity of both the male characters in the program and the male viewing audience. Film theorist Marsha McCreadie correctly notes that the very nature of the image is visual, and therefore, one must be aware of appearance and looking on screen (McCreadie 1983:48). McCreadie takes a similar position to that of Laura Mulvey, Joan Mellen, and Molly Haskell, who communicate a rigorous feminism in their work on film studies. Like Mulvey, McCreadie sees film as a weapon with which to do battle against phallocentricism within social conventions, not to promote it McCreadie 1983:60). As such it is unlikely that followers of this branch of feminist thought would see *Buffy the Vampire Slayer* as a feminist work. Anne Millard Daugherty notes:

> For all efforts taken to negate the traditional male gaze, Buffy's physical attractiveness is, in itself, objectifying [...] the cultural construction of an ideal female – young, shapely, carefully dressed and made up, fashionable, glam-

orous – may be considered in itself as 'oppressive' because it proffers an image which many women feel it is important to live up to and yet is at the same time unattainable for most of use [this] describes Buffy perfectly. She is [...] petite, blonde and always impeccably dressed [...] few women can live up to [this] (Daugherty 2001:152).

Indeed, both the series and the very nature of the characterization promote Buffy as a visual icon, a manipulated and cosmetically produced sexualized toy, representing a false appearance of female power and feminism.

Designer Peer Pressure

"Television is *the* popular cultural form of the late twentieth century. It is without doubt the world's most popular leisure activity," notes cultural studies scholar John Storey (Storey 1996:9). Consequently, *Buffy the Vampire Slayer* has become a household name for teens in western culture airing during prime time when there are sure to be as many young adults watching as possible. The initial series (episodes 1:1-2:22) is geared specifically to a younger audience, incorporating *token teen issues* to ensure its success; Buffy sets out to experience all the same things that teens deal with in 'the real world'. Buffy is from a broken home, thus she and her mom continually deal with single parenting issues; and, as the show revolves around high-school life, common early 'teen' issues addressed in these episodes include dating, school field trips, parental confusion/generational gap issues, parent-teacher nights, writing your Student Aptitude Test's (S.A.T's), sneaking out of mom and dad's house, high-school dances and proms. Moreover, even in season three, the program engages in poignant moralistic messages. For example, "Bad Girls: Take a Walk on the Wild Side" (3:14), illustrates the dangers of peer pressure when Buffy becomes reckless with excessive partying. She is 'out of control' as she drinks alcohol, goes clubbing and ignores the wiser concerns of her gang. The underlying motif is that the pressure of being the Slayer has gotten to her; she wants to be a 'normal teen' – feelings which all teens can relate to. Juxtaposed to this reckless behavior, the rest of the Scoobie gang responsibly contemplate life after high-school, future careers, and debate the harmful effects of alcohol. To push the moralism in the episode, Buffy becomes possessed and regresses to a cave woman when her beer is spiked with a magical potion.

Here, the negative illustration of the use of magic is coupled with the concept of anti-beauty. Buffy becomes the enchantress turned hag when she trespasses into the masculine world of consuming alcohol. As the Slayer, Buffy is already a trespasser, a transvestite of sorts, in patriarchal territory, which is only 'acceptable' because she possesses stereotypical 'feminine' characteristics (mainly her inability to control her own personal life). However, her involvement with alcohol pushes her further into the forbidden masculine territory, and as a result, she loses her physical beauty. The projection of this Medusa figure to the screen represents the traditional monstrous feminine in the fantasy/horror genre. Barbara Spackman discusses this motif, arguing that "the grotesque female body is not a product of inversion [. . .] it belongs to the topos of enchantress turn-hag, a topos that opposes the beautiful enchantress (woman as lie) to the toothless old hag hidden beneath her artifice [. . .]"(Spackman 1991:14). Spackman's choice of language here is important; that is to say that the female body, inverted from the beautified to the hag, is a long time myth, supported by literature and maintained by popular culture – the fear of losing ones physical beauty *is* what gives power and strength to the beauty myth (take for example the classic fairy tale *Snow White* or *Cinderella*, whose plots hinge on the notion of lost beauty and the lengths women will go to keep that particular quality as well as the onslaught of women's magazines produced each month which promote beauty and body changing products). Buffy's cave woman regression reinforces this myth whilst, simultaneously, strengthening the long-standing cliché that women are *not* attractive when they drink.

Other episodes during the early seasons of *Buffy* promote similar, if not more disturbing, detrimental images of body and beauty. In "Some Assembly Required" (2.2), the town of Sunnydale is disturbed by a grave robber with a mission. We soon discover that this supernatural grave robbing force is stealing the body parts of dead young women; the goal is to assemble the parts and construct the perfect female form as a partner for a recently resurrected and now un-dead footballer. The episode plays upon obvious images of malleable women found in stories such as *Pygmalion*, *The Bride of Frankenstein* and the *Stepford Wives* without interrogating them; rather, we literally see the addition and removal of body parts as the grave robber seeks to create a patchwork woman. While the notion of dismantling the female body is highly problematic in itself (and undoubtedly a misogynist one), here it takes manipulation and reconstruction further.

Laura Mulvey has called the male viewing experience 'the gaze'. explaining that the pleasure in looking is made more powerful for the film viewing audience when the object of the gaze sets up a masquerade which expresses a strange underworld of both fear and desire (Mulvey 1989:8). Clearly, the objects (the women) of our gaze in this episode are indeed both desirable and grotesque; in "Some Assembly Required", the bodies of the dead women that are chosen for parts belong only to pleasurable looking girls (classed in terms of beauty), yet the obvious 'deadness' of these bodies should be read as equally unsettling. Significantly, it is the head of Cordelia that is to be the final piece in this Stepford assembly; as the 'head' of the elite and most popular girls at Sunnydale High-school, Cordelia is a character who is entirely consumed by her own 'beauty' and fashionable attire. Here, in taking the body apart, examining individual parts for perfection and worth, the myth of physical perfection is blatantly reinforced. Moreover, one cannot help but draw parallels with this episode of obvious aesthetic messages and contemporary obsessions with plastic and cosmetic surgery. This is especially true when one considers that Sunnydale is a Californian town (the center of western cosmetic surgery and surgeons) and that it is Cordelia's head – more specifically, her face – that is the final piece of the assembly. Indeed, in a world where "Elizabeth Arden's is the most advanced treatment of the century, as if aging required chemotherapy" (Wolf 1991:226), and superficial cosmetic surgeries are commonplace, the Frankenstein imagery and quest for power over the female body portrayed in "Some Assembly Required" makes one wonder: what message is being conveyed to the mass of teenage girls targeted for its viewing?

Sex and Love

If the series takes its token high-schoolism seriously, it works harder to concentrate on what has been culturally inscribed as the 'most important' problem in the young teenage girl's life: love. The first two seasons of *Buffy the Vampire Slayer* center primarily on the concept of love, specifically unrequited love and sexual frustration: "Teachers Pet" (1:4); "Never Kill a Boy on the First Date" (1:5); "I Robot... You Jane" (1:8); "Prophecy Girl" (1:12); "Bewitched, Betrothed, Bewildered" (2:16); "Passion" (2:17); "I Only Have Eyes For You" (2:19); and "Becoming" (2:21-2:22) are just a few of the titles of individual shows that deal exclusively with love. There is a consistent pattern of an unattainable, but still very much desired, love within the group of characters, with struggles between Angel/Buffy, Giles/Ms. Calender, Xander/Buffy, and Xander/Cordelia and Xander/Willow. In fact, every single episode of *Buffy the Vampire Slayer* (during the first two seasons at least, but arguably throughout the entire series), is either specifically about a love interest or issue, or it has a small side plot dealing with the hardships of love. Moreover, sex is not a force of good in the early days of the program. The only people engaging in non-problematic or angst free sexual activity are evil characters like Spike or Druscilla. For Giles, the only male authority figure on the show, sex is a sign of irresponsibility and a lack of enthusiasm in his work with Buffy. Giles is marginalized in his sexual activity; Xander has continual problems with sex, most notably almost being raped by Faith; and Buffy herself has her heart broken when she engages in sexual activity. Importantly, the most significant love dilemma on *Buffy the Vampire Slayer* culminates in the Angel/Buffy relationship.

Buffy is undoubtedly a sexual character. She appears as a normal teen that dates and likes the attention she receives from the opposite sex. She dresses provocatively (almost exclusively in short dresses or skirts throughout the first two seasons) and appears to be in control of her life when it comes to slaying. But eventually, Buffy falls in love. Her relationship with

Angel is both problematic and mysterious from the beginning. We learn that Angel is a vampire and protects himself from feeling emotion for fear of jeopardizing his soul. Thus, the struggle between Buffy and Angel continues for some time while they cope with their growing feelings of sexual intensity; Buffy's character is denied sexual release until halfway through the second season in the episode "Surprise" (2:13). When they finally consummate their relationship, a dark magic is summoned to reverse the gypsy spell and Angel physically runs from the bed screaming. Angel's soul is dramatically destroyed, turning him from good vampire to evil vampire, and literally transforming him into Angelus, his former evil self. Immediately he kills his first human in 100 years – a sufficient message to audiences world-wide that sex is a dangerous and negative act for both young men and women alike. As Roz Kaveney notes "Angelus is not only dangerous in and of himself; he is the principal representative of the menace posed by love gone rancid" (Kaveney: 2001:17). Buffy is forced to kill Angel and in subsequent episodes (after Angel manages to come back to life and be good again), references to her power over him in this way are made repeatedly: "Don't make me kill you again". Thus, we learn that Buffy has the power to dismantle not just Angel's life, but his masculinity; she is evil in this (as all powerful women are)[10]- capable of spiritual neutering and emasculating.

Beyond *Buffy in* Buffy the Vampire Slayer

Obviously, there remains a need for deeper insights into how women are positioned within sexual discourses, and the sexual nature of the Buffy character is no exception. Patricia Waugh notes that the nature of the problem lies in its very portrayal of the female character. She argues that when women are represented within sexual contexts it often proves unsuccessful due to the "regressive emotional investments of romantic love [. . . and] the desire to conform to dominant images of feminine attractiveness" (Waugh 1989:38). While Waugh does not make reference to any specific female character in film or fiction, her contention is useful in this analysis. As noted, early *Buffy the Vampire Slayer* struggles with token teen issues, in particular with her decisions in the game of love. And it is here where her position as female power figure is most strongly in question. While one could conceivably argue that her slaying of vampires and position as the *chosen one* represent a feminist vision of sorts, it is Giles who directs these actions almost entirely in the early seasons of the program and, as we have noted, Buffy does not actually 'choose' this role. As well, her regressive and predictable inability to handle her own love life, or more specifically her sex life, necessarily negates any previous agency. Buffy is an emotional character who in turn characterizes 'traditional' feminine emotions. As Steve O'Brien notes in *SFX*, "[l]ike (the late) *Ally McBeal, Buffy's* an unusual show in that it showcases a woman who's both good-looking yet whose emotions are nakedly on show. Far from the stellarised icons of the past, these are touchable role models, girls next door with better legs" (O'Brien 2002:101). While O'Brien clearly sees this 'touchable' quality as complimentary role modeling for women and teens, I would suggest that the fact that she needs to have *better legs* in order for her emotional outbursts to be acceptable is highly problematic.

But the character Buffy, played by Sarah Michelle Gellar, is problematic in itself. While she exudes innocence and wholesomeness on the series, there exists a dichotomy between the character and the actress. Gellar is the *teen* representative for Maybelline cosmetics and her face appears on several advertisements found in teen magazines promoting the mosaic mask of the cosmetic industry, yet she is a woman in her mid twenties, dressing up as a school girl in both instances. Sarah Michelle Gellar has become one of the leading sex symbols of the late twentieth and early twenty first century. Gellar is clearly a girl who sets fashion trends, dresses provocatively, and is 'boy crazy' in the early series of *Buffy the Vampire Slayer*. As Vint correctly notes, in "the first two seasons [...] Buffy almost invariably wore a short skirt and a spaghetti strap top" (Vint 2002:2).[11] Moreover, she both actively and willingly participates in the beauty myth. Thus, while Buffy is an improvement on previous supernatural female idols on the screen, she is not entirely satisfying as a strong positive role model.[12] Further, the participation and promotion of the beauty myth in the series, in the film, and in the media makes *Buffy the Vampire Slayer* representative of a new wave of designer peer pressure for its youthful fans. Buffy, the character, in the primary text (the series) as well as Sarah Michelle Gellar, the actress, in the secondary texts (media) promote mythical images of 'girls' and 'women'.

In 1997, the same year that the *Buffy the Vampire Slayer* series first aired, Gellar appeared in two films: *I Know What You Did Last Summer*, and *Scream 2*. Both films were of the horror genre and in both, Gellar plays the very typical 'ditzy blonde' that her Buffy character *technically* avoids: while she is the heroine in *I Know What You Did Last Summer* (1997), she is more concerned with her hair (horrifyingly the killer in the film cuts her hair off), her makeup, and her position as town beauty queen in the upcoming pageant than she is with the fact that someone is trying to murder her; and in *Scream 2* (1998), her character is literally the girl who is 'too stupid to not go downstairs,' characteristic of 80's slasher films. Moreover, she solidified her role as one of the most provocative sex symbols when she appeared in the 1999 release of *Cruel Intentions*, a remake of the earlier *Dangerous Liasons* (1988). In the film, Gellar plays a sexually aggressive school girl who uses sex for her own gain and enjoys the power she holds over the male characters in the film; additionally, the plot of this film concludes when the powerful female character (Gellar) is sold out by the male hero, disempowering her entirely, and publicly humiliating her. A true sexual predator in this film, as elsewhere, it is difficult to watch Gellar as the wholesome Buffy after these appearances.

Conclusions

So, can we accept Buffy as a feminist character or *Buffy the Vampire Slayer* as a feminist series? Perhaps the answer is both yes and no. As Sheryl Vint notes: "My struggle in "placing" Buffy as feminist or not is related to the tension in feminism between critiquing and celebrating images of women in popular culture" (Vint 2002:7). While *Buffy the Vampire Slayer* portrays a female figure of some power, it does work against itself in the early series to disempower the heroine of the program. An icon of popular culture, Buffy *has* made an impact and *has* absorbed feminist ideas in the process, despite its skewed result, and she also proves that powerful women do not have to be evil. Equally, however, *Buffy* proves that strong women are still not allowed to be (or get) angry, as well as promoting a dangerous patriarchal ideal of beauty and body. Perhaps *Buffy the Vampire Slayer* should be read as a text that ultimately reflects a cultural ambivalence toward gender, sexuality and identity for contemporary teens. Women do not need to deny being sexy in order to be powerful, nor should 'aesthetically pleasing' women be denied social or political strength, but the deliberate promotion of an emotionally vulnerable visual icon as representative of 'sexy' or 'strong' remains problematic.

Notes

1. The term text here, as elsewhere, is employed to refer to all created works, regardless of traditional definitions of text.

2. I have narrowed my discussion of *Buffy the Vampire Slayer* to the first three seasons of the program for the following reasons: first, because I am interested in *Buffy* (both character and program) as an influence on adolescent female viewers. Buffy's character ages with the seasons of the program and she is no longer an adolescent after the third season. Second, the first two seasons of the program were pilot seasons. They did not have a pre-existing audience base, nor did they enjoy the intense popularity of an established fan base that included adults (and academic adults) who sought to analytically view the program. Finally, as Marti Noxon, the program producer, acknowledges, the initial seasons of *Buffy* were "about cheerleading" and "high-school type metaphors" (O'Brien 2002:92).

3. See http://www.slayage.tv/

4. For example, in a recent article in *SFX*, "I am the Resurrection," Steve O'Brien claims that "*Buffy* [is] one of the few shows on TV that could convincingly call itself feminist, without accusations of patronizing male paternalism" (O'Brien 2002: 90).

5. The *image* of woman is one often portrayed as having a dualistic nature, most notably the 'good' and the 'bad' as seen in the Madonna/Medusa binary construction. Consequently, feminist critics have taken up this problematic notion of image and representation in their analysis of texts. See, for example: Warner, Marina (1985). *Alone of all Her Sex: The Myth and Cult of the Virgin Mary*. London: Random House; Mulvey, Laura (1996). "Pandora" in *Fetishism and Curiosity*. Indianapolis: Indiana UP; Gilbert, Sandra M., and Gubar, Susan (1979; 1984). *The Madwoman in the Attic: The Woman Writer and the Nineteenth-century Literary Imagination*. New Haven London: Yale UP.

6. See also: Mulvey, Laura (1989), *Visual and Other Pleasures*. Indianapolis: Indiana UP; Pally, Marcia (1985). "Object of the Game", *Film Comment* 21:3 (June), pp. 68-73.

7. The upper case is employed here to emphasize the media image that has created Buffy. Cosmopolitan is, of course, a leading women's magazine in which Sarah Michelle Gellar's face is often present as a Maybelline Representative.

8. For example, Aunty Entity in *Mad Max: Beyond the Thunderdome*, Rani in *Doctor Who*, Founder Leader in *Deep Space Nine*, the Borg Queen, the Sisters of Duras and Sela in *Star Trek*, Mystique in *X-Men*, Drusilla, Darla and Layla in *Buffy/Angel*, Hathor in *Stargate*, Alia in *Quantum Leap* or Zelda in *Terrahawks*. Akasha in *Queen of the Damned* or the Wicked Witch of the West in *The Wizard of Oz*.

9. Take for instance Medusa, Medea, Morgan le Fey, Cassandra, Pandora, any evil stepmother or witch of fairy tale.

10. The irony of this statement can be seen in countless 'fantastic' literary references, most notably in Chaucer's Wife of Bath's tale.

11. Vint goes on to argue that the later seasons (4 and 5) see Buffy's wardrobe "mature with her character" (2). However, it should be noted that Vint's examples of this include Buffy's "work out" cloths – a contentious point since these sparse and tight chested work out tops and low rise, loose fitted track bottoms set a new fashion trend among young women 'working out' throughout North America.

12. Previous powerful (supernaturally or fantastically) women on television have been portrayed much weaker and anti-feminist than Buffy. Examples of this include Samantha in *Bewitched* whose main concern in life is to make her goofy husband content and happy, or Sabrina in *Sabrina the teenage witch* who is foolishly wholesome. More contemporary 'visions' of powerful female feminist heroines in television prime time include the sisters in *Charmed* or the problematic Xena in *Xena: Warrior Princess*.

References

Berger, J. (1988). *Ways of Seeing*. London: Penguin Books.

Cixous, H. (1989). Sorties: Out and Out: Attcks/Ways Out/Forays. In C. Belsey & J. Moore (Eds.), *Essays in Gender and the Politics of Literary Criticism* (pp. 101-116). New York: Blackwell.

Daugherty, A. M. (2001). Just a Girl: Buffy as Icon, Roz Kaveney (Ed.) *Reading the Vampire Slayer: An Unofficial Critical Companion to Buffy and Angel*. New York: Macmillan.

Delphy, C. (1984). *Close to Home: A materialist analysis of Women's oppression*. London: Hutchinson and Co.

Kaplow, S. (1973). Getting Angry. In A. Koedt, E. Levine & A. Rapone (Eds.), *Radical Feminism*. New York: Quadrangle.

Kaveney, R. (2001). She Saved the World. A lot. In R. Kaveney (Ed.), *Reading the Vampire Slayer: An Unofficial Critical Companion to Buffy and Angel*. New York: Macmillan.

McCracken, S. (1998). *Pulp: Reading Popular Fiction*. Manchester and New York: Manchester UP.

McCreadie, M. (1983). *Women on Film: the Critical Eye*. N.Y.: Praeger.

Mellen, J. (1973). *Women and their Sexuality in the New Film*. London: Davis-Poynter.

Moran, M. (1999). Anarchic Spaces in Sword and Sorcery Fiction. *Diegesis: Journal of the Association for Research in Popular Fictions*, No. 4 (Summer), 41-50.

Mulvey, L. (1975, 1989). *Visual Pleasures and Narrative Cinema*. Indianapolis: Indiana UP.

Mulvey, L. (1995). The Myth of Pandora: A Psychoanalytical Approach. In L. Pietropaolo & A. Testaferri (Eds.), *Feminisms in the Cinema*. Indianapolis: Indiana UP.

O'Brien, S. (2002). I am the Resurrection, *SFX*, July, 90-102.

Smelik, A. (1998). *And the Mirror Cracked: Feminist Cinema and Film Theory*. New York: St. Martin's Press.

Spackman, B. (1991). *Refiguring Woman: Gender Studies and the Italian Renaissance*. Ithaca: Cornell UP.

Storey, J. (1996). *Cultural Studies and the Study of Popular Culture, Theories and Methods*. Edinburgh: Edinburgh UP.

Vint, S. (2002). Killing us Softly? A Feminist Search for the 'Real' Buffy. *Slayage: The Online International Journal of Buffy Studies*, 5. June.

Waugh, P. (1989). *Feminine Fictions: Revisiting the Postmodern*. New York: Routledge.

Wolf, N. (1991). *The Beauty Myth*. Toronto: Random House.

Dark Comedies and Dark Ladies
The New Femme Fatale

Karma Waltonen

Fallen women were women who had fallen onto men and hurt themselves.
Margaret Atwood

Feminist film theorists continually find themselves in the 1940s, exploring the significance of the femme fatale in U.S. film noir. Contemporary theory allows us to historicize the fascination this figure held for her audience. Yet she is not relegated to the past. The femme fatale is with us still, masked in women's films of the 1990s. That is, we can find women exhibiting the characteristics of the noir femme fatale in contemporary "chick flick" romantic dramas and comedies. I will scrutinize three such films: *Practical Magic* (1998), *Addicted to Love* (1997), and *My Best Friend's Wedding* (1997). All three enjoyed commercial success and were marketed to a female audience, allowing us to imagine the expected audiences' reaction to the fatale. The choice of these films also allows me to explore the fatale in drama, dark comedy, and romantic comedy. Many critics have noted that as these films are part of classical Hollywood cinema, they reinforce old notions of active males and passive females despite the difference in their target audience. That is to say, even in films that are called women-centred and marketed toward a 1990s female American audience, the most active independent woman is still relegated to depend upon the choice of a man. The idea of these films as women-centred is pervasive, though, and makes the films' conventions all the more harmful. By disguising the femme fatale and the old-fashioned messages of these films in 1990s feminist coding, the films encourage the hegemonic acceptance of traditional ideology.

The femme fatale of film noir is a figure who continues to intrigue viewers and scholars alike. Among the critics to define her characteristics is Mary Ann Doane.

In her book, *Femmes Fatales* (1991), Doane asserts that while not all femme fatales fit a rigid definition, it is the male characters' inability to classify or know her definitively that identifies her:

> The femme fatale is the figure of a certain discursive unease, a potential epis-
> temological trauma. For her most striking characteristic, perhaps, is the fact
> that she never really is what she seems to be ... In thus transforming the threat
> of the woman into a secret, something which must be aggressively revealed,
> unmasked, discovered, the figure is fully compatible with the epistemologi-
> cal drive of the narrative, the hermeneutic structuration of the classical text
> (Doane 1991:1).

Unfortunately, Doane's analysis (which is, admittedly, "not really about the femme fatale" (Doane 1991:3)) ends with film noir era texts. As the arche-type of the dangerous eve/salome/destructive mother didn't start with film noir, one could hardly expect her representation to end there. 1990s film critics have been quick to point out the dark lady in our contemporary neo noir and thriller/horror genres. Thus, the femme fatale has already been marked and studied in films such as *Basic Instinct* (1992), *Devil in a Blue Dress* (1995), and *Species* (1995).

As I'll be using primarily Doane's definition of the femme fatale, it is necessary to address how *Femmes Fatales*'s investigations inform my own. Doane's cinematic interpretations are engaged in what Jane Gallop would call "the continual working of a dialectical tension between 'psychoanalysis' and 'feminism'" (Gallop 1982:xii). The oversimplification of the position of the spectator in most psychoanalytic-based criticism has inspired Linda Williams to question the position women are relegated to by traditional theory in her book, *Hard Core* (1999). She cites Doane's assignment of two spec-tator positions women can take as being too limiting and rigid as they as-sume "the operation of ... pure sadism ... and ... pure masochism," making the woman identify herself with either one or the other (Williams 1999:214). Williams is right in asserting that no spectator position can be that simple.

While I don't purport to be able to answer definitively any questions about the position(s) of the (fe)male spectator here, they are worth keeping in mind as my argument focuses on movies that assume a female spectator in their marketing and reception. Nor do I assume to know of any language better suited for discussing agency, power, and dominance in relation to gender and sexuality than psychoanalysis. The women's stories we are to explore are all based on the presumption that the female protagonists are, as psy-choanalysis has told us all along, defined by lack. Laura Mulvey's groundbreaking theory that men fetishize the female body on screen to ameliorate their fear of realizing the female body's lack of a penis is useful. This fear is supposed to be unconscious and the female body, of course, isn't the only thing capable of being fetishized. The penis is never as pow-erful as it's supposed to be – which is why phallic symbols take on so much importance. That is, the symbol has to make up for the faults in the signified or represented. While I can't assert that the female spectator sees the hero-ines of romantic dramas and comedies as lacking a phallus/penis uncon-sciously, I do hold that women are expected to understand that these women are lacking love. Monika Treut, in her essay, "Female Misbehavior," declares, "[r]omantic love is not reality, it is not a socially practiced form of life. It is but the ideal of a dream and of illusionary wishful thinking" (Treut 1995:114). Just as psychoanalysis attempts to define us by our penis, or lack thereof, society attempts to define individuals by a subjected, coded, constructed thing called love.

This is not to say that the lack of a phallus/penis and lack of love are entirely equitable. Men are supposedly reassured when they fetishize the object that lacks a penis. Similarly, the entire audience is supposedly assured when women in film don't lack the capacity to engage in reciprocal heterosexual relationships. Moreover, while the phallus/penis won't be the focus of my investigation, determining which characters have agency is crucial. Both the lack of phallus and of love problematize this issue in film. The psychoanalytic argument, which determines woman as object, must be, at least partially, set aside as it is the woman's subject status that becomes the question for the hero and the film to answer. If this woman can return heterosexual love, she is subject. "Chick flicks," furthermore, encourage women to see the heroine in the subject position, which, as we've seen, must be established by her love status without regard to the phallus/penis. Unfortunately, love, like so many things, is not entirely definable, but we are constructed to recognize its codings when we see them: "Today romantic love is simply that which is missing still. It has become supplement of a lack" (Treut 1995:120). This is especially true in romantic films and especially notable when these films have protagonists whose ability to love is in question.

The Femme Fatale

Doane holds that, like 'woman', the femme fatale is unknowable. Paradoxically, her definition is that she defies easy classification. It is possible and quite useful, however, to identify those aspects of character that filmmakers seem most often to emphasize in relation to the femme fatales of film noir so that we may better understand the fatale of the other genres. Primarily, their sexuality (tied with some aspect of "mystery") is what gets the male protagonists' and our own attention. As Ann E. Kaplan notes in her introduction to *Women in Film Noir*:

> Defined by their sexuality, which is presented as desirable but dangerous to men, the women function as the obstacle to the male quest. The hero's success or not depends on the degree to which he can extricate himself from the woman's manipulations ... often the work of the film is the attempted restoration of order through the exposure and then destruction of the sexual, manipulative woman (Kaplan 1980:2-3)

The man's heroic status is therefore determined by his correct definition of and treatment of the woman. He must name her, discover her unknowable qualities, and ensure that she is punished for her discretions. Thus the hero is often put in a position of secular authority over the woman, usually as a detective, as "Symbolic Order of the law of Patriarchy" (Kaplan 1980:5). These circumstances of the dependence of the male on a woman for definition are by no means limited to film noir, however. Judith Butler reminds us: "Women are said to 'be' the Phallus in the sense that they maintain the power to reflect or represent the 'reality' of the self-grounding postures of the masculine subject, a power which, if withdrawn, could break up the foundational illusions of the masculine subject position" (Butler 1990:45). Obviously these illusions are vital, then, for men to be secure in the gender constructions by which they are defined. Yet the femme fatale refuses to define man in this way, and we must remember that the masculine subject in romance is displaced by the presence of the woman as subject in romantic genres.

What happens when the foundation of the masculine subject position is shaken? Sylvia Harvey, a film noir scholar, reminds us that we've seen the result in the world of noir, in which we encounter "examples of abnormal or monstrous behavior, which defy the patterns established for human social interaction, and which hint at a series of radical and irresolvable contradictions buried deep within the total system of economic and social interactions that constitute the known world" (Harvey 1980:22). Normal human interaction entails clinging to the illusions reinforced when women stay in their place as the reflecting object. The important characteristic for the woman to have, then, is the ability to reflect – she must be readable, knowable, and clear for the man to see himself and his power. And this is precisely the femme fatale's problem. As Janey Place, the author of "Women in film noir," notes: "The primary crime the 'liberated' woman is guilty of is refusing to be defined in such a way, and this refusal can be perversely seen ... as an attack on men's very existence" (Place 1980:35).

When man attempts to read a fatale, what constitutes the body he seeks to know? Usually this body is white. Richard Dyer, in his book, *White*, comments on the importance of a white woman's purity and its ability to be easily discerned, concluding, "White women thus carry – or, in many narratives, betray – the hopes, achievements and characters of the race" (White 1997:29). Western men have long been concerned with white woman's relations to sexuality: "One of the terms that, in Victorian times, most suggested an association of white women with sexuality was that of the 'fallen woman' (cf. Nead 1988)" (Dyer 1997:28). One might ask what the white woman would be falling into. Both Dyer and Doane agree that "[T]he white woman, in her unknowability and sexual excessiveness, does indeed have a close representational affiliation with blackness ... The white woman would be the weak point in the system, the signifier of the always too tenuous hold of civilization" (Doane 1991:213-14). Doane does make the distinction, however, that "the crucial difference [is] that white women constitute an internal enigma

... while 'primitive' races constitute an external enigma" (Doane 1991:212). That is, non-white races are outwardly marked as problematic to the white male hero, while the mask of a white, supposedly pure, face makes the femme fatale all the more powerful in her subversive capacity.

The ability of the white woman to be sexual, to conceal that sexuality, to hide her "true nature" from the man, makes her a danger not only to her white male counterpart, but the white "hold of civilization": "The claim to racial superiority resides in that which cannot be seen, the spirit, manifest only in its control over the body and its enterprising exercise in the world" (Dyer 1997:44). Racial superiority and, as we've seen, the "illusions of the masculine subject position," are therefore entirely dependent upon what's behind the veil of the fatale and whether the man can see it: "Such a stress on sight poses a problem, however, in relation to that which cannot be seen. In a humanist culture, the cardinal instance of this is human personality. No amount of looking at someone gives authoritative access to their inner being. Yet just such scrutiny in search of personality has characterized the past two centuries" (Dyer 1997:104). Dyer points to what Doane sees as woman's problematic position on the Hollywood film screen. The white woman's inner being is all important; man's happiness depends on being able to see what is not possible to see. In regard to the femme fatale, the hero cannot trust what is seen.

Conversely, the audience must see certain things to understand that the woman on screen is not what she seems. Paradoxically, we must identify those clues that indicate a woman is indefinable. Aside from her epistemological disturbance, the femme fatale is also a sexual threat – she initiates sexual behavior, bringing a private behavior (one that no self-respecting white woman should exhibit) into the public realm. She is undeniably attractive, although her whiteness is undercut by visual choices that emphasize shadows and darkness. We are also to understand that she is not an ideal woman in that her sexuality doesn't lead to procreation, or that which justifies the white woman's sexual act: "Consequently, it is appropriate that the femme fatale is represented as the antithesis of the maternal – sterile or barren, she produces nothing in a society which fetishizes production" (Doane 1991:2).

The non-maternal fatale is often contrasted to her counterpart, the 'pure' white woman, who, in Dyer's assessment, is "bathed in and permeated by light. It streams through them and falls on to them from above. In short, they glow" (Dyer 1997:122). That is, the pure white woman, bathed in light, is understood to be exactly what she seems. Her glow is an indication that her inner being is undefiled, that she can love and be loved, while shadows surround our fatale to indicate her impermeability. Lighting is not the only indication of purity. Pure women tend to be blonde ("Blonde hair too could give white women that glow" (Dyer 1997:124)) and costuming choices can also indicate how the audience should read a female's nature. Bernard F. Dick, who studies femmes fatales, explains: "If *la femme noire* first appears in white it is a case of purity in color only; soon her other colors – or color

– are revealed. If she first appears in black, her innocence is even more dubious: She can protest it, but there are still two strikes against her – her attire and her character" (Dick 1995:58). Purity and non-purity, however, are not only tied to the ability to love, but also to the woman's sexuality: "Film noir is a male fantasy, as is most of our art. Thu' woman are here as elsewhere defined by her sexuality: the dark lady has access to it and the virgin does not ... women are defined *in relation to* men, and the centrality of sexuality in this definition is a key to understanding the position of women in our culture" (original emphasis, Place 1980:35). That is, men are drawn to femmes fatales as sexual women, yet we are to understand that their sexuality and lack of light are dangerous. The man must have no doubts about the inner qualities of a woman so that he may define himself against her. Therefore, her sexuality and its ability to cloud the judgments of man cannot be tolerated. This sexuality, or desire for her own pleasure, obviously isn't in the best interests of the man; "Self interest over devotion to a man is often the original sin of the film noir woman and metaphor for the threat her sexuality represents to him" (Place 1980:47). Again, the fatale's interests, unlike her pure white counterpart's, are incompatible with the hero's as they are not his own.

Although the fatale of film noir is undeniably self-centered, Doane reminds us that her behavior is often unintentional: "Her power is of a peculiar sort insofar as it is usually not subject to her conscious will, hence appearing to blur the opposition between passivity and activity ... In a sense, she has power *despite herself*" (Doane 1991:2). That is, the fatale doesn't mean to endanger the male. Though her sexuality is indicative of active behavior, it is beyond her to change this behavior. The fatale is not only blind in her self-centeredness to the male, but is also blind to herself and her destructive nature: "She does not *know* that she is deceiving or *plan* to deceive; conscious deception would be repellent to the man and quite dangerous" (Doane 1991:59). Of course, her unconscious deception proves just as dangerous to the hero, but "this unconsciousness of the woman, her blindness to her own work, is absolutely necessary in order to allow and maintain the man's idealization of her, his perfection of her as an object" (Doane 1991:59). In other words, a conscious evil is easily revealed and avoided while a woman who's unaware of her own fatale capability is more desirable to the male. That which is hidden or mysterious is always more attractive, yet, in the case of the femme fatale, this mystery means she is unknowable, and therefore unavoidably deceitful.

The New Fatale of Romance

Tom Reichert and Charlene Melcher, who write about the contemporary fatale, note: "The femme fatale of film noir is still with us, but she has been updated to reflect the social and sexual concerns of the 1990s" (Reichert & Melcher 1999:288). Not all noir fatales were of the same ilk, and her present incarnation shouldn't be expected to be completely static, either: "[J]ust as the presence of a homicidal heroine does not automatically make a movie a film noir... just as there is a hierarchy of film noir, there is also one of *femme noires* ... But, for the most part, the *femme noire* is a servant of the fates, who lend their spinning wheel but reserve the right of final cut for themselves" (Dick 1995:156). The dark lady has undergone several fundamental changes for the conversion to the genre of romance. For example, Dyer, in his article "Resistance through charisma: Rita Hayworth and Gilda", notes that there were only a few cases in film noir where the fatale was a star (Dyer 1980:96). The leading lady of contemporary romantic dramas and comedies is, by necessity, a star. These formulaic films depend more on what the actors have done before than the film's particular charms to draw in an audience. While the genres of romance, romantic comedy, and dark comedy have unique formulaic elements, the films we're reviewing all fall into formula romance – boy meets girl; there are complications; boy gets girl.

This formula necessitates the new fatale's most important difference from her 1940s counterpart. The genre of romance usually demands a happy ending. The fatale must prove herself worthy of that happy ending by demonstrating that she has the capacity for romantic love. Romance (and the star system it depends on) encourages the audience to identify with the heroes. The female audience must not only see their potential to be independent 90s women in the heroines, but also internalize the patriarchal values which consider this independence ultimately dangerous to heterosexual love. Thus the suffering. There is always suffering in romance. The traditional position of all heroines is one of suffering, yet it is only the fatale who seems to deserve her treatment. Doane observes, "the femme fatale is situated as evil and is frequently punished or killed" (Doane 1991:2). Pure women in traditional romances (think Shakespeare) are often falsely accused by the hero of impurities. The romance ends with their recovery of face and forgiveness for the suffering they have endured.

The modern romantic novel, which often resembles romantic film, allows both the hero and the heroine to suffer: "The expression of this suffering now seems to be a necessary ingredient in the desirability of the genre's male heroes, who must give ample evidence of their feminine and masochistic 'vulnerability' before they can be truly sexy and earn the woman's love" (Williams 1999:219). The fatale of the 1990s in romantic films also needs to suffer to prove that she can love. The romantic heroine, though famous, is no longer Doris Day. Today's romantic film heroine (at least in comedies) is not the desirable virgin; she is a desiring, sexual woman. She is a fatale because she is not readable, her love status is lacking. She can redeem herself if she not only proves that she's capable of love, but that she wants it. The shrew must be tamed. We must note that she is not always rewarded, that the suffering is not always completely ended. This fatale, however, doesn't need to be killed if she can be passively domesticated. Rewarded or not, the suffering domesticates her.

Practical Magic, directed by Griffin Dunne (1998), was marketed towards women, with the ads emphasizing not only the romantic angle, but also the female bonding which became so popular in the 1990s film discourse. In a review of the film, Kevin Maher claims: "[I]t is an attempt at updating the 'women's picture', in this case by injecting the supernatural into the genre" (Maher 1997:54). This film depicts generations of witch sisters, the Owens, struggling to overcome the curse that keeps them from love. Nevertheless, the tag line, "There's a little bit of witch in every woman," sought to normalize the supernatural aspects of the film, while "flattering its female target audience by suggesting that they're invested with a vague glamour sheerly by virtue of being born with double-X chromosomes," according to reviewer Laura Miller (1998). The women's power, by the end of the film, is shown to be within every woman – innate not only in the women of the Owens family – but an innate part of femininity. Not coincidentally, this feminine power is tied to the destruction of the masculine. The matriarch the Owens trace their power to, Maria, lost control of one of her spells, which was, in turn, passed to all the women in her family: "As her bitterness grew, the spell turned into a curse, a curse on any man who dared love an Owens woman ..." The power of the curse is two-sided, however. We learn that "when you hear the sound of the deathwatch beetle, the man you love is doomed to die." Death comes, in theory, only with reciprocal love. Our primary heroine, Sally (Sandra Bullock), is terrified at her destructive potential. Knowing that she cannot cure her innate evil, she casts a spell to prevent herself from falling in love. Thus, she is aware that her femininity is dangerous, out of her control, and ends up rejecting the side of femininity that could prove her pure, i.e. her capacity for reciprocal heterosexual love.

Many critics have noted that *Practical Magic* has a femme fatale. Our secondary heroine, Gillian (Nicole Kidman), plays the role of the seductive woman. Unlike her sister, Gillian is not gifted in her magic and so her power comes out of sexuality alone. She is beautiful, scantily clad, and aware of her power. As we trace her life, we see her as a troubled child who eventually runs away from home, only to move from one man to another. When she returns to the safety of home years later, she threatens the townswomen, warning them to watch their husbands. She is also destructive. Her foreign boyfriend, Jimmy (Goran Visnjic), a "Transylvanian cowboy," ends up dead, not because of reciprocal love, but because the sisters had to defend themselves physically against him, thus killing him. Gillian's strawberry blonde locks don't cover the bruise on her face and her lack of purity means she has no protection when Jimmy comes after her from beyond the grave. She is very effectively punished for her transgressions and saved only by the unconditional love of the more subversive femme fatale, her sister.

Although Gillian embodies blatant qualities of the femme fatale label, the story isn't hers. Our true heroine is the good girl, the subtle fatale, complete with a fatal destructive power aimed at men. Like the classic fatale, however, she embodies the fatale who "has power *despite herself*" (Doane 1991:2).

Practical Magic (Griffin Dunne 1997), Warner.

Sally, as the good girl whose love will destroy, is therefore more dangerous, more subversive than her sister. Sally has long. dark locks and often appears in black. Strangely, though, she is not innately sexual. Her aunts have to put a spell on her to unleash her passion for her first husband, who dies, of course, because she grows to return his love. Yet the audience senses her attraction to the hero when they first meet. Gary (Aidan Quinn), our incarnation of the noir detective, and Sally can't resist each other. Unlike classical noir, the 1990s audience is to understand that the sexual chemistry is not a sign of danger, but a sign that this couple belongs together. The signs are all there. They gaze into each other's eyes and she is unable to deceive him: "I can't lie to him." Just as Sally is contrasted with her sister, Gary is contrasted with Jimmy. Both are cowboys, although Gary is, in many ways, more genuine than Jimmy. Jimmy is a self-proclaimed, posing Transylvanian (Hungarian) cowboy, while Gary is a silver star-rearing officer from Arizona, who knows how to ride horses backwards. While his primary motivation is to unravel Jimmy's disappearance, his goal becomes dependent upon discovering Sally's nature. In keeping with the fact that her destructive nature is unintentional, her feelings are also foreign to her. She is aware of her own epistemological disturbance, telling him that if they were to be together, neither would be sure of her motivations. Gary dismisses her concerns: "Curses only have power if you believe in them, and I don't. You know what? I wished for you, too." Eventually, the injurious power of the women comes to an end, thanks to a modern day cowboy and his refusal to acknowledge the power of innate femininity to destroy him.

Both of our heroines are changed by the end of the film. Gillian is saved and fades from the foreground of this women-centered text. We see her at the end with the rest of the family, participating in the quasi-domestic family rituals she used to despise. Sally, who has acknowledged her powers to the community and her desire for love to herself, becomes just another woman, fulfilling the hopes the audience had for her all along. In this witch story, the evil women, provided they are capable of love, are redeemable, but the sisterhood the movie reputed to stand for is not the kind of love that redeems. Sally must become domesticated, using her powers to make cleansing products and to entertain the neighborhood while her beau looks on, approvingly. Just as this movie bills itself as confirming that there's magic in every woman, it also affirms that there's danger in every woman and this danger must be domesticated by heterosexual love: "Perversely, it seems the whole point of making Sally powerful is to reassure us that she's never going to do anything *interesting* with her power" (Miller 1998). Like Samantha from *Bewitched*, one gets the feeling that Sally's power will be used only on days when she forgets to make cookies for her daughter's class from scratch. The fact that Gary finds her magic endearing (as he feels immune from it) is supposed to be liberating, yet we are left to ponder: "Maybe there *is* a little bit of witch in every woman – but wouldn't it be fun if there were a lot more?" (Miller 1998).

Addicted to love (Griffin Dunne 1997), Warner.

The dark humor of Griffin Dunne's *Addicted to Love* (1997) comes from seeing one of the consummate romantic heroines of contemporary U.S. film play the antithesis of the girl next door. Meg Ryan plays Maggie, who is, as reviewer James Berardinelli summarizes, "a bad girl, although not quite as bad as she'd like everyone to believe. She wears her hair short and unkempt, travels around the streets of New York on a motorcycle, and prefers donning anything in black that exposes her navel" (1997). Distinct from the other fatale we've discussed, Maggie is intent on maliciousness. Film scholar B. Ruby Rich characterizes "the early femmes fatales" as women who "had no explanation for their relentless pain or greed" (1995:6). In contrast, Maggie has an explanation for her behavior as she was used and abused for a green card. Her black leather-donning active bitterness is contrasted sharply to the white-to-the-point-of-transparency grammar school teacher who's the apple of the hero's eye. In this black comedy, though, the "blacker" heroine must win, but only after she's changed her wardrobe and her attitude.

Sam (Matthew Broderick), our hero, chases his girlfriend, Linda (Kelly Preston), to New York after she leaves their small town (and him) for Anton. Obsessed, he sets up a voyeuristic "bohemian hellhole" that would make Jimmy Stewart uncomfortable. Maggie, who's been spying on Anton, the man who betrayed her, imposes herself into Sam's world. Sam is initially reluctant to enable Maggie's revenge, as he sees his obsession as altruistic – he doesn't want to punish Linda, he just wants her back. As soon as Maggie proves useful in hastening what Sam believes is the inevitable end of Linda and Anton's relationship, the arrangement becomes so comfortable Maggie actually smiles a few times: "Even dementia, the film observes, can become a domestic comfort if you've got someone to share it with" (Miller 1997).

The master-plan changes when Maggie starts to turn into Linda. Our first glimpse of Linda is when Sam spies her through his telescope. She glows in the sunlight, lit from above in soft focus. Through the telescope, she is a celestial body, with long blonde hair and lots of white and pastel clothes. Maggie's short cropped, obviously not natural blonde hair, and black clothes are no match for her. The film makes this abundantly clear. Sam and Maggie relieve their frustrations with each other when Maggie puts on Linda's white dress (although Maggie's black bra is visible underneath), only to resume their mission when the costuming returns to normal. The view of Linda in the voyeuristic enterprise illustrates what Doane and Dyer have pulled from Mulvey about the place of the white woman in film. Linda is projected onto a wall (painted white so she shines through better) solely to-be-looked-at. In one particularly poignant scene, Linda (lit from above) is projected onto the wall behind Maggie, her translucence overflowing onto Maggie's opaque form.

Maggie's transformation into someone who can enjoy reciprocal emotion cannot occur while Linda remains the fantasy. For Maggie to rise from her fallen status, Linda must descend slightly from her pedestal. To this end, Maggie differs from the classic (and the new) femme fatale in that her sexuality is not overt. That is not to say that she isn't attractive, but that she seems very unselfconscious about her sexuality and the director chooses not to emphasize it. Her red panties are only revealed "for authenticity" when she plants them to incriminate Anton. Linda, by contrast, is portrayed as surprisingly sexual. Notably, we don't see her sexual pleasure; we hear it in Sam and Maggie's first attempt to add sound to their show. When Sam finally has a chance to get Linda back, he does find visual clues (i.e. a tongue piercing) that reveal her capacity for imperfection.

As Linda grows darker (moving from translucence to flesh), Maggie becomes lighter. She smiles, the lighting changes, her clothes (while remaining unconventional) move further away from black, the hero's gaze lingers on her. When she's had enough revenge, (Anton having fallen from grace), she has a cathartic scene in which they forgive each other. The movie lets the audience see Maggie as a good woman who'd put on a fatale façade to protect herself, the opposite of the unloving fatale who pretends to be pure of heart. In the last scene, before the inevitable embrace between Sam and Maggie, he walks in on her looking through a magnifying glass. When she puts it down, showing her white, angelic face, clothed in a light colored shirt, she takes herself out of the position of voyeur. She is, finally, to be looked at, embraced by, and in reciprocal love with the hero.

My Best Friend's Wedding (1997), directed by P.J. Hogan, allows another romantic comedy queen, Julia Roberts, to show us her dark side. Our fatale seems harmless enough (although we learn immediately that she can't commit to a man) until she finds her destiny – competition. Driven by jealousy, she becomes the fatale we most fear – a woman aware of her seductive powers who will lie and cheat to get what she wants. Our fear is only slightly abated by our awareness that her destructive power is aimed at her female rival, not the hero.

Roberts play Jules, a single, independent food critic who doesn't get along well with other women. Jules recalls in the first scene of the film (after a prolonged musical credit number which, according to reviewer Darren Arnold, "almost seems like a hellish advertisement for marital bliss" (Arnold 1997:51) that she and her best friend, Michael (Dermot Mulroney), made a pact to marry each other when they got to a certain age. Fearful that this time is approaching, Jules finds herself taken aback when Michael announces that he's getting married to someone else – Kimmy (Cameron Diaz). Jules is by far our most evil heroine in the romantic genre. Her destructive powers are well under her own control (unlike Sally's) and her reasons are simple jealousy and competition, without even Maggie's motivation of a woman scorned. Reviewers of the film have shown much more contempt for this heroine, calling her "unflattering" (Arnold 1997:51) and "a scheming bitch" (Barber 1999).

While most critics agreed that the film's "most interesting aspect is how the two main female characters are presented: Hogan wisely eschews the good girl/bad girl dichotomy that has become synonymous with the modern romantic comedy" (Arnold 1997:51), feeling sympathy for both characters doesn't mean they're treated similarly by the film. It is perhaps this comedy that encouraged other directors to blur the line between the fallen and the saved woman. It is certainly this film that inspired *Forces of Nature* (1999) to break out of the pattern of the heroine always getting the hero, yet the dichotomy between good and bad is still very strong. If the audience is predisposed to root for Jules (and in the beginning, she hasn't done anything to change their minds), then they might share her disgust at the first sight of Kimmy. Kimmy is perpetually clad in pink, with short blonde hair. She's upbeat, young, and willing to give up college for Michael. Even though she lacks the voice of an angel, Kimmy is well lit and makes the face of the hero light up as well.

Jules, on the other hand, is sympathetic because of the actress's star power and because she embodies the New Woman that the new romantic comedies tell women they can be: independent, strong, career-driven, attractive, and abhorrent of pink. All that is admirable about this incarnation of woman is undermined by those characteristics that push the limit between independent woman and femme fatale. Jules is well lit and beautiful, but her propensity for strong colors and red locks denote danger rather than autonomy. She is clever and ruthless in her plot to drive a wedge between the lovers: She dresses seductively, changes her behavior more to Michael's liking, lies, schemes, and even turns jealousy to her side. Her conscience is embodied in her gay male friend, George (Rupert Everett), who tries to tell her the truth behind her motivations, yet still goes along with her schemes. Superficially, but not unimportantly, Jules laughs too loud, drinks to excess, and commits what can be seen as one of the most malicious deeds in the late 1990s – she smokes. All of these acts illustrate that Jules is indeed self-involved and conceited. Kimmy comments on these well-known character traits when they're finding a bridesmaid's dress: "You wouldn't be comfortable unless you were distinctive ... You're not up for anything conventional or anything viewed to be a female priority, including marriage, romance, or love."

Jules is not concerned with the welfare of the hero, or even the welfare of her own heart. Although she concedes her defeat and suffers at the end, the audience is not convinced that she ever loved Michael purely or that she is capable of being loved in a suitable way. Critics applauded this film for it's ending because it breaks romantic convention by making our heroine lose the man, a potential danger at the box office. One critic notes, "I'm sure one of the factors behind the film's US box office success is the wickedness of the pleasures it offers; the invitation to become complicit with a woman behaving badly" (Barber 1999). In other words, the audience can give up the pleasure of seeing their heroine win the hero if they've had the pleasure of being bad vicariously through her. The pleasure in watching a bad woman has almost always included the pleasure of her punishment and this film is no exception. Jules not only suffers the humiliation of loss, she is also punished in that, by the end of the film, she believes her life is missing something. For the first time, she is unsatisfied with her life and desires the unattainable romantic ideal. Not only does she appear at the wedding sans the white dress, she now can't feel complete until she has one.

Although the initial musical sequence may seem "hellish" in regard to marriage, the rest of the soundtrack is simply a compilation of old love songs, including Tony Bennett and Jackie DeShannon. These songs not only emphasize the importance of romantic love, they also separate the competing women. Kimmy shows that singing a love song, even if you've a horrid voice, means you're pure of heart. Jules's reluctance to sing along amplifies her fatale status. Moreover, at the end of the film, she gives her song to Kimmy and is left dancing with her conscience, George, to a song of platonic friendship.

Kimmy has won the day, and despite the problems that remain unresolved in her relationship with Michael, we are led to believe she'll have a happy-ever-after-life. If the audience is to experience pleasure by identifying with Jules' bad side, they must suffer with her and learn the lessons she internalizes. In this movie, the line between independent and fatale (both embodied in Jules) is not drawn as distinctly as is the line between feminist (Jules) and feminine (Kimmy). Happiness doesn't come from scheming, but it also won't appear as long as the heroine believes in her own autonomy. Suffering will follow those who don't exemplify those feminine attributes of the pure, white woman: sacrificial, devoted, young, and beautiful.

Doubtless, it has been easy for critics and enlightened views alike to guard themselves against internalizing the anti-feminist messages in 1940s noir films, due partly to the ability to identify the fatales as fatales so readily. We know the dark lady of classic Hollywood is a construct, and our analysis and labelling of her as such enables us to shield ourselves from the implications of the stereotype, and to sometimes reappropriate her image in our analysis. It is much more difficult to negotiate the romantic fatale. How can we enjoy 1990s women's films, which market themselves as supportive of female independence, if independence is consistently punished in the quest for romantic love?

One must not neglect the position of the male hero in these romances. We've seen how, in classic noir, the hero's quest is intimately tied to the discovery of the fatale's nature: "Narrative's containment of the image of the woman is generally mediated by the male character who demystifies, possesses, or sadistically punishes the woman" (Doane 1991:101). In the romance, the male becomes not only the demystifier, but the domesticator, the one with whom the woman must share love to be redeemed. The position of the male is troubling, though, due to the specific nature of the films. Why is it that the male still has the ultimate agency in women-centered texts? Gary frees Sally from suspicion and then returns to her – apparently he had to be the one with the initiative. In the romantic comedies, the basic situation revolves around a man choosing between two women, pushing aside female camaraderie for competition in order to gain a man's favor. Ultimately, through noir and romance, the man has the power to determine the fate of the female.

Many critics have postulated that the femmes fatales of noir emerged as a reaction to women entering the labor force (Harvey 1980:23). While this doesn't directly explain the fatale's presence in neo-noir or romance, we can see, through the hierarchal positioning of both the heterosexual imperative and the masculine subject position, that the reincarnation of the dark lady in the 1990s is yet another way to push her back into the heterosexual, woman-as-subject-only-if-she's-partnered-with-a-man domestic world. The 1940s fatale is often read as male fantasy. Our romantic fatales are supposedly made for women, presumably becoming female fantasy. Of course, these films instruct about desire as much as they reflect it.

The emergence of these figures may point to many social factors. Earlier romances and comedies had "bad" women, but they were secondary characters, not the heroine. That is, earlier women who might be identified as fatales with whom the heroine had to compete, with the 'good' heroine inevitably the winner. That the independent heroines on screen now share properties with the 1940s fatale can be read as evidence of a backlash against female independence. While women in the United States continued to gain access to positions and power once reserved for men in the 1990s, their on-screen counterparts were made to suffer. The push for independent women to enter into long-term, monogamous, heterosexual relationships may also reflect the idea that modern women must 'have it all'. A woman is not seen as successful without a family, or at least a man. The films make this clear. These women might still have the illusion of independence, as they aren't necessarily aproned or fertile, yet the inevitability of romance equates independence with transgression.

References

Arnold, D. (1997). Review of *My Best Friend's Wedding* by P. J. Hogan. *Sight and Sound, 7* (9), 51.

Barber, L. (1999). Review of *My Best Friend's Wedding* by P. J. Hogan. *News.com.* Retrieved March 7, 2000, from http://archive.entertainment.news.com.au/film/70927f.htm

Berardinelli, J. (1997). Review of *Addicted to Love* by G. Dunne. Retrieved March 8, 2000, from http://movie-reviews.colossus.net/movies/a/addicted/html

Butler, J. (1990). *Gender Trouble.* New York: Routledge.

Dick, B. (1995). Columbia's Dark Ladies and the Femmes Fatales of Film Noir. *Film/Literature Quarterly, 23* (3), 155-162.

Doane, M. A. (1991). *Femme Fatales.* New York: Routledge.

Dunne, G. (Director). (1997). *Addicted to Love* [Video]. Hollywood, Warner Brothers.

Dunne, G. (Director). (1998). *Practical Magic* [Video]. Hollywood, Warner Brothers.

Dyer, R. (1980). Resistance through charisma: Rita Hayworth and *Gilda.* In E. A. Kaplan (Ed.), *Women in Film Noir*, (pp. 91-99). London: British Film Institute.

Dyer, R. (1997). *White.* London: Routledge.

Gallop, J. (1982). *The Daughter's Seduction: Feminism and Psychoanalysis.* Ithaca, NY: Cornell University Press.

Harvey, S. (1980). Woman's place: The absent family of film noir. In E. A. Kaplan (Ed.), *Women in Film Noir*, (pp. 22-34). London: British Film Institute.

Hogan, P. (Director). (1997). *My Best Friend's Wedding* [Video]. Hollywood, Tristar Pictures.

Kaplan, E. A. (Ed.). (1980). Introduction. In *Women in Film Noir* (pp. 1-5). London: British Film Institute.

Maher, K. (1997). Review of *Practical Magic* by G. Dunne. *Sight and Sound, 9* (1), 53-54.

Miller, L. (1997, May). Review of *Addicted to Love* by G. Dunne. *Salon Magazine*. Retrieved March 3, 2000, from http://www.salon.com/may1997/addicted970523.html?CP=SAL&DN=110

Miller, L. (1998, October). Hocus Bogus [Review of the film *Practical Magic* by G. Dunne]. *Salon Magazine*. Retrieved March 1, 1998, from http://www.salon.com/ent/movies/reviews/1998/10/16reviewb.html?CP=SAL&DN=110

Place, J. (1980). Women in film noir. In E. A. Kaplan (Ed.), *Women in Film Noir*, (pp. 35-67). London: British Film Institute.

Reichert, T. & Melcher C. (1999). Film Noir, Feminism, and the Femme Fatale: The Hyper Sexed Reality of *Basic Instinct*. In M. Meyers (Ed.), *Mediated Women: Representations in Popular Culture* (pp. 287-304). Cresskill: Hampton Press Inc.

Rich, B. R. (1995). Dumb Lugs and Femmes Fatale. *Sight and Sound, 5* (11), 6-10.

Treut, M. (1995). Female Misbehavior. In L. Pietropaolo & A. Testaferri (Eds.), *Feminism in the Cinema* (pp. 106-124). Bloomington: Indiana University Press.

Williams, L. (1999). *Hard Core: Power, Pleasure, and the "Frenzy of the Visible*. Berkeley: University of California Press.

A Woman's Gotta Do
What a Woman's Gotta Do

Anne Gjelsvik

During the late 1990s, Norwegian cinema experienced a small wave of modern thrillers, most of them featuring female protagonists. One main characteristic of these movies was the central role of female artists on both sides of the camera (two movies based on novels by famous Norwegian writers Anne Holt and Karin Fossum, and at least three thrillers directed by female directors).[1] In these modern Norwegian thrillers, the realistic representation of female protagonists breaks both with the generic representation of the thrillers and the national heritage from feministic movies.

By analysing three of the movies – *Cellofan – med døden til følge* (*Cellophane*, Eva Isaksen, 1997), *Evas øye* (*Eva's Eye*, Berit Nesheim, 1999) and *Salige er de som tørster* (*Blessed Are Those Who Thirst*, Carl Jørgen Kiøning, 1998[2]) – this essay discusses the 'realistic' representation of modern 'working girls' (a journalist, a painter and a police woman) in opposition to genre conventions of the thriller. The three movies have a lot in common besides the female protagonists. *Cellophane* and *Eva's Eye* were directed by two of the leading female directors in Norway, Eva Isaksen and Berit Nesheim. Both directors have several acclaimed productions in various genres on their merit list. Nesheim was Academy Award-nominated for *The Other Side of Sunday* (1996), which also was critically acclaimed, won a number of prizes and was a box office success both nationally and internationally. The scripts for *Eva's Eye* and *Blessed Are Those Who Thirst* (director Carl Kiøning) are based on the commercially successful books by the leading female crime writers Karin Fossum and Anne Holt.

A main topic in this article is the movie's extensive focus on the women's 'private life' and how this private life is essential to the plot and for the choices the women get to make. The movies also dwell more on the 'right' and 'wrong' of these choices (for instance the use of violence, the role of revenge after rape, etc.), thus inviting the audience to participate more actively in ethical judging of fictional actions than most mainstream movies. As the director Berit Nesheim states about the story in her movie *Eva's Eye* (based on the novel by Karin Fossum), "I like that the focus is on 'the why' and not 'the who' in Fossum's crime stories" (Aas Olsen 1999).

My discussion will start with the context of the Norwegian 'women's film',[3] because these new films draw both on heritages from American mainstream genres and on a specific national context, and then again are different from both.

From Wife to Woman[4]

The new female wave in Norwegian cinema coincides with the international women's liberation movement in the 1970s. Norwegian female directors became a central part of the movement both in terms of their own roles and due to their new radical aesthetics, but most of all because of their new focus on female protagonists and female topics. In Norwegian film history four movies are touchstones in this respect: Anja Breien's *Hustruer* (1975), Laila Mikkelsen's *Liten Ida* (1981), Vibeke Løkkeberg's *Åpenbaringen* (1977) and *Løperjenten*, (1981). After these movies, the term women's film became a "word of honour" among Norway's political progressive and cultural elite (Dahl 1996:391), and was used to describe movies with a more realistic representation of women combined with a realistic film style.

Most prominent was *Hustruer* (*Wives*), which became a symbol for the Norwegian women's liberation movement and is recognized as "The Norwegian Women's movie" (Hausken 1992:7). The movie is inspired by *Husbands* (John Cassavetes, 1970), in which three men leave both their families and work to travel and drink on their own. The director Anja Breien posed the question "How would it look if three women did the same thing?" (Hausken 1992:7). *Hustruer* is the story about three women's reunion fifteen years after primary school. Instead of returning to their husbands and children, they prolong the party. The movie follows the women as far as three days into their drinking spree, where among other things they have made the journey with the so-called *Danskebåten* (The Danish boat), a symbol for irresponsible partying in Norwegian. Through the improvised dialogue the movie is a portrait of women captured in the role as 'wife' (Hausken 1997:169-170). Important for the movie's ideological potential was the open ending with its focus on new opportunities for women and female companionship as a key to liberation.[5] One central characteristic is how the collective is highlighted at the expense of the women's individuality, visually done by constantly framing all the women together (Hausken 1997:182). In opposition to the traditional narrative's goal-oriented protagonist, the movie uses the wives as a collective group not knowing where they are going. In terms of representation the ending is particularly interesting; when it's time for separation, the character Heidrun states: "We can't stop now". Afterwards the picture is freeze-framed with the text: "But the movies ends here." The text functions as an assertion that the project of the fictional characters could and should be brought to an ending by other non-fictional women (Hausken 1997:173-175).

Recent developments in the Norwegian society have changed the conception of Norwegian women from wives to women, with almost as many women as men working or taking higher education, and with a high level of political participation (Likestillingssenteret 2001). I will claim that a modern movie with the ambition to mirror contemporary women's experiences needs working women as protagonists.

Since the mid 1980s Norwegian movies have moved toward an internationalisation with an extended production of entertaining genre movies, like action film or thrillers. To what extent are the Norwegian thrillers different than their predecessors, and does the use of female protagonists make a difference? Do the movies reflect the modern situation?

From Wife to Working girl

All three movies are up to date in their presentations of the protagonists, all of them starting by introducing the female protagonists as working women.[6] Our first encounter is with journalist Marianne Hovden in *Cellophane,* who is in the middle of success with a front-page story and the praise from her chief editor. Hanne Wilhelmsen in *Blessed Are Those Who Thirst* is a female investigator who rises from her lover's bed to get back to work, even on Saturdays. Hanne is also portrayed as skilful and dedicated in her work. Eva (*Eva's Eye*) is struggling with her career as a painter. Nevertheless for her (as for the others) the role as working woman is portrayed as most important, almost more important than her role as a single mother. Eva is an artist in spite of her economic difficulties and although she has to take odd jobs to make ends meet, it is obvious that her identity is firmly connected with her work. Her ambition as an artist is the reason for her financial problems, which leads her into violent situations, first as a witness to the murder of her friend and later becoming a killer herself.

It is also illustrative that the women are no longer married. Marianne Hovden's boss gives her the following characterization: "Forget that lady! She is not capable of relationships that are longer than three days!" Both Eva and Hanne have been given "politically correct identities," Eva being a divorced single mother and Hanne a lesbian. Hanne is living in a lesbian relationship, but she is secretive about it toward her colleagues and not totally out of the closet. In sum, all the protagonist's 'unmarried' statuses are interesting and reflect the range of possibilities for modern women in terms of both private lives and careers. But these representations do not mirror the Hollywood cliché of a heroine's sexual availability. Carol Dove describes Hollywood's female lawmen as "seductive women with guns – and vulnerable through that sexuality. Although male movie cops sleep with their enemies on occasion, female law enforcers are routinely placed in danger through a sexual relationship, usually with an opponent" (Dove 2001:82). The sexualization of female heroines which are so often seen (i.e. Lara Croft, Ripley, Ilsa) are much more downplayed in the Norwegian movies and less attention is given to the female body than in modern Hollywood. Yvonne Tasker's study on gender and action film encapsulates this genre as "muscular movies," but the "spectacular bodies" are not adapted in the Norwegian thrillers (Tasker 1993). The Norwegian heroines are neither copies of the male heroes or "hard-bodies" (Ibid).

This is again connected to a lesser degree of physical power and use of violence than in American genre movies. These thrillers are for instance seeking realistic explanations for the use of weapons, in a country where people rarely use guns and the police are unarmed. Because of this situation, the police ask for permission to be armed before the dramatic climax of *Blessed Are Those Who Thirst,* and the heroine of *Cellophane* has to defend herself with a pendulum from the clock on the wall.

Violence and the use of guns appear, in spite of the generic convention, to be more like something women have to do only when in a state of emergency. The traditional description of female heroes "who really are men" is not the case here (Tasker 1993:132).[7] Unless we count curiosity and investigation eagerness as male qualities. The exception is Hanne (*Blessed Are Those Who Thirst)* who also has several traditional masculine characteristics, but on the whole mainly feminine values and experiences are represented.

The use of female protagonists in masculine genre has problematic sides as well according to Tasker.

> The casting of women as the protagonists in the cop movie, the road movie, the science-fiction film and so on shifts and inflects the traditional vulnerability of the hero in such films. This is a set of genres, after all, in which the hero is constantly subject to physical violence (Tasker 1993:151).

The degree of insecurity and vulnerability the protagonists experience differs in the three movies, with the police movie keeping the protagonist the most safe, something I will relate to the fact that the women are safest in their professional roles. Hanne hunts criminals, something she is good at, and it is only her private life she has trouble coping with. But as we know, even the toughest women can have trouble when dealing with both career and private life. I for one can relate to that dilemma through drawing on my own everyday experience.

Audience Engagement

Contemporary film theory has drawn more attention to how common knowledge and everyday experiences come into play in spectator' responses to fiction film. Paul Messari is among the cognitive researchers focusing on the role of perception and the similarities between seeing a movie and seeing in ordinary settings. More than drawing on separate perception skills when seeing a movie, the spectator uses ordinary experiences and the perceptual skills as when perceiving the real world claims Messari (Messari 1995).

On the other hand, the cognitive turn in film theory has upgraded the role of cognition and understanding at the expense of the spectator's engagement and emotional response. But some researchers have successfully combined perspectives including the role of both emotional and cognitive processes in the meeting between movie and viewer. I will draw on some of these methodological perspectives in my discussion of engagement with these female heroines. Among other things, this position examines how some characteristics in a movie lead to some fixed responses shared by many spectators. The American film philosopher Noël Carroll can serve as an example of this position. According to Carroll a filmmaker can construct a specific focus in a movie, which under the right circumstances creates an emotional focus in the spectator. The film researcher's task is to identify which characteristics lead to certain kinds of reactions, and for this she should use herself as a detector. With her own reaction as a working hypothesis, the researcher can study which film devices and characteristics create certain emotions in specific movies. Caroll himself investigates how specific emotions come to life in encounters with different film genres. *Melodrama* creates compassion and admiration (for instance with the heroine's sacrifice in *An Affair to Remember* (1957) or *Dancer in the Dark* (2000)). *Horror* creates fear and disgust, for instance in *The Fly* (1986), where we both fear and are disgusted by the protagonist's transformation into a fly. And finally *suspense* creates the expectation that something evil or dramatic is about to happen (for instance in *The Pledge* (Carroll 1999:21-47). In order to create suspense in an audience the movie needs to establish the audience's concern about the outcome of the narrative according to Carroll. This kind of concern is encouraged through an object of emotion where "an event whose *evil* outcomes are probable and whose *righteous* outcomes are improbable, or at least, no more probable than the evil ones" (Carroll 1999:44). In other words, "morality turns out to be the card that almost every suspense film plays" (ibid). Carroll also claims that the most important level the filmmaker possesses for influencing our assessment of morality, involves character portrayal (Carroll 1999:45). Carroll is also concerned with how movies can shape ethical responses that diverge from our everyday judgement, and I will return to that problem in my closing argument. First some perspective on how fictional characters can both establish the viewer's involvement and encourage ethical judgements.

Engaging Characters

Murray Smith has with his *Engaging Characters. Fiction, Emotion and the Cinema* (1995) provided the most systematic effort to understand the importance of character involvement. Smith argues that our ability to react emotionally toward fictional characters is a key aspect in our experience of and engagement with fiction film. Smith therefore investigates the role of fictional characters in a narration. What guides our reactions and understanding of these characters, and what do we mean by stating that we tend to identify with fictional characters?

Smith draws a line between Aristotle's *Poetics* and modern literature theory in his search for a deeper understanding of what a fictional character could be with the classical question; is the fictional character people or words? (Smith 1995:34). While Aristotle was engaged in both the mimetic relation and the character's function in the narration, several modern traditions tend to rank one aspect above another. These positions claim either that the character is important as a plot construction or in terms of its mimetic relationship, that is, being human. Murray Smith claims both positions to be false. The character is a text element, but at the same time the lifelikeness of the characters is central for our engagement and our judgements of them are based on real experiences. The Norwegian thrillers have their strength in their relation to normal people's experiences, which also are the most interesting part of the movies, both for artists and spectators as far as I can see.

Murray Smith challenges the much-used notion of identification, although the term tends to cover a lot of central experiences (Smith 1995:1). For instance what would my reaction be if I found myself in a dangerous situation like Marianne in *Cellophans*? What do I reckon is most important, my own well-being or the possibility to clear my father's name? Can we defend the rape victim's revenge in *Blesssed Are Those Who Thirst* and could I do the same? Smith argues against the strong version of the fallacious conception of identification as used in psychoanalytic film theory, where identification is understood as a process where the spectator mistakes herself as the protagonist. Smith argues for an engagement with the protagonist containing a conscious understanding of fiction as being fictional, and with emphasis on the spectator's cognitive understanding and judgements. Smith formulates a new theory of engagement based on what he terms a structure of sympathy. For Smith a strong involvement with fictional characters is important for our experience of fiction, but not necessarily with only one character during the course of narration.

Smith outlines three levels in his structure of sympathy. Recognition describes the construction of a character. Alignment describes the process by which the spectator is placed in relation to the characters, in terms of access to their actions. The third level, allegiance, pertains to a deeper understanding of the characters and to our moral evaluation of their actions. The basic level of recognition is based on the mimetic relation and describes the spectator's construction of characters based on the perception of textual element and previous experiences from everyday life. The spectator constructs the fictional character as a continuous and recognisable person. Our possibility to construct individual agents with recognisable traits is connected to the conception of personata schema according to Smith.[8] We tend to believe that

Salige er de som tørster (Carl Jørgen Kønig, 1997) Nordic Screen/Dynamo.

fictional characters have human traits like intentions, emotions and being capable of making choices and judgements (Smith 1995:21, 82-83, 110-139). The construction of characters is not one-dimensional or stable and can undergo changes during the movie, calling for reconsiderations from the spectator. Is the character as we believe her to be, and are we seeing her true self, or do we have to change our view of her? For our engagement to grow stronger we need a stronger attachment with the character's choices etc., and this takes place when we are aligned with the character through the information we are given access to according to Smith (Smith 1995: 142-186). The alignment is produced mainly by two functions, spatio-temporal attachment and subjective access. The first function describes how the narration "may follow the spatio-temporal path of a particular character through the narrative" (Smith 1995:142).

Murray Smith (as does Noel Carroll) emphasises the spectator's conscious choices and judgement, including our moral and ideological evaluation of the character's action. For instance, we can be challenged to accept revenge when the police are unable to punish a rapist, or we may feel sorrow when the victim chooses violence herself, as in *Blessed Are Those Who Thirst*. While the first two levels of the sympathy structure, recognition and alignment, only need the spectator's attention toward the textual elements presented before her, allegiance is reserved for the level where we actively evaluate and give an emotional response toward the actions we are witnessing. It is an important part of Smith's theory that we are able to react differently from the characters, and that we are active in our evaluations all along.

In light of this theory I will argue that as the violent acts of the women in *Baise-moi* (2000) fill me with disgust and tristesse, while others are filled with female courage, they do not automatically cause a transfer of hate and aggression. And as Carroll, I will argue the importance of ethical judgements in relation to suspense dilemmas, and that the need for our own judgements are more urgent the more authentic the genre film seems. In the cases of the Norwegian female protagonist thrillers, the closeness to ordinary women's everyday experiences emphasise the ethical dilemmas.

One of the Boys

Hanne Wilhelmsen (Kjersti Elvik) is one of the boys, going out for a regular beer after a week's work. She drives a big motorcycle, talks rough, smokes a lot and works many late hours. Hanne is originally a heroine created by the best selling crime author Anne Holt, who has portrayed her in six books.[9] *Blessed Are Those Who Thirst* was elected best crime book of the year in Norway in 1998, and the movie got a Norwegian film award for best production. As a writer, one of Holt's strengths is her emphasis on authentic descriptions of people and places. Holt actually has a history herself as superintendent in the police and Minister of Justice for the Labour Party in the Norwegian government and situates her stories in settings she is acquainted with. The literature historian Øystein Rottem writes about Holt: "An eye for the authentic is one of her prime qualities, but she is also skilled in plot construction and creation of suspense. Her books are distinguished by her social consciousness and focus on up to date society problems, and she writes with a critical perspective on social differences" (Rottem 1998). These characteristics place her books firmly in the tradition of realistic and debate oriented art, which also are being criticised by others. One reviewer wrote: "Anne Holt's tendency toward propaganda and her anxiousness to bring the politically correct opinions out to a large audience is once again the problem with her books" (Ekle 2000).

In the movie *Blessed Are Those Who Thirst*, two themes are obvious for the spectator, the lack of justice for rape victims and racism. But it is particularly as a statement for lesbian identity that Hanne Wilhelmsen has come to play an important role. Anne Holt herself is among the most profiled and famous homosexuals in Norway and has been fighting for her right to adopt the child she has together with her lesbian partner. But the author was for a long time reluctant to be open about being gay, claiming this to be part of her private life and of no interest to the public. The conflict between private life and career is also a dilemma for the protagonist in *Blessed are those who Thirst*.

The movie introduces us to a hectic police setting. Hanne Wilhelmsen and her colleagues are enduring hard times with a crime wave in Oslo placing pressure on the short-staffed police force. Two cases are put on Hanne's desk at the same time, and it is the strange 'Saturday-massacres' case that takes her attention. Several weekends in a row people have discovered large quantities of blood at different places around town. The Saturday-massacres case is unique due to the lack of any victims, but also because mystical numbers have been written in the blood. Finally Hanne discovers that the numbers are related to the numbers on young girls' asylum applications, and that a racist cop has killed all of the girls. While being occupied with this intellectually stimulating riddle, Hanne and her colleague Håkon Sand get a new high priority case. The young medical student Kristine Håverstad (Gjertrud Lynge) has become victim of a brutal rape in her own home.

Blessed Are Those Who Thirst is in most respects a traditional crime movie, although stylistically the movie is up to date and 'fresh'. Fast editing and use of repetition are central devices in the creation of the rough style, in particular in the more dramatic scenes. These techniques create a physically uncomfortable state for the spectator that suits the savage actions and also creates suspense and an uneasy feeling that something is wrong with the police attitudes in rape cases and racial topics.

The narrative follows a classical two-plot structure; one following the work of the police trying to solve the two cases, the other focusing on the raped girl and her father's attempt to cope with the situation, the sorrow and the thought of revenge. The movie moves between the main characters allowing, as Murray Smith claims, the possibility of engagement with different characters, being either Kristine and her father, or Hanne and her overlooked partner Cecilie. That the two cases are connected is hardly a surprise for an experienced crime audience, but more important than plot is character development. The movies connect these elements in a strong opening.

The opening sequence consists of three parallel plotlines edited together in a fast montage. Opening with young nightly flirtation, Kristine is walked home by a fellow student. At the same time Hanne shares a romantic meal with her lover Cecilie, and Håkon Sand checks in at a hotel to share the night with his lover Karen, the lawyer. A stranger attacks Kristine as she is entering her apartment, and this is cross-edited with the love scenes between the other two couples. The incident, later described by the police as a particularly brutal rape, thus is tight-knit with beautiful love-scenes in a way that can hardly leave the spectator untouched.

These techniques create an engagement based on revolt and empathy with the victim Kristine, through the creation of a body based understanding of what the rapist destroys and of Kristine's feelings and her loss. Kristine is being tied to her own bed while being raped, with the sound of her bedpost's rhythmic hits toward the wall and the continuous moaning from the rapist. Mixed with intense music (the director's own composition) and the sound of her screams, this collage makes the sequence troublesome for the viewer to endure. The idyll is destroyed both aurally and visually, leaving a membrane of vulnerability over the mood of the movie.

Interestingly, Hanne Wilhelmsen herself is never threatened or vulnerable when at work as an investigator. It is the private room that is in danger, like it is for Kristine when being raped by an intruder in her own home. And so it is for Kristine's father after finding his only child stripped naked and bound after being raped. Kristine's post-traumatic depression leaves her unable to cope with life, friends and studies, leaving her father helpless and almost as wounded as her. While Kristine, the always-correct lawyer Karen and a long row of young immigrant girls become threatened by violence, rape and murder, Hanne is always safe in and at her work.

Flirtatious and tough, she is hiding her private life and not letting her colleagues come too close, although it seems that she would like to uncover her secret. When the police are ordered to work overtime, a male college complains, "My wife is pissed. What does your husband say to this?" Hanne's reply, "She'll get used to it", is an answer with a double meaning and understood in different ways by the spectator and the colleague. Hanne's wife, Cecilie is also pissed, because like she says, "No matter how late I come home from work you are always more late!" To the extent that Hanne is threatened it is by her own feelings that she, as unconventional for a portrait of a woman, is incapable of talking about.

Hanne seems like a bitchy and unemotional woman. When she is called up because of a new 'Saturday-massacre' murder and gets ready to leave, Cecilie shouts, "If you have to go I will kill you!" Hanne's reply is simply,

"Now you have to choose between killing me or joining me!" Cecilie interprets this as a golden chance to meet Hanne's colleagues, but she is at first totally ignored at the crime scene and finally introduced by Hanne as "a very old friend."

Hanne's lack of empathy and caring is evident in her encounter with both witnesses and the rape victim Kristine, but most of all when it comes to her own private life. Hanne is clever, just and tough, but sometimes too tough for her own good. And sometimes too tough for a deeper engagement from the spectator; we admire Hanne, but we disagree with her choices most of all in the way she treats her lover. Although the film places most of the spectator's empathy and understanding on Kristine and her father, the spectator will reveal that Hanne's strength is a mask. The most tender and emotional moment in the movie is when Hanne's coldness cracks and she invites her colleague Håkon to her house for dinner, and by that, admits her love for Cecilie.[10]

The movie (as the books) has created some debate related to the representation of a lesbian protagonist. The opinions have been mixed, with some focusing on the positive potential of having a lesbian protagonist in a mainstream film. Others have been critical to whether the cold Hanne could serve as a positive role model. In my point of view, the healthiest development in contemporary cinema is a wider range of female representations, not seeing women's roles as binary oppositions, perfect ideals or hopeless victims. Women have several qualities; women are like Hanne, both strong and weak.

The debate shows that the fictional characters do engage and are vital in the reception of the movie. But the strongest emotional focus in the movie is still the victim(s), as the biblical quotation in the title refers to. As a rape-revenge[11] movie, *Blessed Are Those Who Thirst* differs from traditional genre films in several respects, most of all in relation to how the revenge is developed over time. The solution is also questioned until the bitter end. Director Carl Kiøning formulates this:

> I want to …introduce the problems, the dilemmas and complications. I want to show the rage in a person possessed with the thought of revenge. I ask the question but without being given the final answer as to whether revenge can be defended (Løchen: 1997).

And the movie succeeds (more than is usual in conventional thrillers) in making these ethical dilemmas the spectator's own dilemmas.

"I Have to Know"

Eva Isaken is a leading Norwegian director and her filmography covers a range of different genres, among them movies for teenagers, comedies and several crime stories, both in film and television. In *Cellophane* it is obvious that both writer Leidulv Risan and the director have wanted to make a mainstream genre film with the ambition to entertain.

The crime puzzle in *Cellophane* has an original connection with women's everyday experiences because it starts with the protagonist Marianne (Andrine Sæther) taking care of her father who is sick from cancer and dying. The spectator understands Marianne as an active career woman, who still tends to her father. At Jacobs's bedside Marianne promises to burn her father's secret papers, but instead of doing so, she and her admirer Peter read them. The papers turn out to be letters claiming her father to be a murderer. This triggers Marianne's curiosity, but as Peter formulates it, "Either you have to live with not knowing or you have to live with what ever you find out."

Marianne *wants to know* and she starts her own undercover investigation, her reason being simply "It is *my dad*!" The investigation becomes a traveling back in time to a place where Marianne lived as a child, but somehow has forgotten. Both the private and professional lives become tangled in a new way, partly because Marianne researches the murder while pretending to do a story for her newspaper on rehab for drug-addicts. At the same time, the connection between private and professional is typical; with the exception of Hanne, the women get themselves into dramatic situations because of their private lives.

The motivations for their actions are strong. The women may not know what to do (Marianne, Kristine and Eva), but why they have to act the way they do is clearly character driven. This is almost contrary to the action hero, whose motivation may be blurred and whose reason for being chosen for a "mission" is a mere coincidence often related to being in the wrong place at the wrong time (Schubart 2002:22).

Marianne is a curious and brave young woman, but lacks the professional investigator's strength and power. For instance, she is hunting a presumed murderer without any kind of protection from others or from weapons. In *Cellophane* the protagonist is situated in a more unsecured environment (than in *Blessed Are Those Who Thirst*) and with imminent dangers. The urban Marianne is not at home in the country. Even the cows represent a threat, literally by causing her to drive off the road and by serving as an insecure hiding place when she is running from the killer. After the car accident, the locals comment Marianne's lacking the ability to make it through the woods on: "Next time you visit the countryside, be sure to wear suitable shoes!" In reply the high-healed Marianne moans: "I hate trainers."

The men in the countryside are mainly portrayed negatively- like primitive hillbillies, a bit creepy and all of them likely to be assaulters, in a way reminding us of John Boorman's *Deliverance*. This is of course to be understood as a suspense grip, as suspense is based on the spectator being insecure and leaving open several possibilities of whom the killer is. A side effect of this portrayal is an urban critique of the rural culture which is presented as consisting of a bunch of men killing wild animals with their cars or being sexually frustrated and fanatically religious. The account of the countryside is actually quite similar to the "Norwegian-American" country-side in *Fargo*.

Marianne is both stubborn and independent. Around her are two different but positively portrayed admirers. Her colleague Peter is the patient suitor who sits home waiting and visiting her sick father (with whom he is not acquainted beforehand) when Marianne is around and about. Peter is the charming caretaker. Jon is the simpler yet mystical and attractive local Marianne is flirting with. The attraction is clearly sexual, as explicitly shown when Marianne gazes at him unobserved as he is fixing her car and the camera is lingering on Jon's behind and oily arms. Even though Marianne herself is made an object of the male gaze (both by Jon and her landlord who is an actual voyeur), the heroine is only to a low degree eroticised.

Marianne's voyeuristic scene continues into a dialog on car reparations that is filled with sexual connotations. The sexual tension between the two is only partly released. The revelation of Marianne's real name and reason for investigation gives Jon the feeling of being deceived. In anger and frustration he kisses her violently and asks her to leave. The romantic dilemmas (choosing between the two) are left unresolved, with Marianne walking into the dark on her own. In the middle of the struggle with the killer,[12] Marianne has lost one of her high-healed shoes. In the movie's symbolic ending there is no prince who comes running with the missing shoe, leaving Marianne at first limping out of the picture, before she finally tosses the other one, continuing barefoot on her own.

Through mainly keeping Marianne on her own, the movie strengthens the spectator's engagement with the heroine. *Cellophane* makes the clearest case for Smith's claim on the techniques for and importance of alignment where the suspense depends on our involvement with Marianne. Our involvement is further increased because the conflict between making it on one's own and the need for independence is recognizable to the female audience. The way careers, love life and taking care of a family are an interwoven mixture of incompatible components is an everyday experience for many modern women. *Cellophane* achieves an engagement with the protagonist more credibly and realistically than Hollywood's heroes and heroines, due to Marianne's familiarity and resemblance with the heroines of everyday life.

Something Else Besides a Mother

More than revealing secrets, *Eva's Eye* is about concealing secrets. The movie is based on the leading Norwegian crime-writer Karin Fossum's book with the same title, and it is directed by one of the leading female directors, Berit Nesheim.

In the movie's opening Eva (Andrine Sæther)[13] is going for a walk with her seven-year-old daughter, when they discover a body floating in the river.

Eva pretends to phone the police, but behind her daughter's back she is actually phoning her elderly father, asking how he has been lately. Why? The answer is given when we go back in time. Eva is in her mid-thirties, divorced and has one daughter. She works as a housekeeper and a security guard to make ends meet. She is an idealistic artist and a down-to-earth single mother still dreaming to live as an artist. One day she meets a childhood friend, Maja, who gives her a tempting and frightening offer – to try prostitution together with her. Being desperate as her debt increases, Eva makes a choice of fatal consequences. The first night in Maja's apartment Eva witnesses Maja being killed. The murder gives her the chance to take all of her friend's savings and so she does, causing someone to hunt her down and finally making her a killer herself.

A book reviewer brings forth how Fossum's story confronts us with the protagonist's ethical dilemmas:

> What would you do if you were alone in a cottage in the mountain at night with a box containing millions and you hear the sound of a man trying to enter and you know that he is after the money? You would run. I know I would, but where? Out in the middle of nowhere? Down in the basement or in the attic? You wouldn't have a chance.

But before Eva is in the situation, she has faced another question even more recognisable: If you needed the money would you take the money and run? Both the director Berit Nesheim and the actor Andrine Sæther are interested in these dilemmas. "The people are the most important is Berit Nesheim's credo, and her goal is to make personal movies" (Aas Olsen 1999).

> I was struck by how original and unpredictable Karin Fossum's story was the first time I read the book. It is a suspense story where the suspense is related more to the characters and to what happens to them than the story itself. The story arises out of a Norwegian everyday experience that everyone is familiar with, which makes it more credible. And I like the fact that the key question isn't "who" but "why".

Eva's Eyes is the story of how any ordinary person can be trapped if he or she makes a wrong choice and deviates just one small step from the safe path directed by one's own conscience. And the movie is challenging because we first get to know Eva and her situation, her troubled economics and her despair over not being able to give her daughter the things she needs, like a backpack on her first day of school. The engagement is in another words created through the level of alignment, making the basis for an alliance with the ethical wrongdoings that Eva comits. Modern attitudes strengthen our view that it is Eva's right to be a single mother *and* fulfil herself through her choice of career. Based on our own or secondary knowledge of single mothers' situations, we construct the character of Eva. Our alignment progresses gradually; we follow her curiosity and thereafter her despair in a hunt for new opportunities. Afterwards our allegiance is challenged when Eva commits murder, an act we cannot sympathize with, but we still want the best for her (perhaps we want her to keep the money and get a fair punishment for the killing). By ingraining the main character in modern women's reality, the movie's foreground is in the ethical dilemmas, even more than normal in the thrillers.

Noël Carroll points to the fact that films often shape the ethical responses that diverge from our everyday moral judgments (Carroll 1999:45). More often than not the protagonist possesses positive virtues and acts morally correct according to the ethical norms shared by the audience (Carroll 1999:44). Interestingly, these actions and judgments are questioned in all three movies in a more explicit way than normally seen in suspense movies.

The relation between fiction and reality is a challenging relation, particularly when related to ethically challenging topics. The fictional worlds have their own ethical standards not always analogous to our own. The movies discussed nevertheless invite us to question the choices made by the protagonists, especially when it comes to the use of violence. Even though all three movies picture women using violence, they also question these solutions. Violence doesn't make a happy ending; every closing is a painful one.

Women are Doing it for Themselves

Twenty female directors have made feature films in Norway since 1990. Among these movies, several are of the most important and most acclaimed productions, both commercially and artistically. They cover a wide range of genres, including personal documentaries (Magrete Olin), animation movies for children (Vibeke Idsøe), one dogma movie (Mona Hoel), movies for young audiences (Torunn Lian and Eva Isaksen) and adaptations of famous literature (Liv Ullman og Unni Straume).

More than being artistically challenging, these three movies represent a central tendency called 'mainstreaming' of Norwegian film. The small Norwegian production tends to move in little waves all the time, and these movies have caused an alarm for making the female directors more invisible than before (Larsen 2002). To become visible one needs to stay in the business over some years, which is a challenge in a small national film production. (The Norwegian film industry has moved from about ten productions a year to about twenty the last few years). Among the most productive directors is Eva Isaksen, who directed *Cellophane*. She belongs to the generation emerging after the women directors of the 1970s and does not want to be labelled with gender. "I have to admit that I am glad that I don't have to wait for a 'women director' sign," she claims. A main point as she sees it is that one should have a variety of goals, both in front of and behind the camera (Hoff

1997). When working on *Cellophane*, both she and the actor Andrine Sæther were conscious about making the Marianne character tougher and moving away from a lot of female clichés. "It is in due course that we get more movies with strong and vigorous women as protagonists. And why shouldn't they be commercial?" (Hoff 1997).

In my opinion these women aren't particularly strong or one-dimensional ideals – they all make bad decisions and show both strength and weakness. Nor are they masculine women or just heroes in women's clothes (Dole 2001). They find their own individual solutions and they do it themselves, without much help, either from other women (like in the 1970s) or with the hands of a man (like in Hollywood). The pioneer women looked for a new feministic aesthetic, new female representations and topics closer to women's ordinary world. In relation to these goals the thrillers seem quite traditional, but nevertheless in my opinion they also represent progress. More than larger than life women we can never match, these are women we already know, showing the type of strength we see in women everyday, women able to cope with different tasks all at once. Instead of showing an easy way out, the movies make us compare and evaluate the actions and attitudes presented in the fictional world.

The lifelikeness of these women makes them more invisible at first sight, but the connection to my own fights in everyday life make them all the more welcome. Like always, for better or for worse, a woman's gotta do what a woman's gotta do, in life as in fiction.

Notes

1. Among these is *Bloody Angels* directed by Karin Julsrud, not included in my discussion here due to the lack of a female protagonist.
2. To make the reading of this article easier I use the English titles from this point.
3. The term *women's film* should not be confused with women's genres, the latter being a term for classical melodramas.
4. This heading is indebted to Liv Hausken's study on *Hustruer*.
5. The *Hustruer* project is unique in Norwegian film history because the director and the actors made two sequels 10 and 20 years later.
6. In *Evas øye* her occupation is presented a little later.
7. Yvonne Tasker discusses this view in her book, but the view should not be understood as her own.
8. Smith refers to Clifford Geertz in relation to the "human-agent schemata".
9. Three of the books about Hanne Wilhelmsen have been adapted to three different mediums (film, television and radio) by the same director Carl Kiøning, all with the same actress Kjersti Elvik
10. Hanne is unable to come out of the closet, and this remains a problem in later books. In *Død Joker*, Cecilie gets cancer, which Hanne is unable to cope with, which makes her working even more.
11. Rape-revenge is a term used about low budget movies mainly from the 1970's that focus on rape and the women's revenge. The most famous is *I spit on your Grave* (1978).
12. The killer is a religious leader and an old friend of her father, who is accidentally killed in the final battle; he drowns in cow manure.

13. Andrine Sæther, one of the most popular actresses in Norwegian film, plays in all three movies as she also plays Cecilie in *Blessed*. Jørgen Langhelle, a leading man in Norwegian cinema, portrays both Jon in *Cellophane* and the killer in *Blessed*.

References

Carroll, N. (1999). Film, emotion and Genre. In Carl Plantinga & Greg M. Smith (Eds.), *Passionate Views*. Baltimore & London: John Hopkins University Press.

Dahl, H. F. (et al) (1996). *Kinoens mørke, fjernsynets lys*. Oslo: Gyldendal.

Dove, C. M (2001). The Gun and the Badge: Hollywood and the Female Lawmen. In Martha McCaughy & Neal King (eds.), *Reel Knockouts: Violent Women in the Movies* (ed). Austin: Texas University Press.

Ekle, L. (2000). Retrieved from http://www.nrk.no/litteratur/1188.html.

Hausken, L. (1992). *En annen historie: En analyse av Anja Breiens "Hustruer"*. *Levende bilder*, nr 4/92 KULTs skriftserie, nr 9. Oslo: Norges allmennvitenskapelige forskningsråd.

Hausken, L. (1997). Kvinner finnes ikke – finnes Kvinnefilmen?. In Gunnar Iversen & Ove Solum (eds.), *Nærbilder*. Universitetsforlaget: Oslo.

Hoff, A. (1997). Kvinner og film – fremdeles 'det annet kjønn' – både foran og bak kamerat? *Film og kino*, 6/97.

Larsen, M. (2002). Film: et mannsyrke. *Dagsavisen*, March 20, 2002.

Likestillingssenteret (2001). *Minifakta om likestilling*. Retrieved from http://www.likestilling.no/ publikasjoner/minifakta.shtml.

Løchen, K. (1997). Full trøkk for norsk krim. *Film og kino* 6/97.

Messari, P. (1995). Visuell Læseferdighed: En teoretisk sammenfatning. *Mediekultur*, 23, 1995.

Rottem, Ø. (1998). *Norges litteraturhistorie: Etterkrigslitteraturen,* Oslo: Cappelen.

Schubart, R. (2002). *Med vold og magt*. København: Rosinante.

Smith, M. (1995). *Engaging Characters: Fiction, emotion, and the cinema*. Oxford: Clarendon Press.

Tasker, Y. (1993). *Spectacular bodies: Gender, genre and the action cinema*. London: Routledge.

Aas Olsen, T. (1999). Tårer for Evas øyne. *Dagbladet*, October 23, 1999.

"Must-see Medicine Women"

Breaking Borders
of Genre and Gender in *ER*

Mervi Pantti

The writers of *ER* have had seven years to perfect their portrayal of women doctors, so we expect them to have it right by now. But they have yet to have a female physician who totally pushes the envelope, challenging authority figures, acting like a know-it-all and stomping off in a huff when things don't go her way. A female Doug Ross would be "must-see TV" (Booth 2001).

The commercial imperative of the television industry, coupled with the demand for programming that is the 'same but different', has led to more and more combined genres in an effort to draw bigger audiences. Genre hybrids such as the phenomenally successful medical drama series *ER* (1994-present day) are calculated to appeal to diverse audiences and capitalise on different markets. As Robin Nelson has discussed television executives have become aware of shifting cultural values and learnt that crossovers of role and genre can do miracles for ratings (Nelson 2000). Consequently they are more willing than before to entertain innovative, non-traditional gender representations of characters during previously conservative prime time television slots. My goal is here to find out what kind of impact this yearning for a mass audience has had in changing images of women, on television, in professional roles traditionally assigned to men. Specifically, I trace the recent hybridisation of genres and their effect on gender representations. This hybridisation can be seen in larger terms as a central aspect of the post-modern age, in which the boundaries between texts, as generally traditionally formulated by programme-makers, have become increasingly blurred, with the inclusion of styles and subjects from other genres and texts.

My case-in-point is an example par excellence: the much celebrated, watched, and discussed medical drama *ER*. Approaching *ER* as a genre hybrid, incorporating the life and death situations of melodrama, the tension relieving humour of sitcom, the excitement of action, and accuracy of documentary, can provide answers to questions about the popularity of the series, as well as about how the images of women are turned out. I discuss the programme in relation to the following dimensions: generic history; genre's form-related features; and representations of characters. I then conclude by suggesting that the series' multidimensional generic features cater for multilayered representations of both genders; and thus provide for a broad platform for both identification and emancipation.

Better Images, Please!

The idea that anyone in authority should decide what is 'better' has become something of a taboo. In much of the recent theorizing and analyses of the media, the notions of 'good' and 'bad' gender representations are practically absent. This is, naturally, in line with that particular tradition that emphasizes 'reading against the grain' and celebrates the polysemy of the text. However, here I wish to take a different standpoint in that I want to address the questions of quality, with regard to a particular genre and a particular series (as opposed to television as a medium), and assess that from the gender perspective. When compared to the earlier medical series, as well as to the medical series targeted at more specific audiences, ER seems to me ideologically 'progressive' both in its portrayal of women and handling of social issues.

Media scholars, including feminist researchers, have long recognized the role of television as a cultural forum for public discourse about social issues and social change. According to Newcomb and Hirsch TV offers "a way of understanding who and what we are, how values and behaviour are adjusted, how meanings shift' by providing 'a multiplicity of meaning rather than a monolith dominant view" (Newcomb and Hirsch 2000:564). Hence, for Newcomb and Hirsch the key task of television is the raising of issues that reflect and bring together a variety of viewpoints in a society (though it is not necessary for TV to have clear solutions for the problems under discussion). Although I agree with the authors that television's emphasis is on presenting a diversity of opinion rather than coherence, I do not believe that it features debate without direction. Television's ongoing debate is conditioned and constrained by its aesthetic conventions and by its social and cultural context.

Television also produces representations of gender through different discourses. These images tell us about the values and norms attached to gender in our culture. In relation to these 'cultural ideals', which are produced by representations, real women and men construct their own identities and construct their histories (De Lauretis 1987:10). The notion of cultural forum thus contains the conflicting nature of these representations and holds that the images of women are far from homogenous and that television does not promote one solid set of values. The conflicting nature of TVs images is most of all due to the fact that television contains different types of programmes, which all tell a story in their own words. However, these stories and the values they produce are bound to an era and therefore change along with cultural change. These inherent contradictions and movements can thus be called television's polysemy (Newcomb & Hirch 2000). In this clashing of different images and ideals, the ideal types of gender representation can be and are broken. Television and its programmes are not the cause of change, but rather, as John Fiske (1987:45) believes, television is in the midst of this movement of changing ideological values.

Whereas Fiske identifies television as the fellow traveller of progressive social change, others have viewed it as conservative and ultimately supportive of the status quo. Todd Gitlin has argued that dominant ideology is produced through prime time (Gitlin 2000). According to him those programming hours contain those images that best are thought to attract large audiences whereas contrasting and controversial viewpoints are perhaps shown in single programmes at marginal viewing times. If ideas, ideologies and values alternative to the mainstream culture are touched upon, they are cushioned with the emotional and the private, which ultimately results in the loss of broader social connections.

Many of the initial feminist dealings with film and television were calls to action that grew out of a conviction that women's oppression was related to demeaning and stereotypical media representations (Brundson et al 1997: 4-5). After the mid 1970s, this social and political criticism was overshadowed by psychoanalytical and semiotic academic analyses. However, the concept of images of women must be still considered crucial for feminist thinking – without necessarily connecting them directly to social reality. The concept entails both audio-visual texts, as well as the definitions, presuppositions and visions they produce about womanhood and the feminine. The impulse behind studying representations of women and other oppressed groups lies, as Richard Dyer says, in the notion that; how different social groups are represented is part of "how they are treated in life" (Dyer 1993:1).

In the 'first wave' of feminist media research, scholars and activists argued for 'better' representations of women, urging television executives to realize changes that portrayed women in less stereotypical ways (see Walters 1995:31). Gaye Tuchman, in her much-cited 1976 essay "The Symbolic Annihilation of Women by the Mass Media", argued that the media was suffering from 'culture lag' by maintaining sexist imagery and sex-role stereotyping even in the face of changing social reality, and consequently reflected only the previously dominant values of society. Tuchman represents a typical first wave image analyst who worked on a prescriptive rather than a descriptive level and saw culture as a reflection of reality.

While fluid representations of gender and the view of (overly) active audiences have taken over in academia, tales of 'good' and 'bad' images of women are still very much part of both popular and academic discourses – though more openly in the former than in the latter. This claim can be seen in the quotation at the beginning of the paper: "a female Doug Ross would be 'must-see TV'". Making judgments is a problematic task for television studies, as after the 'cultural turn' it was seen as an act of oppression and elitism. As Charlotte Brunsdon has written, "film and television studies ... rarely explicitly engages with issues of critical evaluation, except perhaps politically in the varied guises and defences of the 'progressive' and the 'popular'" (Brunsdon 1997:127). While judgments of quality usually must be traced from between the lines, John Mepham has boldly tried to provide us with a recipe for it: "High quality television is television which is excellent as measured by its faithfulness to these principles: the rule of diversity, the cultural purpose of telling usable stories and the ethic of truth telling" (Mepham 1990:51).

With good reason Dyer writes that a great deal of image analysis, typically fuelled by anger or frustration, seems only to demonstrate that there is nothing new on the media front. He argues that studying images needs to be tempered by considerations that get closer to the real political difficulty of representations. This means, first of all, stressing that representations always entail the use of the codes and conventions of the available cultural forms of presentation. Secondly, it means that cultural forms do not have single determinate meanings because people make sense of them in different ways, even if we are, of course, restricted by both the viewing and the reading codes to which we have access and by what representations there are for us to view and read. Thirdly, what is represented in representations in not directly reality itself but other representations (Dyer 1993:2-3). The analysis of images always needs to see how any given image is rooted in a network of other images. Genre history is an essential part of that network: the modern day medical drama draws from the conventions established by earlier medical dramas, which originally drew from the conventions of films, radio plays and novels.

A Most Unsuitable Job for a Woman

Television's medical drama is part of a wide category of medical fiction, which encompasses many genres from science fiction and horror to melodrama and romance (see Moody 1998:9-22). In the history of television's prime-time medical drama the beginning of the 1960s represents its first turning point. The classic *Dr. Kildare* and *Ben Casey* series (1961-1966) became a phenomenon and led network executives to believe, as Joseph Turow (1997:185) has written, that a successful, lasting medical genre formula had been invented. The formula was set in the hospital (instead of the home or other non-hospital settings) and was built around male physicians (typically older man/younger man duo). In the 1960s medical shows were heavily influenced by the interests of organised medicine, which took care to ensure that the physician's image fitted its ideal vision of an all-powerful doctor working in an unblemished high-tech hospital (Turow 1997:193). In the early 1960s, women had minor supporting roles in these shows due to the conventional wisdom among TV programmers that a starring woman would create ratings problems (Turow 1997). The attractive female nurses and romantically suffering female patients served primarily to provide an unlimited reserve of romantic interest for the male doctors.

In the early medical dramas, the doctor is male, wise and caring. An individual who can solve the underlying causes of illness by locating the source of a problem in personal trauma or social circumstances (Hallam 1998:32). Those doctors were very much utopian creatures. Interestingly, this detective-like, compassionate and wholly dedicated healer was reborn as a female at the turn of the millennium. This is the case, for instance, in NBC's feel-good family drama *Providence* (1999-2002), which tells the story of Dr. Sydney Hansen (Melina Kanakaredes), a plastic surgeon who abandons her dashing career to return to her eccentric family and the safe haven of Providence to find fulfilment working in a low-income medical clinic. Like the male medical doctors' concerns in the 1950s and 1960s, Dr. Hansen's concern extends well beyond the treatment of the physical body to incorporate a time consuming investigation of the underlying causes of illness and to a special bonding with her patient.

When *Dr. Kildare* and *Ben Casey* were pulled from prime time in 1966, the first doctor show cycle on American television ended. Nevertheless, the hits had established boundaries for the elements that would work in the medical genre. It meant that "the dramas had to enact high-emotion issues of life and death, not subtle problems of the mind or the politics of the hospital or the medical system" (Turow 1997:97). It also meant that the dramas had to evolve around male physicians, not nurses or female doctors. There were attempts to centre medical dramas on female doctors at the end of the 1970s and 1980s, but as Turow writes: "The fate of these shows ... reinforced the prevailing industry attitude that medical series with women as title characters were poison."[1]

Television eventually caught up with reality in the 1980s. The image of a god-like male doctor having everything under control was replaced by medical teamwork conducted in a chaotic crisis environment. It is not an overstatement to say that John Masius's ensemble show *St. Elsewhere* (1982-1988) revolutionized the medical drama in the same way *Hill Street Blues* (1981) rewrote the cop show. Indeed, *St Elsewhere* was directly modelled on the very successful *Hill Street Blues*. It had a large ensemble cast, the use of the continuing serial narrative, and blended melodrama and comedy with the 'realist' treatment of controversial issues already common to medical dramas. With *St. Elsewhere* the focus of the narrative shifted from professional conflicts to personal relationships, from glorifying the health care system and medical profession to the exploration of the emotional frontier of hospital life. This trend of mixing public and private lives only deepened when *ER* and *Chicago Hope* made their debuts within a day of each other in 1994. The major change in the 1980s' dramas was to introduce the doctor as human being who experiences a large scale of personal and professional problems. Women also fitted to this new category of 'more like us' doctors, and therefore introducing female physicians as part of a large ensemble was a perceptibly less of a ratings risk than a 'poisonous' title character.

Finally, in the 1990s a medical show with a female lead touched a chord: *Dr. Quinn, Medicine Woman* (1993-1998), starred Jane Seymour as a Boston physician who moved to the mountains of Colorado in the 1860s. It developed a loyal following amongst the advertisers' favourite audience; women between eighteen and forty-nine. What's more it did this in the usually deadly Saturday night slot on CBS. As Bonnie J. Dow (1996:164) has described in her analysis of the series, *Dr. Quinn*'s success was unpredicted by industry due to it possessing several risky characteristics. First, it was a soft family drama; secondly, it was a historical western set in the mythic U.S. of the mid-19th century; and thirdly, it depended upon a female lead. In the era of ensemble casts in series about professional doctors a successful drama about an individual heroine's triumphs could be seen as indicating something new about the producers' understanding of who constituted their audiences. *Dr. Quinn* and *ER* can be seen as examples of the respective ways the media has responded to the fragmentation of audiences. Firstly, by tailoring programmes for specific segments and secondly, by reaching for larger audiences through hybrid genres and ensemble cast series.

As Jason Jacobs has pointed out, television's interest in medicine reached "epidemic proportions" in the mid-1990s (Jacobs 2001:23). This epidemic included documentaries, docusoaps, magazine programmes, and of course medical dramas. These dramas were also part of a wider growth in the depiction of professional working lives on television, especially professional women's working lives. Nearly ten years ago Suzanna Walters expressed concern about television's role in the so-called backlash (Walters 1995:134-135). According to her the portrayals of women on television were getting worse both in numbers and in quality: the 'good' woman is mother who stays at home and the career woman is stereotypically portrayed as desperate for a man, lonely and bitter. The absence of women in prime time shows is not the case at the beginning of 21st century. Indeed, much of the current entertainment output of television features strong women, single mothers, career women, and female friends, not to mention the growing output featuring young women with superpowers. The visibility of women in television drama has certainly increased, but whether this is a progressive shift or whether this 'feminization' of prime time entertainment has something to do with feminism needs, of course, to be discussed.

Current broadcast network programming arguably presents a greater variety of representations of women than in previous decades, partly due to changes in gender roles in society since the women's movement. Since *Dr. Quinn* and *Providence* a new female centred medical drama has appeared, namely Lifetime's *Strong Medicine* about two female doctors who share a practice in Philadelphia. This development can be seen as having occurred because the 'new woman' is recognized as a consuming audience member, not just because the networks feel a responsibility to break down cultural stereotypes. Such marketplace driven political correctness even motivated the creation of Lifetime, a cable network dedicated to offering female characters for women to cheer, and "to inspire women and girls to Be Your Own Hero" (lifetimetv.com). The significant proliferation of female characters (e.g. *ER* has five female doctors) in current medical dramas parallels the rise in the number of women entering the medical profession for real. More importantly, it parallels the recognition by television executives that women – particularly those in the much-desired 18-to-49 demographic – support shows starring women.

ER – Exceeding Limits of Generic Conventions

What differentiates *ER* from its ancestors and its current counterparts? There have been several attempts to explain the overall success and boom of the medical drama as being due to actual developments in the health systems of the westernised world. Sabine Krajewski (2002:12) takes the British series *Casualty* as an example: "Since the British health system had gone through major cuts and changes during the eighties, *Casualty* producers hit a nerve with the series. ... The series became a medium for the viewers to discuss and influence these changes." Film Studies Professor Janine Marchessault has noticed the same correlation between cuts to health care and an increase in fictional doctor dramas in America: "The less access people have to health care, the more they consume health culture... not just as a means to escape the harsh realities of cuts to health infrastructures, but rather as a means to escape the loss of access" (Marchessault 2000). The success of the medical drama genre may be in part due to some relation to current social conditions or transformations, however, I do not find it satisfactory to tie the success of *ER* to some general thesis of society or even popular culture. Besides, the above-cited arguments certainly suffer from 'text-blindness'. For instance, the chaotic County hospital portrayed by *ER* can hardly be seen as a utopian substitute for a real life loss.

While the above explanations may be part of the story, they cannot explain the wide appeal of this particular 'ratings buster' show or its durable viewer loyalty. The explanation may be more fundamental; *ER* provides pleasure that comes from offering television that is the 'same but truly different' while at the same time exceeding previously clearly distinguished gender norms based on male/female binary opposition (see Nelson 2000:62-73). Traditionally gendering has been located in dichotomous thought-patterns: The key male/female binary opposition has been echoed in series of other binaries, such as reason/emotion; masculine deduction/feminine intuition; public sphere/private sphere and rational detachment/emotional involvement. The female emotionalism has historically been situated on one side of the binary divide, the male rationality on the other. In *ER* watching Dr. Greene trying to bond with his daughter or Dr. Weaver making her hard-headed, autocratic decisions we have examples where those dichotomies are broken.

Every Thursday night 35 million Americans, and for example near to a fifth of the Finnish population watches *ER*, where it sits amongst the twenty most popular programmes.[2] *ER* is the most awarded, praised and expensive medical drama to date – at the time of writing about to start its ninth season in Finland. As widely circulated legend has it the creator of *ER*, trained doctor and best-selling author Michael Crichton, waited twenty years for his idea for the show to be broadcast on the small screen. The script was bought by Steven Spielberg and was finally accepted as a two-hour pilot project by NBC, who believed that the names Spielberg and Crichton would sell the series. In addition *ER* would become known for its formal experimentation (e.g. the forcefully promoted live broadcast episode), hectic pace, long stedicam shots, documentary look, complex medical jargon and sarcastic humour. The hospital is no longer imagined as a place of peace and harmony as in the 1960s series but as a tense environment disrupted by uncontrollable, yet generically predictable events of which the gurneys shooting through the swinging doors are the most visible symbol.

ER has thus gained a reputation for realism. Director Rob Holcomb has defined the premises of the series set by the pilot: "People came and went, and not all the stories were finished, because in real life, you're not always going to be there to see how something finishes up. But we gave the audience a taste of something real. That was the mission" (Pourroy 1995:14). *ER* can be called 'docu-real' fiction which refers to the entertainment programs that self-consciously showcase documentary units or modes as part of their narrative and plot and documentary looks as part of their mise-en-scéne. What is at work with the documentary style is, amongst other things, that it serves to highlight prestige drama at the time of diminishing market share. Plus it tends to overturn conventional taste-culture hierarchies that normally assign documentary to the higher but smaller, taste cultures of PBS and 'pure' entertainment to the lower but far broader taste cultures (see Caldwell 2000:259-292). Despite *ER*'s realistic status, vigorously emphasized in the promotion, it retains a strong melodramatic impetus that arises from focusing on the doctors' personal and professional dilemmas. As Julia Hallam has pointed out, another important even if less commented on 'house style' of the series is the use of saturated colours, low-key lightning and the melodramatic use of soft focus lenses – techniques which are hardly documentary (Hallam 1998:41).

A medical series may lean on soap opera, melodrama, sitcom, adventure or even action film styles depending on a variety of factors, e.g. the producers' aim and their need to reach certain segments of the audience. This genre mixing, even if not a new phenomenon as such, is nowadays more and more the norm both in the film and television industries as it may attract the so called and greatly desired cross-over audiences. Rick Altman argues that Hollywood producers tend to avoid rigid genre classifications, as those might turn off potential viewers (Altman 1999:123-143). Instead, they aim at bringing together features of previously successful series, and mix as many segmented genres as possible. However, when we deal with the hybridisation it is important to remember that they are not reducible solely to the economic principles that give rise to them. There may be also the potential emancipatory aspect to be taken into the consideration. As Yvonne Tasker writes: "developments such as genre hybrids may serve *economic* concerns, … whilst simultaneously functioning as complex cultural forms" (Tasker 1998:11).

An illustration of this 'genre cocktail' logic can be found for instance in *ER*'s eighth season episode "Partly Cloudy, Chance of Rain" in which Dr. Kerry Weaver acts like a full-blood action heroine: She vaults into a wrecked ambulance and performs an emergency C-section for a seriously injured woman, while overhead a damaged power pylon showers sparks, and a torrential rainstorm pounds the accident site. Conversely in another eighth season episode "Start All Over Again" Dr. Susan Lewis's first day at work begins as a slapstick comedy: Lewis and Dr. Carter are about to deliver a baby when the bed starts rising because the woman's broken water is leaking onto the pedal. Lewis runs off and returns with a ladder. The doctors climb up and successfully deliver the baby.

Ideologically, *ER* is about professionalism, but professionalism as seen in its everyday realization through personal relationships. We have issues of individualism and teamwork, and the wider social and political issues of gender and race relations in the workplace, as well as topical 'hot' issues and the recognizable 'cold' issues of bureaucracy, cost cutting, and rationalisation. The significance of these processes is emphasised in the fact that for a hospital these may have life or death consequences. In the ninth season starter "Chaos Theory", chief of staff Dr. Robert Romano is in the process of transporting four critical surgical patients to another hospital. A nurse on the phone is told the other hospital will only accept one patient. Romano takes the phone from her and speaks to the person on the phone. He tells them that they will take all four: "You tell your chief of staff that Robert Romano is sending over four patients, all of whom I expected to be treated like his own mother without the inappropriate touching." Here, at stake are two things: on one hand, the social criticism expressed in the (touching) commitment to the professional code to help anyone in need; on the other hand, the typical narrative device of using humour as relief from a tense narrative. For a medical drama, humorous storylines or one-liners fulfil that task by relieving the audience from the tension created by serious topics, gory accidents and unjust fates.

In *ER*, even the most tragic elements are often paired with black humour make the peak dramatic scenes tolerable. Later in the same episode the helicopter rotor cuts off Dr. Romano's arm during a hectic evacuation procedure. We are confronted with blood, vomit, and depictions of unbearable pain leading to his unconsciousness. When he regains consciousness in an emergency room he notices familiar faces: "Aaaghh, I'm at County…" he moans with dismay. The chief of staff is terrified of being treated in his own hospital. So, in addition, this scene offers also an excellent example of the *ER*'s (entertainingly) critical view on America health care system. *ER* is speaking to a particular cultural and political moment when the publicly funded health system is threatened by the neo-liberal politics not only in United States but also in Nordic welfare countries.

For many viewers, emotional influences and impacts, such as humour, are important attractions when they select a programme to watch. The use of storylines that produce a variety of emotional extremes as a guideline for constructing fiction is a 'pragmatic' decision. Torben Grodal writes: "The practical reason for making emotion-evocation a principle of generic construction is probably that, to produce fiction for a global market, the producers very often need to create clear-cut and relatively universal narrative motivation" (2000:161-162). Surely it is easier to communicate expectations of good laughs or blood-chilling thrill to a mass audience than it is to communicate an 'interesting narrative'. The main genre-formulas are often constructed to produce certain emotions, by allowing the viewer to simulate one from a set of fundamental emotions. Hybridisation, of course, enables a wider range of emotions. This feature, coupled with fast-paced editing, snappy, fast spoken dialogue and multiple story lines each having its own emotional tone, creates the emotional roller coaster called *ER*. Only in special episodes, like the eight-season episode "On the Beach" as Dr. Greene lives his final days and dies does the emotional tone remain unchanged.

Until the early eighties, dramatic shows tended to have one basic story line per episode. In a medical series this meant meeting a patient, portraying the disease and finishing with a satisfactory life affirming solution. That style changed in 1981 with the Steven Bochco's *Hill Street Blues,* which introduced the strategy of multiple story lines. This new storytelling style typically told three or four different interwoven stories in the course of an episode. The innovative aspects of a programme are important in attracting viewers and in accounting for their success; this is clearly seen as new series are marketed through their 'groundbreaking' innovativeness, whether it is a setting unlike others (a funeral home in *Six Feet Under*), never-seen-before characters (*Queer as Folk*) or a new style of storytelling. With *ER*, as producer John Wells has said, dramatic television was reinvented once again: "[W]e usually have anywhere from nine to eighteen stories running in any episode. We wanted the pace to move in a way that would hold the audience's interest. The joke around here was that *ER* is the show for the era of remote controls because there is no need to channel surf: All you have to do is hang around for a minute or two and you're going to see another story" (Pourroy 1995:19-20). Probably *ER* can be best explained as 'flexi narrative' (Nelson 1997:32), meaning that variable number of stories is being told at the same time and in order to keep the tension and to create a sense of action they are cut into fast changing segments: If one storyline is not pleasing, the viewer does not have to wait long until another is taken up again. The new aesthetics of short segments, fast-pace editing and more fluid camera movements also work to arrest 'distracted' viewers moving through the channels.

The short, distinct segments also allow viewers to enter the programmes and make sense of them at various points.

Robin Nelson claims that the format of a television programme is closely connected with the distribution of power and ideological content: "Flexi-narratives do not seek to channel a singular ideology but are plural in their very structures in recognition that audiences comprise a range of people with differing perspectives. ... Whilst, then TV drama texts are by no means in-nocent in their discursive positions, flexi-narratives particularly evidence a model of negotiation of a range of meanings rather than an inoculation theory of ideology" (Nelson 1997:41-42). The multilayered characters of *ER*, as I see it, are in themselves illustrations of the not fixed set of values regard to gender roles.

Angels with Dirty Faces

"It is a soap displaying a very exceptional set of super doctors," says Sabine Krajewski (Krajewski 2002:71) about *ER*. The current staff of ER is multi-gendered and multiracial: in the primary roles are four Caucasian females (Kerry Weaver, chief of emergency medicine; Elizabeth Corday, associate chief of surgery; Susan Lewis, attending ER physician; Abby Lockhart, intensive care unit nurse and former medical student), one Asian female (Jing-Mei Chen, Attending ER Physician), three Caucasian males (Robert Romano, chief of staff; Luka Kovac, attending ER physician; John Carter, chief resident), and two African-American males (Gregory Pratt, medical intern; Michael Gallant, medical student). From a brutal 'counting heads' approach to diversity – which is one of the Mepham's (1990:51) three rules of quality – *ER* passes the test for one criterion. All primary cast members usually have their own storyline in every episode. In this 'democratic' sharing of stage and point of views, *ER* sets itself apart from ensemble dramas in which a large cast functions mainly as a 'chorus' for a main character (e.g. *Ally McBeal*). However, the abstract idea of diversity, as Geoff Mulgan has pointed out, leaves unanswered questions about how good or bad such diverse programmes are (Mulgan 1990:27).

A hero needs trouble, and in medical drama there is plenty of it. Trouble comes running with EMTs pushing gurneys and shouting "BP one-forty over ninety, tachy at one-sixty, gave him three hundred cc's of saline!" However, unlike Krajewski's claims, *ER* does not display "a very exceptional set of super doctors" but a set of exceptionally ordinary doctors. *ER* doctors raise questions regarding the traditional heroism of TV doctors, substituting in its place a vision where the identity of the doctor characters (both male and female) is complex, flawed, and ambivalent. As doctors whose everyday world of *ER* is one of cracking chests, intubating and giving internal heart massage they are also heroes. And the fact that they are underpaid and overworked public hospital doctors only adds to their heroism. Most importantly, how-ever, they are fallible humans like us. The notion of identification is crucial here. Grief, conflict and crisis, the stuff that melodrama is made of, is also an essential part of our identity and our experience. It is the mistakes the hero makes, which makes the doctor human and thus more easily identifiable. A hero must be morally good, but not too good and not by any means perfect. Here one can detect an interesting difference between *ER* and the medical dramas targeted specifically to women, as the latter tend to glorify their main characters. This is particularly evident in *Dr. Quinn* where the heroine's moral excellence is emphasised by contrast with overly stereotypical, chauvinistic male characters. A similar set-up can be found in the 'black medical show' *City of Angels,* in which African-American and Hispanic doctors are portrayed as morally superior in contrast to the conniving and incompetent minority of white doctors.

It can be argued along the lines of Dyer that without an understanding of the way images function in terms of genre or narrative, there cannot be an understanding of why these images are realised in a certain way (Dyer 1993). This just might be at stake when Deborah Philips claims "there is currently no woman doctor in a British or American medical television drama who is not somehow represented as handicapped" (Philips 2000). Philips refers to the physical damage of Dr. Weaver's leg and to the 'otherness' (Britishness) of Dr. Corday. These arguments do not hold when inspected in terms of genre or narrative. All the doctors regardless of their sex are somehow handicapped. For example Dr. Corday had to retrain because she was foreign, but Croatian physician Dr. Luka Kovac had to begin his career at Country General by moonlighting, and is also haunted by the deaths of his wife and young child in war. Whilst Dr. Weaver walks with a crutch, Dr. Greene had a fatal brain cancer, which before his death meant he had to attend competency hearings. Nurse Lockhart was assaulted by her neighbour and redeveloped a drinking problem and correspondingly Dr. Carter developed an addiction to drugs after being assaulted and stabbed.

Both female and male characters can be understood as located across several positions within the show. They can be portrayed, for instance, as the healer hero (sometimes tragic), as the family member (both of ER and of a family of their own), and as the victim. They frequently move between these textual positions both inside one episode and along the longer arch of the narrative. In "Chaos Theory", for instance, Romano plays the role of the victim, Corday the role of the family member (missing home, namely her work community, across the Atlantic), and Lewis is given the prestigious role of the tragic action hero. Lewis fights alone on the roof of the quarantined and deserted hospital to save her dying patient. She leaves the patient to run downstairs to find supplies. She yells for help, but gets no reply. Back on the roof she returns to find that the patient needs defibrillation. When the jammed elevator finally works Lewis pushes him inside, all the while trying to do CPR. She yells again for help, and still none comes. Finally an edit shows Gallant entering the scene. Lewis is sitting on the floor, exhausted and we see the desperate, lonely battle she fought on her face. She does not say a word. The patient is dead. In film and TV the idea of masculine and feminine genres is a problematic one, but different 'analytical gazes' frequently produce them. Mixing genres in *ER* means transposing 'masculine' and 'feminine' roles across gender borderlines. In the example above Lewis' heroic failure is worthy of being compared to doomed soldiers in an action sequence.

In addition, not only are all the characters in *ER* 'handicapped', but also their misfortunes and sufferings are the central component of the drama. The importance of being unhappy is well exemplified in the confession of John Masius, the creator of the *Providence*. The series' main plot line seems to be Dr Hansen's innumerable troubles in finding a suitable partner. "The day Syd gets married is the day the show is over," Masius said (Garfinkel 2002), and that is exactly what happened: after its fifth season *Providence* ended with special two-hour wedding finale. Finding peace with oneself (which usually means finding a perfect spouse) may create a 'positive character' but it does not create exciting drama.

ER is a character driven rather than a plot driven text. The development of character is critical to audience interest in serialised fiction, as most people remember characters long after plot details have escaped their memory. According to the director Holcomb, much of *ER*'s appeal was derived from the way its characters were revealed: "In years past … the storytelling tended to be very pedantic. The story needed to have such exacting explanations made in order to make it credible that oftentimes the audience lost the ability to see the main characters. With *ER* it was apparent that the characters were revealed through the fragmented narrative" (Pourroy 1995:8). Accordingly, in *ER* characters are revealed in glimpses. Part of the pleasure of our consumption of *ER* is concerned with how the characters develop and also the way individuals change in response to events and personal relationships.

Having set up certain roles, and having allowed the audience to settle into the prejudices and presuppositions generated by them, the series then systematically forces the audience towards reassessing them. All of the regular doctor characters are taken upon a journey of personality development and revelation, and with each twist and turn the audience must constantly re-evaluate those prejudices and presuppositions. There are fleeting moments when we are able to see new sides of the character. In "Chaos Theory" uncompromising, authoritative, harsh and no-nonsense Dr. Weaver is in several scenes portrayed against her 'type'. First, as evacuation is taking place Dr. Lewis tells Dr. Weaver that everyone did the best that they could do under the circumstances and waits for the usual verbal lashings waiting. Instead, Dr. Weaver lets her know that she is happy about the way they handled everything. Secondly, after two weeks of being quarantined in the hospital are up, Dr. Pratt makes his way to the door while bragging that he coped with no problems. Dr. Weaver tells him that Dr. Gallant has just called in sick and that Dr. Pratt can cover Dr. Gallant's shift. Dr. Pratt looks shocked and then Dr. Weaver tells him that she is just kidding. On her way out, Nurse Lockheart asks Dr. Weaver to approve her timecard, which shows two weeks of overtime. Dr. Weaver does not look happy but neither does she protest sharply, as was expected by Lockheart's character.

Dr. Weaver's complex character development is seen even more clearly if we trace her story line over a longer period of time. She came out for the viewers, and for herself, in seventh season through her relationship with the hospital psychiatrist Kim Legaspi. In the eight season, she developed a relationship with fire fighter Sandy Lopez. After a few false starts, the women go out on a date that results in a break-up when Lopez discovers Weaver is not out at work. Weaver asks Lopez for a second chance, Lopez drops by to visit her in the *ER*, and then, in a pivotal episode titled "A River in Egypt", she outs Dr. Weaver at work by kissing her in the *ER* lobby. When Dr. Weaver later protests angrily, she claims that she "did a favour." A few weeks later, Dr. Weaver goes to find Lopez and admits, "You're right – you *did* do me a favour." Passionate kissing follows. The physical attraction displayed between Dr. Weaver and Lopez equals a standard heterosexual relationship on *ER* and on television in general, and is not downplayed as it is in many other ensemble shows with lesbian characters. Since at work Dr. Weaver is primarily dominant, authoritative, and confidant, this relationship has the effect of letting the viewers see another side to her, namely her fears, her doubts, and her struggles.

Richard Zoglin has described the differences that create *ER*'s success and set the series apart from other medical shows: "The doctors don't look very glamorous, wear frazzled expressions and five-o'clock shadows. Doctors have little time to make speeches about the wonderful work they do" (Zoglin 1994). Zoglin is referring to the male characters but the same thing can be said about the current five female characters. Sexualization has been a central element of western culture's definition of womanhood, and it is still an important component of female heroic representation. Female action-adventure heroes (for example in *Dark Angel* and *Alias*) may kick male butt, but they are also model-beautiful and sexily clad. This post-feminist emphasis on upfront feminine beauty and sexuality is missing from the relatively unglamorous and down-to-earth female doctors in *ER*.

A character component that is also absent in *ER*, as opposed to much of current prime time fiction, is the emphasis on 'woman's difference'. That is, the idea of the inherent qualities of womanhood such as 'maternal thinking'. There is no equation between woman and mother, or the glorifying of motherhood. Of course, the series does not dismiss the discussion of combining work and family – an issue that has been essential to 'post-feminist television' (e.g. Walters 1995:122). There is notorious 'juggling' of work and family, but the work/family dilemma is presented as a problem for men too. In "I'll Be Home For Christmas" single parent Dr. Benton hands in his resignation because Dr. Romano refuses to change his work schedule so that Benton does not need to work nights and weekends. "Newsflash!" Romano exclaims. "This is an urban trauma centre. Until people start planning their MVAs and GSWs better, you are not going to be punching a time clock. That's not me being a hard-ass. That's the job." Consequently, Hallam argues that "currently in *ER*, there is no separate sphere of domesticity that offers relief from the constant [masculine] pressure of professional demands, no 'feminine' vision that offers an alternative mode of thinking or being to the imperative of career success" (Hallam 1998:43). The gender neutrality of *ER* can be seen as women are placed on the other side of a binary divide, which leaves categories intact. Alternatively, this gender blindness may be seen as a process of producing new representations of what it is to be 'female' and 'male' by blurring their boundaries (Nelson 2000:66).

Interestingly, the female-targeted medical series seem to prefer more distinguishable gender 'norms'. Not only are the women doctors more attractive in the traditional sense in for example *Providence* and *Strong Medicine*, but they are also 'softer'. Doctors Stowe and Delgado in *Strong Medicine* are often governed by emotion. In the season finale, Dr. Stowe weeps after she loses a newborn during childbirth and seriously contemplates leaving medicine. Dr. Delgado inserts a feeding tube in a woman who has started a hunger strike in protest at the death sentence hanging over her. The conflict between force-feeding her patient and watching her wither away becomes very stressful for Dr. Delgado and she breaks down in tears. This is something you do not see Drs. Weaver, Corday and Chen doing in *ER*. Writer John Wells explains this in 'realistic' terms: "Generally speaking, doctors in medical shows have been nice, earnest people who are very talented…and they stay with the patient throughout the course of an hour-long episode. But in reality, doctors' lives are not much like that. I've had a lot doctors tell me, 'I can stand here a hold patient's hand, or I can go help two or three other people'" (Wells cit. Pourroy 1995:19).

Mixing Genres, Blurring Genders, Pleasing Audiences?

As problematic as the idea of masculine and feminine genres is, genres are frequently produced by different 'analytical gazes', even if with the hybridisation between programming that was traditionally considered gender-bound have become more fluid. In *ER* the concentration on characters, which is typical for 'feminine' melodramatic narratives, has not been at the expense of action, as Nelson states in discussing the flexi-narrative format for drama (Nelson 1997:23). *ER* mixes genres traditionally seen as feminine and masculine, the personal and emotional with action-oriented storylines. More importantly, it circulates 'masculine' and 'feminine' positions both in the long-term development of the narrative as well as during one episode to the point that these roles lose their gender specific significance: the roles of the healing hero, nurturing parent or weeping victim are no longer gender bound.

John Mepham sees television as "the most influential locus of social self-reflection" (Mepham1990:62). He links the concept of quality to usable stories and to the ethic of truth-telling, which does not privilege as such any particular genre or claim that there is one Truth. According to him low quality stories would simply recirculate received definitions of what is possible and impossible, of what is 'normal' and 'abnormal'. I see the female doctors of *ER* as truly strong women because their representations do not rely on stereotypical 'female' behaviour – or good looks. I want to claim that the 'counter patriarchal' pleasures provided by the *ER* arise from offering a broad range of answers to the question 'What is possible for me?' that viewers face all the time in their increasingly complex and open-scripted everyday lives. In *ER* everyone makes incorrect decisions, gets caught in conflict and achieves occasional fulfilment. These rare moments are perfectly described by the voice-over of the woman doctor in another medical series, *Providence*: "Every once in a while you participate in a miracle. Deliver a baby. Start someone's heart. And in those moments you know exactly who you are and why you do what you do." Furthermore, in *ER* every one moves from being central protagonist to being quite marginal, and even, if we wait long enough, to disappear altogether. This constant rotation of roles is something other than 'the role reversal strategy' seen in action/adventure series, which places women on the other side of a binary divide. The latter ultimately, as Nelson has pointed out (Nelson 2000:73) leaves categories of 'maleness' and 'femaleness' unbroken. On the contrary, *ER* intentionally or not shifts, overturns changes and rewrites the previously normal gendered practices of medical drama. It can be said that it invites viewers to question the validity of some gendered practises as 'normal', which is not to deny that some viewers may read *ER* stories in a way that affirms established gender norms.

Contemporary American commercial television has been increasingly aimed at women. One of the main reasons lies in assumptions about who spends the money in the household and whom advertisers wish to address. Seeing women as preferred spectators parallels with Lynn Joyrich's argument that melodrama is the preferred genre for the television (Joyrich 1992:229-233). The melodramatisation of the medium means that social dilemmas are represented as private, usually in terms of the family (or of the surrogate family). According to Joyrich this strengthening of the melodramatic form of television is not without some positive benefits: the tendency of melodrama to reflect on values, morals and the meaning of life touches audiences at uncertain times (Joyrich 1992:335-336). On the other hand, it is exactly the emphasis on emotions that Gitlin sees as cushioning social problems and paralysing people from dealing with them (Gitlin 2000). The prime-time principle of least objectionable programming can be viewed as weakening once the hybrid, multiple-protagonist drama series such as *ER* began to triumph over the prime time in the 1980s. 'Quality dramas' like *ER* constantly tackle complex social issues and try to present at least two sides to an issue. Still, it has to be remembered that when it comes to exceedingly controversial topics, mainstream values generally prevail in the end.[3]

Prime time images of gender are constructed according to genres and programming types, and are affected by the whole production culture; from the values of the programme-makers, to their conceptions of audience and, of course, the resources at hand. Thus, these diverse images amount to the polysemic potential of television as emphasised by Newcomb and Hirch (2000). This means a wider scope for interpretation and therefore larger demographics. The problem with writing for television is that ideas go out of date very quickly. Market forces change with social attitudes, and on the cutting edge of these changes are television executives hoping to catch the next social tide. The increasing visibility of competent women within the television has begun to correspond with real changes in women's lives. *ER* embodies the increasing hybridisation of television, happening both in cheap factual entertainment (see e.g. Brunsdon et al. 2001) and in prime-time drama with gigantic costs and production values. This process of mixing genres and rotating roles can be seen as due to the programme-makers' conception of audience as internally fragmented into diverse, demographic groups according to gender, age, sexuality, ethnic or national/regional identity. Hence, competition over viewers does not necessarily mean offering least objectionable programming, which more likely than not would leave the representations of gender unbroken. Even if the primary cause for the placing of women in roles traditionally reserved for men in genres such as medical drama may be commercial, the frequent appearance of representations of strong women on television may play a crucial role in changing minds, and ultimately politics, too.

Through television, contemporary feminine and masculine ideologies and female and male identities are being 'imagined'. The benefit of *ER* is that it provides a site through which a variety of groups can negotiate a whole series of social changes. Not only are the women doctors redefining female identities, but the show also creates space for the reinterpretation of men's roles as well as alternative sexual identities. *ER* opens a terrain within the polysemy of television texts, one that enables both women and men to embrace alternative subjectivities. By imagining and showing a world where gender positions are anything but inert, it questions the stability of the boundary between the masculine and the feminine.

Notes

1. The first show with a female doctor's name in the title was ABC's *Julie Farr, M.D.* (1978-1979) starring Susan Sullivan as obstetrician. The show was cancelled after four episodes (three more ran the next year). CBS was next in line trying a medical drama with a female lead: *Kay O'Brien*, a story about a young surgical resident (Patricia Kalember) balancing her professional and personal lives, was born in 1986 only to pass away eight weeks later.

2. Other medical series currently running in Finland are American shows Scrubs and City of Angels , Australian show *The Flying Doctors*, British shows *Casualty*, *Holby City* and *Peak Practice*, and German show *Fieber: Heisse Zeit für junge Ärzte.*

3. For instance, abortion is frequently treated in American prime-time television in such a way that the "winning side" is anti-abortion. A case of *ER*: Dr. Chen finds adoption, instead of abortion, to be the best solution — which at least from a secular Northern European point of view seems as an act of masochism.

References

Altman, R. (1999). *Film/Genre*. London: British Film Institute.

Booth, B. (2001). The softer side: Women doctors on TV. *American Medical News,* April 16, 2001. Retrieved 2003 from http://www.ama-assn.org/sci-pubs/amnews/pick_01/prca0416.htm.

Brunsdon, C. (1997). *Screen Tastes: Soap Opera to Satellite Dishes*. London: Routledge.

Brunsdon, C. & J. D'Acci, L. Spiegel (Eds.) (1997). *Feminist Television Criticism. A Reader*. Oxford: Clarendon Press.

Brunsdon, C. et al. (2001). Factual Entertainment on British Television: The Midlands TV Research Group's '8-9' Project'. *European Journal of Cultural Studies,* Vol. 4, 1.

Caldwell, J. (2000). Prime-Time Fiction Theorizes the Docu-Real. In James Friedman (Ed.), *Reality Squared: Televisual Discourse on the Real*. New Brunswick, New Jersey, and London: Rutgers University Press.

Dow, B. J. (1996). *Prime-Time Feminism: Television, Media Culture, and the Women's Movement since 1970*. Philadelphia: University of Pennsylvania Press.

Dyer, R. (1993). *The Matter of Images: Essays on Representations*. London and New York: Routledge.

Fiske, J. (1987). *Television Culture*. London: Methuen.

Garfinkel, P. (2002). As Doctors on TV, Women Still Battle the Old Clichés. *New York Times*. Retrieved February 24, 2002, from http://www.earth-netone.com/asdoctorsontvwomen stilbattletheoldclichspageone.htm.

Gitlin, T. (2000). Prime Time Ideology: The Hegemonic Process in Television Entertainment. In H. Newcomb (Ed.), *Television: The Critical View*. Oxford: Oxford University Press.

Grodal, T. (2000). *Moving Pictures: A New Theory of Film Genres, Feelings, and Cognition*. Oxford: Clarendon Press.

Hallam, J. (1998). Gender and Professionalism in TV's Medical Melodramas. In N. Moody and J. Hallam (Eds.), *Medical Fictions*. Liverpool: John Moores University.

Jacobs, J. (2001). Hospital Drama. In G. Creeber (Ed.), *The Television Genre Book*. London: BFI.

Joyrich, L. (1992). All that Television Allows: TV Melodrama, Postmodernism, and Consumer Culture. In L. Spiegel & D. Mann (Eds.), *Private Screenings: television and Female Consumer*. Minneapolis: University of Minnesota.

Krajewski, S. (2002). *Life Goes On. And Sometimes It Doesn't*. Frankfurt am Main: Peter Lang.

Lauteris, T. De (1987). *Technologies of Gender: Essays on Theory, Film and Fiction*. Bloomington: Indiana University Press.

Marchessault, J. (2000). Doctors & Diseases: Why Do We Watch? Focus on Research. York University. Retrieved winter, 2000, from http://www.yorku.ca/ycom/focus/past/winter-fa-00/story4.html.

Mepham, J. (1990). The Ethics of Quality in Television. In G. Mulgan (Ed.), *The Question of Quality*. London: British Film Institute.

Moody, N. Introduction. In N. Moody & J. Hallam (Eds.), *Medical Fictions*. Liverpool: John Moores University.

Mulgan, G. (1990). Television's Holy Grail: Seven Types of Quality. In Geoff Mulgan (Ed.), *The Question of Quality*. London: British Film Institute.

Nelson, R. (1997). *TV Drama In Transition: Forms, Values and Cultural Change*. London: Macmillan.

Nelson, R. (2000). Performing (Wo)manoeuvres: The Progress of Gendering in TV Drama. In B. Carson & M. Llewellyn-Jones (Eds.), *Frames and Fictions on Television: The Politics of Identity within Drama*. Exeter & Portland: Intellect Books.

Newcomb, H. & Hirsch (2000). Television as Cultural Forum. In H. Newcomb (Ed.), *Television: The Critical View*. New York: Oxford University Press.

Philips, D. (2000). Medicated Soap: The Woman Doctor in Television Medical Drama. In B. Carson & M. Llewellyn-Jones (Eds.), *Frames and Fictions on Television: The Politics of Identity Within Drama*. Exeter & Portland: Intellect Books.

Pourroy, J. (1995). *Behind the scenes at ER*. London: Ebury Press.

Tasker, Y. (1998). *Working Girls: Gender and Sexuality in Popular Cinema*. London and New York: Routledge.

Turow, J. (1997). James Dean in a Surgical Gown. In L. Spiegel & M. Curtin (Eds.), *The Revolution Wasn't Televised: Sixties Television and Social Conflict*. London & New York: Routledge.

Walters, S. (1995). *Material Girls: Making Sense of Feminist Cultural Theory*. Berkeley: University of California Press.

Zoglin, R. (1994). Angels With Dirty Faces. *Time* magazine, October 31, 1994.

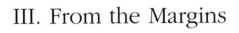

III. From the Margins

Hold It! Use It! Abuse It!
Ilsa, She-Wolf of the SS and Male Castration

Rikke Schubart

Most infamous of all female villains is Ilsa from the notorious *Ilsa, She-Wolf of the SS*. Blond, beautiful, bosomy and fully dedicated to pain and perverse pleasure, Ilsa has made it into film history as a pure example of *the evil dominatrix*. A woman whose mission in life is to please the male masochist by acting out his most taboo fantasies. Not a heroine in the traditional sense, yet a strong, active and aggressive female protagonist who has become mythical within western culture.[1]

Her cruel acts left little to the imagination (one of the first scenes in the film is the castration of a screaming male prisoner!) and the film provoked three reactions: First, audiences for exploitation movies embraced Ilsa with such an enthusiasm that a movie filmed in nine days with a budget of 150.000 $ became a cult phenomenon worldwide. Actress Dyanne Thorne was buried in fan mail and today still receives hundreds of monthly fan letters.[2] The economic success of *Ilsa, She-Wolf of the SS* (Don Edmonds, 1974) spawned three sequels: *Ilsa, Harem-Keeper of the Oil Sheiks* (Don Edmonds, 1976), *Ilsa, The Tigress of Siberia* (Jean LaFleur, 1977) and *Ilsa, The Wicked Warden* (Jess Franco, 1977). The last is an unofficial Spanish sequel with Dyanne Thorne. Ilsa's popularity is undiminished: Today the four films have been re-issued on DVD, beautifully restored in uncut versions including commentary tracks with Dyanne Thorne, director Don Edmonds and producer David Friedman. In 2000 the fan publication *The Ilsa Chronicles* was published and out of print a year later (Venticinque & Thompson, 2000).

The second reaction was from mainstream audiences and reviewers who absolutely hated and rejected the movie. The ardor of their condemnation equaled the enthusiasm of the former group. "The movie is so nauseating that it is impossible even to hint at it's specific scenes without making my typewriter stink," a Danish reviewer wrote and deemed the film "perverse, sadistic pornography of the most sickening and exploitative kind" ("Stinkende premiere," 1976). In an interview a cinema owner described how he had to operate the movie projector himself, because his film operator refused to watch the film (it is necessary to look at the projected film with short intervals to ensure that it is in focus). The director eventually removed the movie from the program, commenting: "Ilsa was so disgusting and her methods of torture so repulsive that the audience was sick" ("Nazifilm om SS-tortur tages af plakaten fordi publikum bliver dårlige" ["Nazi movie about SS torture is pulled because the audience gets sick"], 1976).[3] Dyanne Thorne lost personal friends and though her husband was co-producer, her mother-in-law left the pre-screening in disgust. Even today, reviews of the DVD's mix cult praise with uneasiness: "To have never seen an *Ilsa*-film is to have truly been deprived the joys of one of the last great exploitation film sagas," one review opens while another begins with the confession: "I actually watched this one a couple of months ago and have been wrestling with how to write a review about it ever since" (Major, 2002; "Ilsa, She-Wolf of the SS," 2002). (Incidentally, all comments are made by men; I have not come across a review, commentary or article on the *Ilsa*-films written by a woman).

The third reaction provoked by the *Ilsa*-movies was from film research. It was – silence. An utter silence, that to my knowledge is only broken now. The *Ilsa*-films do not figure in mainstream movie guides such as Leonard Maltin's *Movie & Video Guide*. They are not listed in a prison movie companion such as James Robert Parish's *Prison Pictures From Hollywood: Plots, Critiques, Casts and Credits for 293 Theatrical and Made-for-Television Releases* (1991). They aren't even included in the chapter on wip-movies in Bev Zalcock's *Renegade Sisters: Girl Gangs on Film* (1998). And the few academic articles on wip-pictures – incidentally all written by women – do not mention the *Ilsa*-movies at all.[4]

This third reaction – silence – is significant because it tells us that something is 'wrong', even by the standards of exploitation movies.[5] Of what nature, then, are the 'sickening', 'perverse', 'nauseating', 'disgusting' and 'repulsive' pleasures that have turned *Ilsa, She-Wolf of the SS* into the ultimate see-if-you-dare movie? What are the pleasures celebrated by fans, condemned by critics and muted by researchers? A word running through reviews, comments and articles is 'sadistic'.[6] A word I have *not* found is 'masochistic.' And yet this is where I want to locate the taboo fantasies and pleasures of the *Ilsa*-chronicles.

A Parade of Atrocities

First a summary: *Ilsa, She-Wolf of the SS* laid down the archetypical structure of the series, and I shall use this film as my main point of departure making references to the other three in the series (hereafter called *She-Wolf, Harem-Keeper, Tigress* and *Wicked Warden*).[7] The film opens with a written warning:

The film you are about to see is based upon documented fact. The atrocities shown were conducted as "medical experiments" in special concentration camps throughout Hitler's Third Reich. Although these crimes against humanity are historically accurate, the characters depicted are composites of notorious Nazi personalities; and the events portrayed, have been condensed into one locality for dramatic purposes. Because of it's shocking subject matter, this film is restricted to adult audiences only. We dedicate this film with the hope that these heinous crimes will never occur again.

Presented as a legitimization of the story that will unfold, the text is accompanied by a speech by Hitler ending with repeated Sieg Heil's. The camera then cuts to a bedroom and pans slowly across the bourgeois interiors: white silk ballet shoes hanging on a hat stand, flowers, rococo bed table, two mirrors wherein we see a couple making love intimately, a radio playing classical music, and finally a close-up of the woman saying: "Not yet, no, please." The man, we understand, ejaculates. "You should have waited," she mumbles. The woman has her orgasm in the shower and then awakens her lover: "Time to go." The camera zooms back from a hand with dark-red nail polish to Ilsa in her black SS-uniform. "But you promised I didn't have to go back to camp!" Two female officers take the man away. Strapped to an operating table he is castrated by the three women, the final cut made by a smiling Ilsa: "My little man, I kept my promise – you will never leave the camp again!"

After these introductory eight minutes titles roll across the screen as new female prisoners arrive to Medical Camp 9, where Ilsa, an SS-officer and a doctor, is in charge. Prisoners are presented naked to Ilsa who divides them into two groups: One to be sent to German camps as prostitutes, the other "to serve the Third Reich." During the inspection one woman, Anna (Maria Marx), stands out as proud and defiant. She will become Ilsa's favorite torture victim. Afterwards the women have their genitals shaven by a female nurse.

Next new male prisoners arrive at the camp. They too are inspected by Ilsa, first in the court, then naked in the men's barracks. "You call yourselves men? I see no manhood between your legs!" Again, one prisoner stands out from the rest. "Size is not everything," the blond Wolfe (Gregory Knoph) replies. He is an American and will become Ilsa's lover.

Life in camp is short and unpleasant, consisting of sex, torture and death. In the women's barrack the prisoners are in various stages of terminal illness, infected with diseases by Ilsa. Their leader, Kala (Nicolle Riddell[8]), is horribly disfigured by syphilis, and Anna immediately talks about escape. During Ilsa's daily inspection of her experiments we see a woman killed in a decompression chamber, another woman has an open wound in her thigh alive with maggots infected with typhus, a third woman is boiled alive in a bathtub. Equally worse off are the selected few who are used in Ilsa's private experiment to prove that women can withstand more pain than men. In Ilsa's torture chamber a woman has her toenails plucked with pliers. When Ilsa discovers Anna's plan to escape, Anne is subjected to several days of torture in Ilsa's special room. The women not used for experiments are punished for minor sins by being gang-raped by male guards or flogged to death by Ilsa's female duo, two female soldiers who serve only Ilsa.

Although the men are not used as objects of medical experiments, their fate is no less enviable. While digging a grave Wolfe and Mario (Tony Mumolo) discuss the strange nature of Ilsa, who castrates her lovers. "Castrate? Why?" Wolfe exclaims. "Perhaps it is her way of punishing a man who makes her feel like a woman yet fails to satisfy her cravings for more. Who knows? Only one thing is certain: Once they have served her, it's the end of him as a man," says Mario, himself a victim of Ilsa. "My God, did you kill her?" Mario later exclaims, when Wolfe has survived a night with Ilsa. Wolfe explains his secret: he can hold back ejaculation for as long as he wants, thus satisfying a woman again and again. "You wanna know something: That never-control just about drove her up the wall," Wolfe boasts.

Breaking the routine is the visit of a general coming to inspect Ilsa's results. She throws a lavish dinner party in his honor with a table laid with food and a naked female prisoner, who balances on a block of ice with a noose around her neck. During dinner Ilsa is awarded the Heinrich Himmler Cross and while they toast and laugh the block of ice slowly melts and the woman is strangled. Later Ilsa offers herself to the general, who begs her to urinate on him. She does so, clearly disgusted, and next morning immediately sends for Wolfe. "I need a real man!" As part of their sex games he ties her to the bed, steals her gun and starts the planned revolt. In what is the film's only action sequence – involving the use of fired guns, explosions and slow-motion (in a film aesthetic which is otherwise transparent and primitive) – the prisoners take over the camp and execute their guards. Wolfe and Rosetta escape, while the rest stay and have their revenge. Amidst the uprising German tanks arrive and destroy the camp. A blond officer, who had attended the dinner party, executes Ilsa in her bed and calls head quarters: "General, your orders have been carried out. Camp 9 has ceased to exist. You may tell the Reichführer that the allies will find ... nothing. They will never know." Last picture freezes Wolfe and Rosetta outside the wire looking at the burning camp. On the soundtrack a boy's choir sings a happy song in German.

Setting and period change in the sequels; in *Harem-Keeper* we are in the Arabian desert in the seventies; *Tigress* places Ilsa in Stalin's Gulag during the fifties and in Canada in the seventies; and *Wicked Warden* has her in the seventies but now in South America. Recurring traits are: Her role as dominatrix, torturess and leader of an 'institution'; her two female servants; and her destruction at the end of each film.

Perversion: A Revolt Against the Order of Things

Wip-movies usually tell two stories: The first is a plot of suppression, rebellion and liberation where female prisoners rise against their oppressors to win freedom and self-respect. The second story is a string of perverse situations such as lesbian sex, shower-scenes, torture-scenes and rape-scenes.

The two stories – the dramatic plot and the erotic fantasies – are intertwined, the one justifying and motivating the other.

In *She-Wolf* the first story almost disappears, leaving the second story – the string of perverse situations – to dominate the narrative. More than a drama, the film reads as an inventory of taboo fantasies and this explains the frequently reported unease from watching the film. We find the stereotypical wip-narrative in the arrival of new female and male prisoners to the camp, their maltreatment and their final uprising. However, the plot is so thin and the 'heroic' characters of Wolfe and Anna so poorly developed, that they fail to engage us emotionally or cognitively. Instead we are left with the perverse fantasies.

According to Freud all sexual activities that do not lead directly to heterosexual genital intercourse are 'perverse' in their diversion of sexuality from its primary aim: procreation. In her book *Male Subjectivity at the Margins* (1992) American film scholar Kaja Silverman discusses perversion as not only a diversion from genital intercourse, but furthermore as a subversion of the hierarchical structure on which social order is built. "Perversion (..) subverts many of the binary oppositions upon which the social order rests: it crosses the boundary separating food from excrement (coprophilia); human from animal (bestiality); life from death (necrophilia); adult from child (pederasty); and pleasure from pain (masochism)." Perversion is a revolt against the order of things – but paradoxically simultaneously a confirmation of this very order. In the denial of order is confirmed it's existence: "It is crucial, then, that we grasp the double nature of perversion, that we understand it as simultaneously a capitulation and a revolt" (Silverman, 1992, p. 33, 32). Even though perversions appear radical, they are not sites of political subversion.

She-Wolf may be interpreted as one long fantasy enjoyed by the man, who in the opening scene falls asleep and wakes up to his lover dressed as an SS-officer. This ties in with the ending where every trace of the camp – and thus of the fantasy itself – is erased. Burning down the camp and killing guards as well as prisoners removes all evidence of the atrocious acts and serves as a repression of the historical or 'collective' memory. "They will find... nothing." It also conveniently serves as the audience's repression of its perverse pleasures, thus relieving them from feelings of guilt. This explains why prisoners must die with the guards; in the world of perversion, everyone is equally guilty. No matter their role or function, they are all part of the perverse structure.

In *She-Wolf* the subversion of binary oppositions is everywhere. The opening scene establishes the radical nature of the subversion where every element is turned into it's diametrical opposite: First in the filmic *genre*, where a pseudo-documentary opening is subverted into sexploitation. Then in the *iconography*, where the bedroom becomes the torture chamber below Ilsa's private quarters, the soft bed turns into a hard operating table, bourgeois wallpaper becomes bare grey walls. Then with the *characters*, where the formerly willing mistress becomes a harsh tormentor and the lover a male victim. Also the *sexual aim*, phallic victory – ejaculation – ends in phallic defeat – castration – and potency is transformed into impotence. Finally, a *high culture aesthetic*, marked by classical music and the ballet shoes, is transformed into it's extreme opposite: the primitive, un-adorned and pre-cultural world of torture. The confrontation between bourgeois culture and primitive violence is repeated in the dinner banquet-scene, when the camera cross-cuts from the naked woman, silent and immobile on the ice block, to the elegantly dressed dinner guests toasting in their crystal glasses.

The *Ilsa*-series employs this subversion quite consciously. The producer, David Friedman, had his name removed from the film when seeing the final cut, and only admitted to the film twenty years later. Friedman had earlier produced gore films such as Herschell Gordon Lewis' trilogy *Blood Feast* (1963), *2000 Maniacs* (1964) and *Color Me Blood Red* (1965), but "those were made for fun, no one took them seriously," he comments on the audio track of *She-Wolf*. Friedman immediately stresses, however, that the *Ilsa*-films were also intended as not serious, they were "fun" to make and the team had a "great" time during the nine days of filming. He is clearly right: as most exploitation movies *She-Wolf* employs several tongue-in-cheek elements to serve as comic relief amid the tension. Wolfe's remark that "size is not everything," and the cheerful music accompanying him as he self-satisfied struts from Ilsa's bedroom after having survived a night without being castrated, are 'funny' elements within the nightmare world. However, the real world took *Ilsa* seriously when it premiered, and the mixing of the historical Nazi-setting with the perverse fantasies was perceived as an unheard-of provocation. And it was. Earlier movies to link Nazism and perverse eroticism were Lee Frost's much lighter *Love Camp 7* (1967) and Luchino Visconti's serious drama *The Damned* (1969). *Ilsa* pushed wip-prisons from the dark eroticism of Pam Grier's Philippine pictures to a new violent level and inspired the 'Nazi sex & death' sub-genre.[9]

Male Masochism

Some perversions are more subversive than others. Sadism, Freud notes throughout his writings, is a biological part of the libido and therefore poses no threat to the sexual and social order. It serves "the need for overcoming the resistance of the sexual object by means other than the process of woo-ing" (in Silverman, 1992, p. 34). Otherwise with masochism, which Freud describes as "mysterious" and "incomprehensible" in "The Economic Problem of Masochism" and views as the most dangerous perversion because it subverts the pleasure principle itself by having pain as it's primary aim:

> If pain and unpleasure can be not simply warnings but actually aims, the pleasure principle is paralysed – it is as though the watchman over our mental life were put out of action by a drug. Thus masochism appears to us in the

light of a great danger, which is in no way true of its counterpart, sadism (Freud, 1980, p. 159).

Freud describes the *manifest content* of the masochistic fantasies as "being gagged, bound, painfully beaten, whipped, in some way maltreated, forced into unconditional obedience, dirtied and debased" (Freud, 1980, p. 162). He comments that these fantasies leave a less "serious impression" than "the cruelties of sadism." (I wonder: Is this because they are 'softer' than sadistic fantasies or because their pain is aimed at the subject himself and not at an external object?). We might find a motive for this comment in Freud's explanation of the *latent content* of the masochistic fantasies: "[T]hey place the subject in a characteristically female situation; they signify, that is, being castrated, or copulated with, or giving birth to a baby" (Freud, 1980, p. 162). Recurring in Freudian psychoanalysis is a binary opposition between libido/ Death instinct, masculine/ feminine, sadistic/ masochistic, active/ passive, men/ women, strong/ weak. This is the natural order of the two sexes as perceived by Freud – and this is exactly the order that masochism subverts. Thus it is easy to understand why Freud rejects masochism as "mysterious." Mysterious indeed, because it places the male in the role that sadism usually reserves for women: The passive, painful role of the victim.

I shall not deny that sadism is part of the pleasures of the *Ilsa*-movies. But it is not the central pleasure. Instead, the parallel between Freud's description of masochism and the scenarios of *She-Wolf* is striking: A male victim is whipped to death by a topless woman (one of Ilsa's servants) and when dead he is hung in an exhibitionist manner outside Ilsa's quarters; another is urinated on, lying on the floor; a man is castrated by three beautiful, smiling women; the manhood of naked men are inspected by a cold, beautiful woman dressed in uniform. And so forth. These scenes continue in the American sequels; in *Harem-Keeper* a man is beaten publicly by two naked women who, with the approval of Ilsa, tear off his genitals. In *Tigress* a man is eaten alive by a tiger, another has his arm chopped off by a chainsaw, a third is speared through the mouth. All these scenes belong within male masochism.

Here I am not concerned with the psychological reasons why men become masochists – Freud presents this as the boy's repression of a homosexual attitude towards his father, the wish 'to be loved by the father' repressed into the fantasy 'to be beaten by the father', which again is further repressed into the conscious fantasy 'to be beaten by the mother'.[10] It is this last fantasy we see played out in the 'beating scenarios' where a woman equipped with "masculine attributes and characteristics" punishes her male victim. Whether male masochists repress homosexual desires or not, will not be discussed here. Rather, I am interested in the 'silence' with which male masochism is met when it is quite flagrantly portrayed as in *She-Wolf*.

Is Freud correct to assume masochism to be a 'feminine' perversion due to its self-inflicted pain and passivity? I think not. The German psychoanalyst Theodor Reik and the French film theorist and philosopher Gilles Deleuze both disagree in their respective studies of masochism. In *Masochism in Modern Man* (1941) Reik concludes from his patients that men are more masochistic than women, and that male fantasies are more "orgiastic" than the "aenemic" female fantasies. "The woman's masochistic phantasy very seldom reaches the pitch of savage lust, of ecstasy, as does that of the man (..) One does not feel anything of the cyclonelike character that is so often associated with masculine masochism, that blind unrestricted lust of self-destruction" (Reik, 1941, p. 216). In Reik's view the intensity, the lust and the aggressive savagery are 'masculine' traits, turning pain into an active rather than passive component.

Attacking Eyes and Genitals: Images of Castration

Of the "female situations" Freud mentions in masochism – castration, copulation, birth – only the last strikes me as specifically female. The first, castration, is on the contrary a conspicuously *male* situation. About castration Freud writes: "Being castrated – or being blinded, which stands for it – often leaves a negative trace of itself in phantasies, in the condition that no injury is to occur precisely to the genitals or the eyes" (Freud, 1980, p. 162). But Freud is mistaken. The genitals and the eyes are *exactly* the objects being attacked in masochistic fantasy.

To take the eyes first: Throughout the *Ilsa*-series damage is inflicted on eyes. In *She-Wolf* the leader Kala has half of her face disfigured by syphilis, including the eye, and Anna's left eye is mutilated. In *Harem-Keeper* the right eye of a female victim has been pulled from its socket and eaten by a man. And in *Wicked Warden* one girl has the hollow of one eye covered by grey scar tissue. The mutilation itself is not shown, but the resulting wounds and scars are displayed in close-ups and graphic make-up. Eye injuries are only inflicted on women, and they serve as warnings to a male audience, displacing castration anxiety onto a female body.

An act *not* displaced onto female bodies is castration itself. Let us look at one of the masochistic fantasies Reik reports from a male patient:

> To an ancient barbaric idol, somewhat like the Phoenician Moloch, a number of vigorous young men are to be sacrificed at certain not too frequent intervals. They are undressed and laid on the altar one by one. The rumble of drums is joined by the songs of the approaching temple choirs. The high priest followed by his suite approaches the altar and scrutinizes each of the victims with a critical eye. They must satisfy certain requirements as to physical beauty and athletic appearance. The high priest takes the genital of each prospective victim in his hand and carefully tests its weight and form. If he does not approve of the genital, the young man will be rejected as obnoxious to the god and unworthy of being sacrificed. The high priest gives the order for the

Ilsa - She-Wolf of the SS (Don Edmunds, 1974), Aeteas.

execution and the ceremony continues. With a sharp cut the young men's genitals and the surrounding parts are cut away (Reik, 1941, p. 41).

Reik points to a number of characteristic features in masochism: The aggressive *demand* for punishment; the ritualized and theatrical nature of the *elaborate fantasies* where the punishment occurs; the *suspense factor* of delay and anticipation; and the *exhibitionistic* character of the display of suffering.

Let us now return to the castration scene of *She-Wolf*. In the torture chamber the lover awakens and finds himself strapped to an operating table, surrounded by Ilsa and her two female guards. They are wearing white blood-spattered coats; the two guards are naked underneath, thus underlining the erotization of the scene. "When a prisoner has slept with me, he will never sleep with a woman again. If he lives, he remembers only the pain of the night," Ilsa tells the man. She instructs the women to castrate him and then orders them to leave. "I will finish it!" Holding the instrument in full view of the camera, she slowly walks around the victim, the camera tracking her: "There is a doctor Baum in Berlin. He believes that inferior races prove their inferiority through part of their body. And can you guess what part that is? The part that makes man. The doctor has a collection which proves his theory and yours will be sent to him." She then cuts of the penis, shown in a semi-total shot where we see the screaming man from the side, his body shaking violently, and Ilsa with her back to the camera, cutting. She turns around and the camera zooms in on her smile: "My little man, I kept my promise, you will never leave the camp again," she laughs sadistically.

The similarities between the former masochistic fantasy and the castration scene are striking: a) *Inspection and measuring*: Like the young men inspected by the priests in the fantasy, Ilsa also chooses her lovers during her inspections. And just as the genitals of the men are weighted and approved or disapproved, Ilsa measures and judges the genitals of her male victims. (At a point Wolfe asks Mario: "Mario, did she cut off your..." "No! Would have spoiled the doctor Baum's theory"). b) *Delay and anticipation*: In the fantasy the mutilation is delayed by the ceremony, thus raising the anxiety level of the holder of the fantasy. Likewise, the castration is delayed by Ilsa circling her victim and giving her speech, which anticipates the act. c) *Detail and ritualization*: The fantasy is imagined in great detail, adding music, a number of participants, colours, etc. Ilsa's castration is also displayed in great detail – as opposed to the castration scene in *Foxy Brown* – complete with blood on the white coats (where does this blood come from? The castration has not been performed yet), close-up on all participants and music. The camera is here 'neutral' in contrast to a later scene, where German soldiers gang rape a female prisoner, shown in slanting and fragmented takes. All these features serve the exhibitionistic character of the fantasy, the display of shocking mutilation.

'Final Boys' and the Masochistic Gaze

To determine whether such castration scenes are sadistic or masochistic we need to examine the point-of-identification being offered. About the masochistic fantasy Reik notes that "whether the phantasy is primarily masochistic or more sadistic in character must rest on information as to the person with whom the patient identifies." Reik's patient fantasises about being a spectator, identifying "usually not [with] the one who is just being castrated but with the next, who is compelled to look on at the execution of his companion. The patient shares every intensive affect of this victim, feels his terror and anxiety with all the physical sensations since he imagines that he himself will experience the same fate in a few moments" (Reik, 1941, p. 42).

The viewer, likewise, is 'compelled to look on' at the castration, and in *She-Wolf* we expect Wolfe, the male character with whom the male audience identifies, to be 'next'. Reactions to the film indicate a similar identification with the victim position: On the commentary track there is uneasy silence, then humorist Martin Lewis (who is interviewing the director, producer and star) comments: "With this picture you are not laughing, this is a shocker." As Ilsa, however, laughs and holds her instrument high, the interviewer asks star Dyanne Thorne: "Ilsa, why are you laughing here?" The uneasiness is a break in tone from the otherwise humourous conversation that treats the movie as a 'fun' cult phenomenon. The movie itself foregrounds this masochistic point-of-view. In *She-Wolf* with close-ups of the screaming man begging for mercy, in *Harem-Keeper* with a reaction shot where a man next to Ilsa turns away from the castration with nausea.

What, then, is the reaction of the male audience?[11] An anonymous reviewer on the net comments on the difference between torture in 'standard' wip-movies and torture in the *Ilsa*-movies:

> In these settings [a Nazi slave labor camp or Japanese wartime prison] we seem to cross the line from the taboo/power narrative into the arena of full-blown degradation. Is there really a large market for that? Maybe it is just me, but I think there is a qualitative difference between standard women-in-prison movies and movies like *Ilsa*. WiPs usually play on the common male fantasy of having power over a large number of beautiful women in which torture (often whipping with the woman's cries being played at the line between excitement and pain) is part of establishing the D/s relationship. In *Ilsa* torture is lovingly presented in great detail as an end in itself. Although Puritans of both the left and right might not see the difference, it seems pretty clear to me ("Ilsa, She-Wolf of the SS," 2002).

In wip-movies torture has a purpose – to have power over women – whereas in the *Ilsa*-movies it seems purposeless – torture as "an end in itself." This is exactly the difference between the role of pain in sadism and masochism: In masochism the pain is turned against the subject, which in this case is the viewer. He chooses to understand the movie as "a dare, or a challenge, or a gross-out contest." Other reviewers agree, commenting that this is "gory, sleazy wallowing in nauseating excess," that "the basic appeal of *Ilsa* is a parade of tortures" (Scheib, 2002) and that "this one is certainly not to be watched by the weak of stomach" (Steltz, 2002). The 'nauseating' element is perceived as a 'quality' of the movie, and it requires 'guts' to watch it.

Within film theory spectatorship has been perceived as male, sadistic and voyeuristic (in the Mulveyan tradition). Silverman, however, points out that in masochism the viewing position is less sadistic and controlling than it is "a vantage point from which to see and identify with the whipping boys" (Silverman, 1992, p. 50). To be a spectator to pain means to be gripped in the anxious anticipation of being 'next'. "This is a very disturbing movie," is a repeated comment in reviews. Disturbing not only due to its sadism, but also – and especially – due to its masochistic pain and viewer position.

Writing about the horror movie American film theorist Carol Clover introduced the now famous concept of the 'final girl'. The final girl is the victim who survives being stalked during the last half hour in slasher films such as *Halloween* and *Friday the 13th*. It is through this victim's terrified eyes the male audience experiences fear and anxiety, a process that Clover calls "cross-gender identification." Based on the reaction to horror movies – fear – she assumes a male audience's identification to be with the victim, which is usually a female character. Clover argues that "crying, cowering, screaming, fainting, trembling, begging for mercy belong to the female" and are "coded 'feminine'" (quoted in Creed, 1993, p. 125). To keep a traditional masculinity intact, the 'feminine' emotions must be experienced vicariously through a woman, so that it is possible to share her feminine fears, yet distance oneself from her female body: 'I am scared like her, but this happens to her because she is a woman. It will not happen to me.' This final girl is a stand-in for male identification, and the violence of horror is usually understood as symbolic castration. Thus the final girl in the slasher movie is threatened with castration by a knife-wielding psychopath.

The positions of male monster and female victim are reversed in the *Ilsa*-movies: Here a man is placed in the role of 'final girl', and a beautiful woman makes the threat of castration.[12] But – as in the horror movie – the masochistic viewing position is foregrounded by the film.

Ilsa: *Femme Castratrice*

It is now time to meet Ilsa, the *femme castratrice* of the series. As portrayed by American actress Dyanne Thorne she could not fulfill the wet dream of male masochism more perfectly.

Several reviews note the convincing performance and arresting face of Thorne: "Dyanne Thorne is a frightening Amazon of a woman. She plays a

Nazi commandant like she was one and she even looks the part. Although she is amazingly endowed, her hard facial features literally draw your attention away from most everything else" (Matherly, 2002). Indeed, the harsh features of her face are more striking than her body, and her tight lips, penetrating gaze, over-acting and weird German accent, which would be camp in any other context, underline the nature of the fantasies: The ambivalent masquerade of masochism.

Ilsa travels through time and setting, from the Nazis in Germany to Stalin's Gulag in Russia, from the Sheik's Arabian desert to the South American jungle. The figures around her change, but she remains the same. Dressed in a uniform – a standard prop in masochism – and high heels. The fetishism is developed further after the success of *She-Wolf*, where her costume is fairly simple (although one wonders why she wears riding pants since the camp has no horses). In *Harem-Keeper* she wears a desert costume with mini-shorts and long boot-stockings and she attends the Sheik's feast wearing a tight black outfit held together by red string and holding a chained greyhound in each hand. Her two black servants, Satin and Velvet, have helped her into the outfit and tightened all the strings, thus emphasizing the 'costuming' of Ilsa. American film scholar Gaylyn Studlar, writing about the costuming of Dietrich, notices the use of 'striptease' and masquerade as "erotic metamorphoses" in masochism. The costumes are used to "fetishistically idealize the woman as they are used to play out the masochistic rituals of punishment and disguise" (Studlar, 1990, p. 236-7). Thorne is equipped with guns, sables, dildos, spurs, and various whips – a short black horsewhip, a white rod, and a long brown animal whip. All phallic attributes of the dominatrix.

The mixture of cruelty and coldness that Austrian author Leopold von Sacher-Masoch admired in his women and that Gilles Deleuze took as the title of his study of masochism, characterizes Ilsa. She seems indifferent to the pain she inflicts on the women, but smiles sadistically during male castration. Pain, it seems, is not so much the point, as the object. "They are his to do as he wishes, she is lucky it was not worse," she coldly comments, as the male doctor laments the Sheik's maltreatment of his mistresses in *Harem-Keeper*. Her coldness in contrasted by the hot sadism of the Sheik, who smiles and laughs excitedly when Ilsa demonstrates her vagina-bomb on an unconscious girl, whose abdomen is blown to pieces. The gimmick is a bomb placed deep within the vagina, exploding at the height of intercourse. The Sheik can thus send a beautiful female bomb as a gift to his enemies. Later Ilsa ties the Sheik to the same operating table and has the girl, who is equipped with the bomb, make love to him. As our hero, Adam Scott (Michael Thayer) enters the torture room, she is surprised that he looks away in disgust from the remains of the Sheik.

The uniform, the beautiful but harsh appearance, the fierce pride and the cold cruelty are all features of the dominatrix, who is literally a 'castrating bitch.' She is a hypersexual creature, fully devoted to her job, and always in search of her own satisfaction. It takes a special man to satisfy this woman, and the 'final men' are special in regard to potency and performance. In contrast to The Greek in Sacher-Masoch's novel *Venus in Furs* the heroes in the *Ilsa*-series are not sadistic. They represent an ideal American masculinity – active, strong, optimistic, politically devoted to democracy – but are then also equipped with 'unusual powers'. "I discovered that I can hold back for as long as I want to," Wolfe explains to Mario. "I still can. All night if necessary. I guess you can call me a freak of nature. Sort of human machine. A machine that can set its control to fast, slow or never."

Originally the part was to be played by Phyllis Davis, who had been the lead in the wip-movies *Sweet Sugar* (1972) and *Terminal Island* (1973), but she left the production in protest to the 'golden shower scene.' Instead 42-year old Dyanne Thorne (fifteen years older than Davis) got the role. She had been a Las Vegas-dancer and acted in low-budget exploitation movies such as *Blood Sabbath* (1972) and *Wham Bam Thank You Spaceman* (1972). Her age, her over-acting and her campy 'star persona' now successfully united in the role that would make her immortal.

The Utopian Reading: Ilsa as Feminist?

How shall we understand the figure of Ilsa: Is she a strong woman representing the subversion of patriarchy and of male aggression? Does she turn stereotypical gender roles upside down?

On the movie's commentary track Dyanne Thorne without hesitation characterizes her Ilsa-character as feminist: "This is the first [film], where they had a female villain and also this is the first one where she was, like, the leader of the feminists if you will, which many of the magazines had said, this was the first feminist. See, even with this particular scene [the male castration scene in *She-Wolf*] the victim was the male, and the three females standing there were in total control."

As mentioned earlier I have not found any academic articles on Ilsa. However, in the articles on wip-films written by women, the idea of female strength and independence is taken as a sign of feminism. Pam Cook is the first (writing in 1976) to suggest a subversive content in this genre, focusing on *Terminal Island* (1973) which is the only wip-film directed by a woman, Stephanie Rothman. In *Terminal Island* the women manage to reform the men that initially abused them on the prison-island where male and female prisoners have been abandoned. "They cannot in any sense be described as feminist films," Cook admits, but points to "contradictions, shifts in meaning which disturb the patriarchal myths of women on which the exploitation film itself rests" (Cook, 1976, p. 127). A decade later a German article by Birgit Hein in *Frauen & Film* locates a subversive content in the portrayal of lesbian sexuality and women's use of violence in *Mädchen in Uniform* (1931,

Leontine Sagan), *Ausgestoßen* (1982, Axel Corti) and *Chained Heat* (1983, Paul Nicholas):

> Ich war gleich beim ersten Film von den Frauen begeistert (..) Sie prügeln sich nach allen Regeln der Kunst. Sie gehen ganz selbstverständlich mit Schußwaffen und Messern um. Sie sind hinterhältig und skrupellos. Sie sind sehr geil aufeinander und, wenn es darauf ankommt, sehr solidarisch und mutig. [I was infatuated with the women from the very first film (..) They fight excellently. They are familiar with the use of guns and knives. They are sly and without scruples. They also turn each other on sexually and, when neccessary, stick together and are brave] (Hein, 1987, p. 22).

Hein notices that lesbian sex and violent behavior subverts traditional gendering of female sexuality as passive, clean and delicate. Finally a recent article by Suzanna Danuta Walters (2001) discusses the aggressive women as representing a repressed image of "woman-as-other" within patriarchal order. "Female criminality, female violence, female desire – so firmly negated by mainstream popular culture – here emerge in all their overblown glory. Not only do these bizarre films explore the unexplored with humor and a certain postmodern verve, but they often allow women to be victorious over the forces of male violence" (Walters, 2002, p. 121).

Conclusion

Is Ilsa a feminist? Like in the perverse fantasies, that depends on which point of view we prefer. Certainly, within the context of the films and their reception by both mainstream and exploitation audiences, she was not perceived as a feminist. She was first and foremost constructed as a commercial element, a break with all taboos, which was so radical as to command our attention. In the world of exploitation cinema, attention means money. Ilsa marked an innovation of the wip-movie in the portrayal of her as both dominatrix and protagonist. Her figure displayed a masochistic element, that had until then been a subtext in the films of Pam Grier.

Perverse fantasies work by the subversion of order and transgression of taboos. Thus the extensive use of 'power scenarios' where unequal or inappropriate partners have sex: Master-slave, Nazi-Jew, doctor-patient, adult-child, boss-employee, etc. The perverseness explains the subversion of order which the above feminist readings of wip-pictures all note. But is such subversion politically progressive? Silverman rejects the utopian reading of perversion, and points out that for instance the revolt against patriarchy within masochism is post-Oedipal and not, as Deleuze presents it, pre-Oedipal. In other words, masochism is well aware of its 'perverseness.' Likewise the producers and consumers of exploitation movies. "It's only fun," as Don

Edmonds claims. In his *Eroticism* French philosopher and author Georges Bataille writes: "The transgression does not deny the taboo but transcends it and completes it. (..) Organized transgression together with the taboo make social life what it is" (Bataille, 2001, p. 63, 65).[13]

The function of the *Ilsa*-series is the display of a perversion – male masochism – that is taboo and therefore fascinating. With the figure of Dyanne Thorne the series achieved status as cult and a must-see among young men, where it became part of modern-day male initiation rites. In these rites the playful exploration of alternative sexual traits (sadism, masochism, cannibalism) and the subversion of social order is acted out in the 'safe' setting of watching an exploitation movie. But this transgression leaves no rupture. On the contrary. My experience is that the men who have enjoyed the 'nauseating' and 'sick' pleasures of Ilsa turn out in the end to be – quite normal. Perversion has been experienced as one step in the proces of experiencing and constructing masculinity. And this, in turn, says more about the nature of 'normal' masculinity than about the 'disgusting' nature of Ilsa.

Notes

1. This article is part of a research project funded by the Danish Research Council for the Humanities about strong women in popular cinema entitled *Woman in a Man's World: A Study of Heroines in Male Film Genres*.

2. Interview with Dyanne Thorne in Venticinque, D. & Thompson, T. (2000), *The Ilsa Chronicles*. Huntingdon: Midnight Media, p. 57.

3. Even if people were 'sickened' by Ilsa there was an audience. The three American *Ilsa*-films all premiered in the Danish cinemas at the time of their production, as did other American wip-films such as *The Big Doll House* (1971), *Black Mama, White Mama* (1972), *Chained Heat* (1982) and *The Concrete Jungle* (1983).

4. I have come across four printed articles and one paper: Pam Cook, "'Exploitation' Films and Feminism", *Screen*, vol. 17, no. 2, summer 1976, p. 122-127; Birgit Hein, "Frauengefängnisfilme, *Frauen & Film*, no. 43, December 1987, p. 22-26; Anne Morey, "The Judge Called Me an Accessory", *Journal of Popular Film & Television*, vol. 23, summer 1995, p. 80-87; Suzanna Danuta Walters. 2001. "Caged Heat: the (R)evolution of Woman-in-Prison Films" in Martha McCaughey & Neal King. *Reel Knockouts: Violent Women in the Movies*. Austin: University of Texas Press; Omayra Cruz, "Between Cinematic Imperialism and the Idea of Radical Politics: Phillipines Based Women's Prison Films of the 1970s", paper presented at the SCS Conference in Denver, Colorado, 2002.

5. Exploitation cinema is the 'bastard child' of cinema, an uncivilized lower stratum of cinema history. However, since the advent of 'new' Hollywood and feministic film theory, exploitation films have become a source of inspiration to researchers. Directors such as Herschell Gordon Lewis, John Waters and Russ Meyer have been re-evaluated as innovative in their portrayal of strong women, perverse sexuality and a provocative aesthetics of camp, kitsch and trash. Films such as *The Texas Chainsaw Massacre* (1974) and *I spit on your grave* (1977) are even embraced by feminist film scholars as close-to avant-garde cinema. But not Ilsa.

6. "This brutal and shameless exercise in depravity and relentless sadism..." Venticinque & Thompson, 2000: 4.

7. *Ilsa, The Tigress of Siberia* was not yet released on DVD when I wrote this article and I was ununable to find it on vhs. References to this movie are based on the summary in *The Ilsa Chronicles*. All four movies are avialable on DVD in 2004.

8. The names of the characters vary in spelling and most of the credits are pseudonyms. The prisoner Rosetta – the only woman to escape Camp 9 – does not figure in the end-credits of the films and is not mentioned in *The Ilsa Chronicles* or on IMDB.

9. After *She-Wolf* in 1974 came *SS Girls, Women's Camp 119, SS Experiment Camp, SS Camp 5 Women's Hell, Achtung! The Desert Tigers, Horrifying Experiments of the SS Last Days, Gestapo's Last Orgy, Nazi Love Camp 27*, all produced in 1976.

10. For a thorough discussion of Freud's writings on masochism see Silverman, *Male Subjectivity at the Margins*, chapter 5, an edited version of the article "Masochism and Male Subjectivity." About homosexuality in male masochism Reik comments: "There cannot be any doubt as to the existence and efficaciousness of the passive-homosexual idea in masochism – but much doubt as to its prevalent importance. It does not show up regularly nor is its importance always the same" (Reik, 1941, p. 206).

11. On the commentary track to *Wicked Warden* Dyanne Thorne says that she has received many letters from women thanking her that the *Ilsa*-films have saved their marriage. I may be conservative, but my guess is that if women watch these films they do so on male initiative. When asking around I have not encountered one woman who had viewed an Ilsa-film, whereas many male friends, colleagues and acquaintances surprised me by having watched one or several. My private asking is not a survey poll, but the result is supported by the fact that during research I have not come across any female comments on the *Ilsa*-films.

12. The Spanish sequel is an exception to this rule. It follows the traditional sadistic path of wip-movies with female victims, evil lesbian wardens who are killed in the end and male sadistic voyeurism

13. Georges Bataille, *Eroticism*, p. 63, 65.

References

Bataille, G. (2001). *Eroticism*. London: Penguin Books.

Clover, C. (1992). *Men, women and chain saws: Gender in the modern horror film*. London: BFI.

Cook, P. (1976). 'Exploitation' films and feminism. *Screen, 17*, no. 2, summer, 122-127.

Creed, B. (1993). *The monstrous-feminine: Film, feminism, psychoanalysis*. London: Routledge.

Cridland, J. (1976, March 1). Angående filmen 'Ilse'. *Helsingør Dagblad*.

Crowther, B. (1989). *Captured on film*. London: Batsford.

Cruz, O. (2002). Between cinematic imperialism and the idea of radical politics: Phillipines based women's prison films of the 1970s. Paper presented at the SCS Conference in Denver, Colorado, 2002.

Freud, S. (1980). The economic problem of masochism (1924). In J. Strachey (trans.), *The standard edition of the complete psychological works of Sigmund Freud* (vol. XIX, p. 157-170). London: Hogarth Press.

Hein, B. (1987). Frauengefängnisfilme. *Frauen & Film, 43*, December, 22-26.

Ilsa, She-Wolf of the SS [anonymous review]. Retrieved May 12, 2002, from www.prisonflicks.com/ilsa-shewolf.htm.

Major, W. Ilsa, She Wolf Of The SS. Retrieved May 12, 2002, from *Boxoffice Magazine Online*, http://www.rottentomatoes.com.

Matherly, B. Ilsa: She Wolf of the SS. Retrieved May 12, 2002, from www.daily-reviews.com/i/bmilsa1.htm.

Morales, E. (1995, August 15). Mama Said Knock You Out. *Voice*.

Morey, A. (1995). The Judge Called Me an Accessory. *Journal of Popular Film & Television, 23*, no. 2, summer, 80-87.

Nazifilm om SS-tortur tages af plakaten fordi publikum bliver dårlige [Nazi movie about SS torture is pulled because the audience gets sick] (1976, December 16). *Ny Dag*.

Parish, J.R. (1991). *Prison pictures from Hollywood: Plots, critiques, casts and credits for 293 theatrical and made-for-television releases*. Jefferson: McFarland & Company Inc.

Reik, T. (1941). *Masochism in modern man* (later editions retitled *Masochism in sex and society*). New York: Farrar, Straus and Company.

Sacher-Masoch, L. von. *Venus in furs*. In *Masochism* (pp. 141-293). New York: Zone Books.

Scheib, R. Ilsa, She Wolf of the SS. Retrieved May 12, 2002, from http.//members.fortunecity.com/roogulator/horror/ilsa1.htm.

Silverman, K. (1992). *Male subjectivity at the margins*. London: Routledge.

Silverman, K. (1988). Masochism and Male Subjectivity *Camera obscura, 17*, 30-67.

Steltz, C. Ilsa, She Wolf of the SS. Retrieved May 12, 2002, from www.dvdangle.com/reviews/.

Stinkende premiere [A stinking premiere] (1976, April 26). *Aarhuus Stiftstidende*.

Studlar, G. (1990). Masochism, masquerade, and the erotic metamorphoses of Marlene Dietrich. In J. Gaines & C. Herzog (Eds.), *Fabrications: Costume and the female body* (pp. 229-249). London: Routledge.

Venticinque, D. & Thompson, T. (2000). *The Ilsa Chronicles*. Huntingdon: Midnight Media.

Walters, S. D. (2001). Caged heat: The (R)evolution of woman-in-prison films. In M. McCaughey & N. King (Eds.), *Reel knockouts: Violent women in the movies* (pp. 106-124). Austin: University of Texas Press.

Zalcock, B. (1998). *Renegade sisters: Girl gangs on film*. Creation Books: London.

Xena: Warrior Princess Out of the Closet?

A Melodramatic Reading of the Show by Latin American and Spanish Lesbian and Gay Fans

Walter Alesci[1]

The New Zealand-American series *Xena: Warrior Princess* gathered the necessary ingredients in order to attract interest from different social groups in the countries where it was broadcasted. It didn't need much time to gain so-called 'xenites' – online fans of Xena. Xena, a purposeful and strong woman played by Lucy Lawless, figured in a fiction that didn't present much originality: action, comedy and (melo)drama in a temporal mix of antiquity and medieval. However, the warrior had characteristics that made the audience suspicious: was Xena a woman with conducts associated to masculinity?

In the series Xena is accompanied by her friend Gabrielle (Renée O'Connor). Their affectionate association did not originated only from the text of *Xena: Warrior Princess* (from hereon called *Xena*), but also from the producers of the show and from the actors, who started adding ambigious hints to the sexual nature of the relationship between the two women and thus began a 'game' with the audience, that lasted all six seasons of the series (1995-2001). This cocktail based on permanent contradictions split the audience between those who approved of the relationship between Xena and Gabrielle and those who opposed it.

The Internet was the media elected by the American fans for the foundation of a 'Xenaverse'. In this public form of actions and interactions, xenites from all over the world started to open virtual communities, chats, and discussion lists. The artistic production didn't wait long, and most prosperous was the writing of fan fictions (stories) based on *Xena*, which generally chose different paths from the development of the original product. Fans knew that characters and scenarios belong to their creators, but nonetheless they asserted the right to create new ideas and make interpretations.

The Latin American and Spanish fans connected to this Xena fandom movement and undertook the same cultural practices other xenites did. In this way a Xena fan community appeared and within this space lesbian[2] and gay fans introduced a queer aspect due to the fact that the series showed situations related to those lived by homosexual fans. The construction of homosexual subjectivity in these societies has analogies with the series' supposedly hidden or clandestine content. Therefore, this particular audience felt addressed by a program that made them feel passion and affection for their heroine.

In terms of impact, the narrative is incorporated into their daily lives and, progressively, changes certain habits. I want in the following to discuss how the fiction creates acceptance, resonance, and/or resistance in homosexual fans. The textual and extratextual discourses of *Xena* allowed me to confront fans to the parallel discourses elaborated by the fans. From their actions and interactions of consuming I will reconstruct the forms in which the imaginary homosexuality of these fans is constantly reassured in *Xena* without the series displaying any open signs of rupture.

The first part of this article, from the field of feminist media studies, uses critical speech analysis and the theories of Judith Butler about gender as performance to understand the diffusion of media contents which carries a distinct ideology.

The second part, through ethnographic exploration, gives context to the interaction between habitus, field and capital which reveals the map, tactics and meanings of practices of lesbian and gay fans from Spain and Latin America regarding *Xena*.

A third part explains the melodramatic sense the fans capture form the fiction they are fascinated by. The Latin[3] queer fandom experiences include resistance tinted with suffering, alliances, identification, happiness, projection, activism (and also alienation), fight, upsetting, freedom and desire to keep wanting and loving *Xena*.

I. The Heroine in Search of Redemption

Our warrior was introduced in three chapters from the adventure series *Hercules: The Legendary Journeys*. Xena's plans was to kill a titan and to do this she destroyed everything on her way. But the warrior princess also saved a baby and Hercules decided to be merciful and, after Xena's sexual surrender, exhorted her to consummate a *mea culpa*.

> *Hercules:* I wish you'd let me help.
> *Xena:* You already have. You unchained my heart.

Once again, *man* is given the principles which constitute humanity, and his reason makes him capable of absolving and reconducting the *woman*. And that's because since ancient times violence in the public (and private) sphere has been a masculine attribute, feelings a feminine responsibility. Therefore, the female hero began her path to exonerate her sins, and won her own series, *Xena: Warrior Princess*. But the past is always present and never lets her forget who she was and what she had done. Redemption will come at the end, but to get it she must pay a high price: Constant suffering and abnegation, marks that define the acts which constitutes her very gender identity. "Media texts do not present messages about our culture; they ARE culture" (Rakow 2001).

Feminist media studies have prioritised a text analysis which reinforces the reproduction of *distorted realities* or *unrealities,* which circulate in media communication and on the Internet. The culture industry reinforces a syncretic collective imaginary, where old ideas and femininity myths prevail, and this industry allows their continuation as the basic sustenance in a patriarchal society.[4] This position assures and maintains the audience's ideological competence.

Xena, Lesbian Princess. Oops! Warrior Princess

The heroine faces opponents on her quest to bring peace to the villages. On her trip she meets Gabrielle, and together they discover the reason for them being united. Now, if I assert that Xena is lesbian in a society where heterosexuality is obligatory and institutionalised, this would submerge her in a transgression field or in absolute subversion. Because the power mechanisms disseminated on the social net which is in charge of maintaining, reinforcing and reproducing heterosexist domination[5] would punish Xena's sexual orientation for being unnatural. "'The relationship should transcend all of that,' Ms. Lawless said about the question of their sexuality. 'It is about love, and sexuality is certainly a small part of love. We don't want to be definitive about it. It's one of those things, neither confirming nor denying'" (Lopez 1997).

Is she or isn't she heterosexual? Is she or isn't she a lesbian?

The different speeches (puzzles) within and outside the series constitute the game established by the producers of *Xena* and the communication media for the audiences and the fans. But against the dominant speech emerge resistant speeches[6] within the global oppression context. But media hegemony should nevertheless be understood as absolute, because there is no closed work. A critical analysis about hegemonic speeches as well as contra-hegemonic ones will sediment the basis for the argumentation which assumes a lesbian performance in *Xena* from the premises *is or isn't* she heterosexual or homosexual.

Butler (1990, 1993) has expressed her position in her theory of performance, which claims that all categories and identities exist as ideals. By confronting and reconciling the ideal with the real, a *performance* is obtained as a result. We recognize gender as a constant representation of acts and, at the same time, we see that the gender representation is its own construction. 'Gender' is what one assumes, perpetrated under coercion (man and woman under imposed labels), but with the ability and the keenness to subvert (possibilities of insurrection and resistance) his or her performance within the social and cultural field.

Sub What?

The lesbian/gay audience in the United States began to realize the ambiguity of the friendship between Xena and Gabrielle. Then, voices raised and proclaimed that in the series there was a *subtext*. The producer Renaissance Pictures and the actors chose permanent contradiction as their strategy. Precisely because of this 'detail' in the series' plot, two groups of fans were established: *Sub-texters* and *anti-subtexters*, which also today quarrel off- and online.

> "I still don't see what you see in her" but Tapert insists, "We're not really playing to that audience. There is a love relationship, meaning there's no question that Xena and Gabrielle love each other and are willing to lie down their lives for each other. But I don't neccessarily want to say that they have a sexual relationship, either. There's no question that it is a story of the love between two characters, but, if there's a sexual relationship between them, it's none of my business" (Scapperotti 1999).

> Rob [Tapert] and I [R. J. Stewart] came to understand that this is what made the series work, the relationship of these two women. It was more than just the sexual things that people talk about. It was the relationship. It's something we just stumbled on. We hadn't planned it, but we love the positive feedback we get and, yeah, we play on it and have fun with it (Sherwood 2000).

Love… Forbidden Love…

The image of the confused kiss between Xena and Gabrielle in the chapter *The Quest* and the scene with them in the bathtub in *The Day in the Life*, was interpreted by not only many *xenite*-sites but also by the media as a confirmation of the speculations about lesbianism in *Xena*. The producers of the series, however, kept within the *game* with hints to the audience:

> *Playboy:* What's Xena's vacation fantasy?
> *Lucy Lawless:* A biennial sailing trip to Lesbos (Rensin 1997).
> *Male Audience Member #1:* Are you proud to play a lesbian?
> *Lucy Lawless:* Well… uh… actually, I don't define my character, Xena, as a lesbian. I like to think of her as a fierce warrior who travels… ("Saturday Night Live," 1998).[7]

In *Ides of March* Xena is condemned to be crucified together with Gabrielle. Shortly before they meet the same faith as Jesus of Galilea they exchanged last words because they are unaware of their posterior resurrection.

> *Xena:* Gabrielle, you were the best thing in my life.
> *Gabrielle:* I love you, Xena.

The producers went even further. *Dejà vu all over* is one of the clearest examples of recalcitrant homophobia[8]: "This love cannot be!" The action occurs in the future from the characters, which is our present. Annie (Lucy Lawless) is a Xena fan and believes in the warrior's reincarnation. Her husband Harry (Ted Raimi, who plays Joxer in the series) tries to dissuade her from such madness. Later on, in a previous life's office where we meet also Doctor Mattie (Renée O'Connor), the three protagonists join in the cosmic trip that will resolve anterior identities. Annie is shocked to learn that she was Joxer, Mattie was Gabrielle and the sceptical Harry, no other but Xena. However, because the outcome could be read as homophobia and discrimination of gender, fans preferred to allude to this as *subtext*. Annie (Joxer in the past) leaves Harry so that he and Mattie (Xena and Gabrielle in remote times) can get back together again, because life gives them a second chance to be happy: heterosexuality.

[Possible present with passionate kiss]
Mattie: Harry… it's funny. I do feel strangely attached to you.
Harry: What do you remember?
Mattie: It's been a long time.
Harry: It's been too long… friend.

The inclusion of ambiguous gay and lesbian characters has stimulated censorship and homophobia among executives and advertisers, and paradoxically, in the same productions that have incorporated these characteristics. Nevertheless, a procession of links in *E.R., Buffy, Babylon 5, All My Children*, have been read from a *subtextual* perspective. Although, the most controversial ones have been, perhaps, those of the characters from *Star Trek.*[9] On the episode *Rejoined* (28/10/95) from *Star Trek: Deep Space 9*, an act with similar homophobic characteristics as *Xena* has happened. A kiss between two women seemed to be a lesbian kiss, but it wasn't… Jadzia Dax and her companion had been a heterosexual couple in a previous incarnation and, when they die, take over other bodies. In *Xena* the warrior had patented her election for Gabrielle. The labyrinths created by the audience, which offers the heroine volatile seductions to men, are stratagems to hide the 'secret'.

II. Join Xena! Chronicle of the Actions and Interactions of Lesbian and Gay Fans in Spain and Latin America

Xena was no exception when it comes to a disordered emission of chapters on television channels in many countries. The fans drew on the internet with more assiduity, and subscribed to pay channels to receive it through *USA Network* in Latin America and *Calle 13* in Spain. The phenomenon involves a modification and an impact on the social habits of the subjects in their daily lives, especially in consuming habits. The cultural practices constitute per se a very solid Latin online fandom of *Xena*, which still functions today even after the series have ended, as a process of convergence between the traditional (television) and the modern (internet).

The audiences elect products from the media to make their creative appropriations through the tactics of circumstantial, momentarily and furtive conditions. Especially lesbian and gay fans from Spain and Latin America transform the experience of watching *Xena* within a rich and complex participative and interpretative culture. The circulation of the program's textual and visual discourse provides the enthusiasts with tools to the construction of social and cultural innovation of its own. Furthermore, the fans will use resistance mechanisms to certain elements which become detached from the series, the producers and even the heroine, in order to develop into *xenites*.

Princess Warrior, Welcome to the Ambiente. *The Series in Context*

One important explanation for the success of *Xena* with lesbian and gay fans is the famous *subtext*, which can be considered an analogy to how homosexuality is lived in these countries. A cultural referential from the lesbian/ gay perspective can obtain higher validity and acceptance in the *Ambiente* when the argument presents areas where a *subtextual* interpretation takes place. Because homosexuality is lived as subtext in Latin America and Spain, it must not be too evident. To be part of the Ambiente means to define an amount of practices in the subculture LGBT (lesbians, gays, bisexuals, transsexuals, transgender and travesties) that moves around marginal zones in a society that expels or turns invisible alternative sexualities.

> What hurts me is not the fact that I am a homosexual, but that it is thrown on my face as if it was a plague... (Chavela Vargas, Costarrican-Mexican singer, symbol of the fight and assertion for LGBT).[10]

> The lesbianism in Spain is still in the catacombs... (Mili Hernández, ex-militant from a Spanish association of LGBT).

> The reality of the lesbian woman in the country is that the woman cannot say she is lesbian, because in this moment: la cruz de por vida (...) The truth is that many of the lesbians and gays in this country carry a double life, most of them get married, have children and live parallel relationships (Gina Rodríguez, member of an association of LGBT from Honduras).

To understand the ideological context is the only way to interpret the meaning people give their actions in complex social situations. For that, an observation in a natural scenario and the data collected in interviews can help to set a conceptual map of the reasons leading lesbian and gay fans to live homosexuality in a distinctive way.

In these societies it has not been an easy task to acquire basic rights for the LGBT community. Neither should one underestimate the achievements of these people, the courage and will to fight untill the end. The so called "death squads" or paramilitary groups still murder innocents for their homosexuality in the streets of Brazil, Ecuador, El Salvador, Colombia, etc. ("Violence unveiled: Repression against lesbians and gay men in Latin America," 1996). In Spain, for instance, the government has turned the country into the most homophobic in the European Union by voting against the International Lesbian and Gay Association (*ILGA*) in order to join the group of non-governmental organizations which advise within the United Nations.[11]

Xena is My Life, My Life is Xena... Fans in Situations

The initiative to study *Xena* happened when I discovered a Latin Xenaverse and became aware that speaking about audience reception specified passivity. I used an ethnographic approach, between March 2001 and December 2002, to handle the action and interaction processes of lesbian and gay fans in Spain and Latin America with the series.

My proposal was evocative for the fans, who were exhilarated to confess their attitudes and motivations about the program. In general, their replies were enthusiastic and I achieved an appointment face to face with two lesbian fans from Barcelona. Cruella has a fan fiction website in Spanish and publishes a volume of those writings every week. This writing channel has created an exchange with other Latin American sites. Meanwhile, Jenny is a moderator of a Xenite site and has also her own site. But in this case I decided to follow (indirectly) the relation she established with *Xena* and ended our meeting after some months. The remaining interviews, I have done through e-mail, telephone, chat and talk- show.[12]

The recognition of similarities in the analysed subjects and their affinity upon the reading of the series, which convert them into fans, allow us to think about daily habits which contribute to constitute the field as a universe of signification. A player, according to Bourdieu (1993), defines his position in the field accordingly to his accumulated capital, and his position gives him an amount of tactics to bet and to increase or maintain his capital. This articulation between the objective and subjective can lead to think that the meaning as well as the message built from the series for the lesbian and gay fans in Spain and Latin America constitutes a process of consolidating of their identities.

i. Identity and fanatism

I'm from Spain, work a lot and study, I can barely write the fan fictions and dedicate myself to Xena and Gabrielle... I'm a Xenite-Subtexter-Bardo and I won't stop being because someone has ended the series (Lobezna, actress, 20 years old, Madrid, Spain).

This subculture is defined by the consuming styles and the preferential cultural forms which correspond to one of the characteristics that constitute the fact of being a fan. A statute which is not constructed in occasional form, but exists in certain patterns, legitimated and with consensus, which contribute to delimitate the perimeter of pertinence. Therefore, this consuming is certainly productive, from its perspective of representation, given that it obeys a cultural practice, coherent with the concrete and symbolic appropriation of a determined product.

ii. Identification, memory and interpellation

Xena seemed to me ... impressing. She was a super-warrior woman, who went ahead and on top of it was playing for a love story. It was a homosexual story, but it was more common to see her among boys and not among girls (Eugenio, 26 years old, actor, Buenos Aires, Argentina).

From this show on there are many women who got out of the closet, because thanks to Xena a group of people have met and we have done ´kedadas' [fans' reunions] (Cruella, 35 years old, designer, Barcelona, Spain).

The recognition process that the fans go through is given by the analogy they make with their daily lives. This recognition is key to understand the motivations, projections and, mostly, identification of these audiences with their heroine. The show is a valid and real testimony of its importance for the definition of their identities. The *active* actions are generated from the world of significations and from a cultural memory which link them to the admired heroine.

iii. Intensity and melodrama

Fans that participated on the talk show: Ana (25 years old, student), Jenny (33 years old, journalist) and Aurora (34 years old, administrative clerk).

Host: I've brought something for you... Have you seen it yet? [Clip from "A Friend in Need 2" (Season 6, Series Finale) with Xena and Gabrielle passing water/kissing].
Aurora: No, it hasn't been broadcasted here yet...
Jenny: Uffff...
Host: Why this "ufffff..."
Jenny: That's the final chapter when they kill Xena and I haven't seen it and I don't know if I want to see it....
Host: Shouldn't had finished like that...

Xena: Warrior Princess (Schulian & Tapert, 1995), Universal.

Jenny: They are telling you this love is not possible...
Ana: If the other sequence had been Gabrielle committing suicide...
Host: And if they got out of the closet, better....
Ana: This would have been ideal... Because for me it was a big step ahead to recognize my lesbian condition...
Jenny: When I realised the end, I deleted myself from the discussion list, got very ill, it was a great disappointment...
Host: To have been a fan of Xena, do you believe it helped you to write this book? [Book of self support for lesbians called *Más que amigas* (*More than friends*) published in Barcelona, Plaza & Janés, 2002]
Jenny: It allowed me to know a world of lesbians that I didn't know at that time. My life is a "before Xena" and an "after Xena".

These melodramatic readings are interesting, given that ideas and emotions expressed in the talks positioned the readings the fans made of *Xena*. Even if they express that producers are saying "no" to lesbian love, none of the participants express that there is homophobia. What motives do they have to doubt themselves as victims of the patriarchal segregation? What are the causes to not notice such oppressive mechanisms?

iv. Gender performance in fans and Xena

There is much homophobia still, so they are a bit like Xena, once in a while see themselves obliged to have an apparent male interest, not to seem too lesbian (...)So I don't believe that the question is a mere accumulation of rights, but to fight for that the people accept the sexual diversity. I identify myself with the gay cause and with the feminist cause, as a woman and victim of machismo (Elenis, 20 years old, college student, Madrid, Spain).

Xena lived her relationship similar to what happens to us, because of the prejudice. At the end I liked it better, she took on and defined it better (Luriana, 38 years old, engineer, Rio de Janeiro, Brazil).

The considerations attained regarding the gender performance have been conceived in a space with the use of force by dominant heterosexuality in these societies, which obliges gays and lesbians to exile themselves in foggy frontiers from the genre constructions in order not to be discovered. They establish a special link with the princess warrior, a coming and going, a mutual self-reproduction.

We can ask, from the perspective of Butler (1990, 1993), wether the repeated acts which constitute Xena's performance are in conformity with an expected gender identity or question this expectation? The great disjunctive planted in the show and its derivations (protagonists and producers declarations), allow lesbian and gay fans to participate in this puzzle, which creates what they call *subtext*. In one reading Xena hides the performance character of the gender and thereby delivers what society expects from her. In another reading Xena treasures the performance acts of gender which constitutes her lesbian identity because it is outside the margins imposed by a homophobic and heterosexist society.

Fight for Gay Pride *in the Latin* Xenaverse

The cultural practices of Latin lesbian and gay xenites contribute to a community with typical tones of context, providing it with exchange channels, fans reunions, in contact and the richest artistic expressions which connect them, in the case studied, with the homosexual performance of their favourite heroine.

The fan fictions constitute the most sentimental and passional fibre of a Xena fanatic, and stories interlace intimately searching for a point of union between their lives and the life of their venerated.

> Despite the joy felt for seeing her brother so in love with her friend, couldn't stop feeling some sadness: Gabrielle would never be hers again. To accept from Destiny this alternative of life had painful consequences (Fragment of *Buenas noches Gabrielle*, written by Cruella,[13] 35 years old, Spain).

Last chapter of the show left everyone shocked and imprisoned by the deepest sadness. Emotions and devotion to Xena crystallized among a group, who called themselves 'post final fan fiction of *Xena*',[14] and through this came an uprising:

> Late afternoon came forward but Xena and Gabrielle had completely forgotten about it. The twin souls were back together, in body, mind and heart. A long life together awaited them (fragment of *Sucesos Posteriores*, 112 pages by Ximena, 23 years old, pharmacy student, Buenos Aires, Argentina).

> Agony imprisons my soul and drowns my senses. Why don't you come back to my life? Is this punishment? (fragment of *El amor supera el tiempo*, by F.F. Morgan, 38 years old, computer science teacher, Santiago, Chile).

> Letter written by Gabrielle after Xena's loss: I have no more hope. I have no desire to search through the rubble of my ruined heart. I can't shed another tear for love, because you have taken all my tears long ago... (fragment of *Nunca Adiós*, by José Miguel, Spain)

Xenapolis[15] is a discussion lists which originated from the show. Here diverse opinions can been found, which have produced high tension levels when speaking about the *subtext* which interweave the personal lives of many fans.

> From Guerrera (Spain): Since my brother got out of the closet, I have let go that I am a lesbian. Now I don't have to pretend in front of my parents! :)

From Pili (Mexico): I'd like to be able to do the same, but my parents are quite religious and I don't want them to loose their hope and be angry at me… How nice that they know it! Although I don't actually know up to what point this is nice.

From Paty (Spain): For the homophobic in Xena's mediocre web should know that there are people who are not lesbians and support the subtext!!! I have left a message at the forum and the reply was: "My web of Xena is the best of all, the ones who wrote it are sad and bitter lesbians, which can't stand to know that Xena and Gabrielle are friends… In my web I have shown that lesbians can't stand a different point of view which is not subtexter… the lesbianism is a disease and Xena is not a lesbian."

"Cyber queer spaces are necessarily embedded within both institutional and cultural practices, and are a means by which the lesbian/gay/transgender/queer self can be read into the politics of representation and activism confronting homophobia" (Wakeford, 2000). *Xenapolis* functions for gay and lesbian participants as a cyber queer space. The exposure of such vital themes as the fight for defending ones gender identity acquires a gay/lesbian online activist relevance. Furthermore, the place enables lesbian and gay fans to manifest and sensitise others about the harm caused to them by an oppressive culture which imposes an obligatory heterosexuality on them. These actions have a multiplying effect since it spots instigators of gender discrimination and brings conscience to the rest about homophobia.

III. We Have our Finger Crossed that Xena Gets Out of the Closet!

This work has tried to draw some considerations from critical discourse analysis and audience ethnography about the identification and appropriation processes taken by gay and lesbian fans in Latin America and Spain by the show *Xena* and from such processes, the creation and circulation of products (with a new identity) generated from a television fiction.

A program that wasn't only entertainment but for the devotees, somehow, part of their lives. Therefore the heroine was taken to such a personal level for her implicit behaviour, that it became more than just consuming. *Xena* reproduced the experiences of Latin lesbians and gays. For that, the actions of the warrior princess, the fight for her free performance, gave clues to explore the Ambiente and the codes which allowed to be or not part of it. In the same way, beyond the interviews conducted to fans, messages and creations were overwhelming and precise to show how they live and suffer.

In a society dominated by value, (re)production and cultural heterosexist and homophobic imagination, lesbian and gay fans of a show slide over a subversion which constitutes the performance and constitution of its gender identity. Xena does not wish to be made visible by her producers, but her loyal xenites (from the Latin context) make them visible and see her as well. Therefore, the hegemony of the media (conceived to be read from one way only) is never total or exclusive.

Melodrama: Latin Passion

"*Mestizajes* of which we are made...The melodrama [in Latin America] mixes a little bit of everything, social structures and the structures of feeling. The melodrama is much of what we are – fatalists, inclined to machismo, superstitious – and what we dream of becoming – stealing the identities of others, nostalgia, righteous anger" (Martín Barbero 1993).

The drama of excess as a vision of the world penetrates Latin regions, overcoming the cements of the permanent construction of the collective memory. This cultural expression is rooted in all societies. But it is not just part of artistic expressions such as theatre, literature or movies, but also constitutes a way to think about one's existence. Therefore, it is not casual that, in order to maintain and reproduce dominant values, the patriarchal hetero-hegemonic apparatus uses strategies of interpellation through melodrama. The communication media is the best warlord to consume this task since communication media flood the daily routines of the people.

The melodramatic nuances explored by *Xena* is what has most strongly penetrated on the analysed cases. Latin lesbian and gay fans were struck by the *subtext*, because the heroine and her companion Gabrielle instigated the utopia of eternal love, joined by a surrounding which took over and fed this illusion. Then these disciples had certain expectations: Xena? Would she ever get out of the closet? Would she finally end up with her beloved Gabrielle?

The fans multiply the intrigues and the *subtext* familiar to them, and live their homosexuality from that representation. But Xena is not allowed to love Gabrielle. The gay and lesbian xenites from Latin America and Spain consummate the melodramatic appropriation. The production, on the other hand, redeems Xena from her sin, and in exchange she goes on with her life and separates from her loved one.

Brooks (1976) has researched how melodrama turns sacred by the dominant values in order to preserve the ideological basis of the bourgeoisie. Through sentimentalism, the polarization of the good and bad, from the must be or not be, melodrama interpellates us to glimpse the commitments we are obliged to fulfill in our daily lives.

Why Won't Xena Ever Get Out of the Closet?

What will Xena do to get out of the closet? Was she ever in it? The implicit homophobia of the series resulted in discourses, inside as well as outside the show, which were intended to manipulate the audience through an almost ecclesiastic rhetoric which absorbs from the *Papal Bull*. And, as in every parabola, the end includes a morale or instruction we must follow. The following interview[16] is proof of what I have been trying to demonstrate until now:

> *Ted Raimi:* There are always little looks that they give each other (...) Are they gay? Are they not gay?
> *Robert Tapert:* I'd say they are sexually experimented.
> *Host:* They teased the audience and each other.

"Homophobic discourses operate strategically by means of logical contradictions. The logical contradictions internal to homophobic discourses give rise to a series of double binds which function – incoherently, to be sure, but nonetheless effectively and systematically – to impair the lives of lesbian and gay men" (Halperin 1998). This concept of Halperin enlightens our consideration of the contradictions in which Renaissance Pictures was willing to travel. The producers declared they were playing with the audience, especially with the fans reading the *subtext*. It is possible Renaissance Pictures declared themselves a winner, but its ignorance was to think that every game has an end and overlook the possible resistance that lies in, for instance, *role games*.

> [Clip of the Marching Xena's lesbian group. All dressed up as Gabrielle or Xena].
> *Host:* Who are these people?
> *Ted Raimi:* Fantasy and science fiction fans are generally of a pretty secluded nature. You know, to put it kindly.
> [Later on, when showing other clips]
> *Host:* Yes, that sort of a bang. The show climaxed with Xena at last confirming her sexual orientation.
> [Clip from "A Friend in Need 2" (Season 6, series finale) with Xena and Gabrielle passing water/kissing].
> *Lucy Lawless:* I couldn't believe it. I came and I went: She's gay!
> *Host:* But their love affair was cut short, literally.
> *Lucy Lawless:* It was a cool show. I'm very proud of it.

Queer Resistance

The cultural dimension that the Internet has taken in the convergence process with television offered Latin lesbian and gay fans a platform for new cultural and social practices which they called Xenaverse. The online communities have the possibility to battle the system of traditional media, and such empowerment contributes to defend gender variations.

The difficulty is that xenites are not always conscious of the homophobia they are permanently exposed to. This has to do with the social context they are immersed in. The melodramatic reading which they make and the cultural components that define them, ensures that the emotional prevails. "Readers are not always resistant; all resistant reading is not necessarily progressive reading; the people do not always recognize their conditions of alienation and subordination" (Jenkins 1992).

In spite of that, the frequent chats with fans and the different attitudes they have lived together concerning the television fiction, have taken me to justify some questions. It is interesting, that although they define themselves as unconditional Xena followers, none of them consider her a lesbian or gay icon. In this issue we find the rupture with the character. Xena becomes one more in the group and responds to the same camouflage conduct of homosexuality in a society that oppress and subjugate homosexuality. *Xena: Warrior Princess* kills and annihilates the heroine, but the fan fictions and other lesbian and gay actions ruptures (fractures and breaks) this hegemonic report. When the show ends, more websites with a queer line have opened, the production of post-final fan fictions and the messages referring to the subtext doubled in Xenapolis.

The new experiences on the Internet are signs of resistance in a media, which could have become a new closet. I don't believe it is so today. My interviews and the mails from the discussion lists indicate that interactivity has been integrated into quotidian life. The show has created a new space and a battle has begun.

The melodramatic reading which Latin gay and lesbian fans have made of *Xena: Warrior Princess* have created alternative texts and discourses which have resulted in new identities and interpretations. This is not just meaningful artistic production, but also opinions and ideas about how gender is constructed. These *actions* and *interactions* are part of a protest against and a response to a hetero-hegemonic, patriarchal and homophobic society, that tries to alienate us culturally, socially and sexually.

Notes

1. This research is dedicated to the memory of my love, Walter Aguilar. I will always be thinking about you.
2. Because of a political matter, I have emphasized the relationship between *Xena: Warrior Princess* and lesbians, as well as the authority to speak of them.
3. The term Latin will be used to refer to Latin American and Spanish without distinction.
4. Feminist theory has been in charge of explaining, in a global and historical way, the discrimination and subordination faced by women. Patriarchy implies a distribution of power: Men keep the monopoly of it and assure the consensus, hegemony, and coercion as well as the visible and invisible violence against women.
5. Heterosexuality is defined as normal and beyond discussion. Any alternative sexual orientations found at the margins of this representation system are considered inferior and immoral. This power, awarded from a repressive patriarchal system, erects itself as hetero-hegemonic.
6. The *resistant reading* model, defended by intellectuals from the field of cultural studies (Hall,1980; Morley 1980), decolonises, frees and ruptures the oppressive voices in the

media. This rupture comes about when the work is considered in a way which makes possible a plural reading (Williams, 1980).

7. Lucy Lawless hosted NBC's *Saturday Night Live* on October 17, 1998.

8. Homophobia constitutes a form of intolerance towards lesbians, gays, bisexuals, transsexuals or transgender and travesties (*LGBT*). The lesbian suffers a double discrimination: contempt for being a woman and for being homosexual. Homophobia is sustained and reproduced by hetero-hegemonic societies regulated by a binary man/woman system.

9. David Sinclair is a gay American fan of *Star Trek* with a fan and queer assertion site. "I do not see myself as an activist. For me, the fight to get non-heterosexual characters on *Star Trek* has been lost a long time ago. My site exists as a repository of information to make sure that the bigotry, lies, and duplicity, as well as the valiant efforts of the GLBT *Star Trek* fans will not be forgotten."

10. Vargas, Ch. (2002). Y si quieren saber de mi pasado. Madrid: Aguilar.

11. On April 30 The United Nations Committee on Non-Government Organizations voted against recommending UN consultative status for the ILGA. Canada, France, Germany, The Netherlands and the USA supported ILGA's inclusion while Egypt lobbied Arab, muslim and catholic nations to reject the group. Spain was the only European Union country to vote against ILGA. International Lesbian and Gay Association, May 6, 2002, from http://www.ilga.org.

12. This experience was conducted on a TV set with fans from Barcelona, and I extracted characteristics from this format to reinforce the study about the melodramatic reading from this particular group.

13. Used under permission, available in site Versión original: http://versionoriginal.cjb.net/.

14. Used under permission, available at: El Mundo del Subtexto de XWP: http://www.angelfire.com/ca4/ subtexto/.

15. Its activities began in September 6, 2001, days before the end of *Xena: Warrior Princess*. There were 330 members, the language is spanish and the place has been moved at the end of 2003 to a new website with a lesbian profile under subscription: la_villa_amazona_subscribe@yahoogroups.com. Psico from Colombia and Jesse from Chile were moderators of the list as well as of the Saturday chats. These fans don't define themselves as lesbians, but defend the relationship between Xena and Gabrielle on their sites: El Mundo del Subtexto de XWP: http://www.angelfire.com/ca4/subtexto/ and y Guerrera y Barda: http://www.guerreraybarda.50megs.com.

16. Lucy Lawless (protagonist of the series), her husband Robert Tapert (producer of the series), Renée O' Connor (Gabrielle) and Ted Raimi (Joxer), participated in the english show *Top Ten Sex Bombs TV Show* months after finishing the television success (Channel 4, UK, November 17, 2001).

Sustaining the Definitive Bitch from Hell

The Politics of *Dolores Claiborne* Within a Feminist Genealogy[1]

Sharon Lin Tay

Given the Freudian-Lacanian version of psychoanalysis that is dominant in film theory, attempts to investigate or theorise women's representations in the cinema reach one conclusion or the other. Cinematic women either represent a version of femininity that adheres to psychoanalytic codification, that is, a version of femininity in possession of passive desire and that is submissive to the paternal metaphor; or, as a menacing form of transgression against the patriarchal Symbolic. This is especially owing to the influence of Barbara Creed's work on the monstrous-feminine that is informed by Julia Kristeva's conception of the abject. The successful propagation of this discourse essentially infiltrated (and permeates) feminist film criticism. In other words, the language used by Creed, Kristeva, and Lacanian psychoanalysis became the shorthand, or the default language, with which to discuss female transgression in the cinema. This vocabulary of abjection, female excess, the Other, the doppelganger, the woman in the attic, became the currency with which instances where female behaviour does not square with psychoanalytic prescriptions are discursively traded. These instances, where female mis/behaviour is considered in terms outside of psychoanalytic discourse, include the Gothic woman's film, otherwise also known as the 1940s paranoid woman's film; the modern horror film, in particular the slasher movie; and in conversations on misbehaving women in contemporary mainstream films such as *Fatal Attraction* (Adrian Lyne, 1987), and *Thelma and Louise* (Ridley Scott, 1991).

While it may be gratifying to consider female transgressions as threatening to the Symbolic order, this recourse to the monstrous-feminine is problematic because it relegates female transgressions to the beyond of discourse. As a result, such a strategy has the effect of eliding any political imperative that may be present in feminist film theory, for where could feminist film theory be located politically if it is already outside of discourse? That is, arguably, the fundamental difficulty in feminist (film) theory's conceptualisation of sexual difference. This article considers an alternative framework with which to consider female transgression apart from psychoanalytic codifications. It also sug-

219

gests that the Freudian-Lacanian paradigm in film theory might be past its usefulness, providing an impetus to go beyond psychoanalysis in film criticism and theory. This paper considers these theoretical implications through the textual operations of *Dolores Claiborne* (Taylor Hackford, 1995) as a contemporary Hollywood film which gestures towards the beyond of psychoanalysis in film theory by its constructive use of female anger towards a feminist politics in theorising film. It also shows how the film's flashbacks, via the philosophy of Gilles Deleuze, work to transcend the psychoanalytic preoccupations with childhood traumas, primal scenes, and repressed memories.

In the film, Kathy Bates and Jennifer Jason Leigh play an estranged mother-daughter pair. They are divided because of Selena's (Leigh) memory of childhood abuses and traumas. The film's story centres around Selena's eventual exorcism of Oedipal hauntings related to her father's abuses towards herself and her mother, Dolores (Bates). Selena returns to the island on which her estranged mother still lives after receiving an anonymous fax informing her that Dolores is accused of murdering her long time employer, Vera (Judy Parfitt). Years ago, Dolores was suspected of causing her husband, Joe's (David Strathairn), death although she was not indicted due to a lack of evidence. For this, her daughter blames and spurns her while the detective who failed to close the case, John Mackey (Christopher Plummer), remains on her heels. Selena's unhappy return to the island opens up old wounds and the past comes back to haunt the present in the form of flashbacks that pervade the film and that are visually coded as more real than the present in terms of colour and brightness.

"Sometimes Being a Bitch is all a Woman Has to Hold on to"

Dolores Claiborne brings together various cinematic tropes and genres that relate to female transgression and anger. Casting Bates and Leigh in the main roles references the actors' previous roles in earlier backlash films as psychotic women.[2] Leigh's previous role as the murderous and obsessive flatmate in *Single White Female* (Barbet Schroeder, 1992) and Bates' role as the crazed woman in *Misery* (Rob Reiner, 1990) serve as inter-textual references in *Dolores Claiborne* to establish the film in a post-backlash mould. The above expression with which this section begins is the mantra to which Dolores and her difficult employer, Vera, hold on. All three women, including Selena, repeat the refrain to one another throughout the course of the film in varying contexts. This refrain that is repeated time and again in *Dolores Claiborne* marks the film as the terrain where female anger, expressed as being a bitch, is validated, privileged, and of particular sustenance to the three female characters involved.

Validating female anger, as opposed to interpreting the emotion as monstrous abjection and outside of discourse, translates into the political potential of female anger as an expression of resistance. Apart from overturning the psychoanalytic interpretation of female transgressions as monstrous abjection, validating manifestations of female anger in mainstream cinema has political implications. In an essay about the representations of rage and resistance written in the aftermath of the Rodney King beating and the subsequent public rebellion, Judith Halberstam considers the failure to productively involve female anger in political protest:

> The failure of non-violent resistance to register anything but the most polite disapproval, I suggest, is the effect of a glaring lack of imagination on the part of political organizers, and an overemphasis upon "organization" itself that often produced determined efforts to eradicate expressions of rage or anger from political protest (Halberstam 2001:249).

Instead, Halberstam proposes that media manifestations of imagined female violence be used as acts of political resistance. However, this strategy to affirm female anger and vengeance differs from mere role reversal (with male violence) and that which achieves nothing constructive:

> But role reversal never simply replicates the terms of the equation. The depiction of women committing acts of violence against men does not simply use "male" tactics of aggression for other ends; in fact, female violence transforms the symbolic function of the feminine within popular narratives and simultaneously challenges the hegemonic insistence upon the linking of might and right under the sign of masculinity (Halberstam 2001: 251).

For Halberstam, the potency of imagined female violence manifested in the media lies in the threat of its potential to materialise in the mind of a perpetrator of assault. If indeed female victims have cornered the market in the matter of sexual assault, that market place will experience change if would-be aggressors realise, via cinematic manifestations of female rage, the potential of these victims to retaliate.

The construction of imagined female anger, threat, and power outside of the terrain of sexual assault might function in similar ways that make female anger more politically useful than the versions of monstrous abjection to which psychoanalysis repeatedly returns. Co-opting female anger by politically resisting the pathology of female anger while challenging the absoluteness of feminist film theory's psychoanalytic paradigm function as a two-pronged attack that is politically and theoretically compatible. Halberstam writes that the place of rage "is a location between and beyond thought, action, response, activism, protest, anger, terror, murder, and detestation" (Halberstam 2001:247). In other words, this place of rage springs up in the in-between spaces to enact resistances that defy all manner of codifications that invalidate female anger and deny political resistance. *Dolores Claiborne* illustrates the potential of female anger and resistance in filmic manifestations for furthering the political imperative in feminist film theory.

Dolores, Selena, and Vera are three female figures in *Dolores Claiborne* who are marked out by the anger they respectively express. However, the difference between the qualities of Selena's anger from that of the two older characters reveals the necessity of understanding the potential of female anger for feminist purposes. Dolores and Vera, who murdered their respective husbands, live in relative isolation from the town folks. The two women's difficult personalities express anger that is directed outwards towards an unjust patriarchal world that leaves them with little choice but to kill their respective husbands. While Vera murdered her adulterous husband to escape an unhappy fate as a neglected wife, Dolores killed hers to save her daughter from more sexual abuse. Dolores' recalcitrance in her dealings with the detective and other town folks who harass her is defensive by nature. Their isolation, cantankerousness, and implied unpopularity is evidence of how few choices these two women have apart from taking on qualities of bitchiness to survive. In other words, the model of womanhood that Dolores and Vera represent does not coincide with the proper (modest and passive) version of femininity that psychoanalysis espouses. The feminist philosopher Rosi Braidotti compares the perspectives of Freud and Deleuze in her recent book, *Metamorphoses,* and applies them to feminist theory: while Freud translated his main problematic "into an economy of excess and lack, aiming at equilibrium," Deleuze's philosophy predicates on sustainability in a universe that has already progressed beyond the prospect of restoring equilibrium (Delueze 1989:146). Freud's psychoanalytic economy does not apply to *Dolores Claiborne's* narrative, given that the rot has set in too far for the eventual restoration of a patriarchal Symbolic and an appropriate version of femininity. Playing up the bitch, on the other hand, is a survival tactic that Deleuze would approve, one that is predicated on sustainability and that cultivates "the capacity to sustain and to endure" (ibid.). Dolores and Vera sustain themselves through their hard-edged personalities and grit in order to endure the oppression of a patriarchal Symbolic that has evidently failed and become abusive. As Anneke Smelik (quoting Andreas Burnier) observes about female aggression, "[m]asculinism is a terrible problem, and feminism is an almost equally terrible response to it" (Smelik 1998: 119).

The feminist text of *Dolores Claiborne* resides in the mutually sustaining relationship between Dolores and Vera. Vera, as a difficult, miserly, fastidious, and pretentious socialite, is not immediately identifiable as a feminist role model. However, she recognises the drawbacks of being a woman in a patriarchal world and uses that knowledge to her own advantage. Despite her flaws, she identifies firstly with her sex; perhaps the most rudimentary of feminist statements. Vera insists that Dolores calls her by her first name when the latter breaks down at work with the knowledge that her husband is interfering with the young Selena. Vera hints openly at having murdered her husband and instigates Dolores to do the same because "it's a depressingly masculine world we live in," so much so that "an accident, Dolores, can be an unhappy woman's best friend." In such desperate circumstances where murdering one's husband is a woman's only recourse, being a bitch is really all a woman has to hold on to.

On the other hand, Selena's anger is self-destructive and predicated on Oedipal hauntings; or rather, her failure to accurately render the past into an acceptable story with which she could live. Despite the Vassar education and the high-flying career, she sleeps with her boss to get ahead professionally, is estranged from her mother, chain smokes in an era when smoking is no longer fashionable, and is dependent on anti-depressants. Selena epitomises the failure of achieving the version of femininity that psychoanalysis advocates and that in which she invests. She interprets the abuses she and Dolores suffered at the hands of her father in grossly mistaken Oedipal terms. She grieves about losing the opportunity to become Daddy's girl, believing that Dolores killed Joe before she had a chance, without any awareness of the incest of which she was so close to becoming a victim. The ways in which *Dolores Claiborne* rectify Selena's memory of the past enable the film's textual operation to sustain a series of feminist-becomings that also unravel the psychoanalytic premises of feminist film theory.

Constructing *Dolores Claiborne*'s Genealogy

Dolores Claiborne acknowledges its ancestry in the gothic woman's film, to the extent that parallels may be drawn between the opening sequence's images with those from *Rebecca* (Alfred Hitchcock, 1940) and other gothic woman's films of the 1940s. The film opens with a shot of the sea, after which the camera moves uphill to reveal a big white house that stands on top of a hill and that which over-looks the sea. Through a series of five shots that dissolve into one another, the camera moves closer to the house, enters through the glass on the front door and fades to a shot of the stairwell where a shrill off frame voice is heard saying, "No, Dolores, let me be!" Shadows on the wall by the stairwell show some sort of struggle taking place and a woman rolls down the stairs and lands on the bottom of the stairs, the force of her body breaking the banisters. The camera moves up the stairs from the body at the bottom and Dolores descends the stairs. The shot then cuts to a close-up of Dolores Claiborne who appears breathless as she looks down at the figure at the bottom of the stairs.

Point of view shots follow and very quickly, Dolores cocks her head very slightly to one side. Given Kathy Bates' previous role in *Misery*, this close-up is one of either shock or menace. The shot then cuts to the kitchen sequence where the whistling of a boiling kettle, unsteady overhead shots, knives falling out of a drawer, and Dolores' general ransacking of the place reference Kathy Bates' previous role of the mad woman in *Misery*. Dolores sees a rolling pin at the corner of the kitchen, picks it up, and exits. In the next shot, she returns to the figure at the bottom of the stairs and prepares to smash the rolling pin down on Vera. At this moment, she pauses and the medium shot shows Dolores with rolling pin held high above her head and tears in her eyes as she looks down at the crumpled figure on the ground. A voice-over indicates the entrance of the postman who registers shock at the scene and to whom the scene looks like a murder.

Up till the medium shot of Dolores holding the rolling pin with tears in her eyes, this opening sequence references many films, usually of gothic origins, where foul play invariably takes place on stairwells inside a house. One thinks of *Gaslight* (George Cukor, 1944), *Sleep, My Love* (Douglas Sirk, 1948), *The Spiral Staircase* (Robert Siodmak, 1946), *Psycho* (Alfred Hitchcock, 1960), and even *Frenzy* (Hitchcock, 1972). The medium shot of a tearful Dolores holding up the rolling pin in effect changes the tone of the film up to now. It signals that despite appearances, Dolores is not the psychotic Annie Wilkes of *Misery*, thereby severing the film's association with the earlier backlash films. The big white mansion on the hill is also not the gothic house of terror that eventually morphs into the Terrible Place of the slasher film. As Laura Grindstaff observes in her analysis that centres on the film's narrative, *Dolores Claiborne* misleads by situating the opening sequence at Vera's mansion, "for there is another, decidedly humbler house in the film that, far more than the Donovan mansion, bears the imprint of past evil" (Grindstaff 2001:150). On the other hand, Grindstaff notes how the film functions like the 1970s rape-revenge film *I Spit on You Grave* (Meir Zarchi, 1978) because the woman's anger is proven right, she gets her revenge, and gets away with it in the end (Grindstaff 2001:167). This represents not only a departure from the strategy of pathologising angry women in backlash films such as *Fatal Attraction* (Adrian Lyne, 1987), it also sustains *Dolores Claiborne* as a recent Hollywood film with its feminist genealogy in the gothic woman's film and the rape-revenge genre, amongst others.

Beginning with the house on the hill that is the gothic repository of all family secrets and horror, the film proceeds to resist all the gothic elements that it acknowledges in its generic make-up. The sinister house is not the big mansion, but the humble dwelling of someone who serves in the big house. The villain is far from the dark, handsome, and brooding master of the house, threatening the illusion of the handsome mysterious brute that is Heathcliff in Emily Bronte's *Wuthering Heights* (1847, reprinted 1985). Joe is the alcoholic, unattractive, and good-for-nothing husband of the woman who serves in the big house. That *Dolores Claiborne* cuts across the social-economic class structure of the gothic woman's film demystifies the family secrets and horrors that are disguised by opulence and grandeur, so pervasive in the 1940s genre. In addition, that the horror is displaced from the big house to a much humbler one relegates the gothic space that is imperative for the playing out of family secrets and hauntings in the gothic woman's film to secondary importance.

In effect, the acknowledgement, and subsequent relegation, of gothic space in *Dolores Claiborne* to relative insignificance heralds a new trajectory for

Dolores Claiborne (Taylor Hackford 1995), Columbia/Castle Rock.

thinking about cinematic manifestations of the gothic. If one stops thinking of the woman's gothic film in terms of spatiality, containment, and recuperation, one is then able to think of feminist potential, in some sort of neo-gothic and post-psychoanalytic sense, in terms of time, movement, and productive possibilities. While *Dolores Claiborne's* genealogy reveals a progressive trajectory towards a feminist ideal of positive difference that is not predicated on negating the masculine, its textual operation reveals further ways in which to circumvent psychoanalytic hauntings via innovative uses of the flashback that employs, and extends, Deleuze's understanding of the flashback.

Rectifying the Past

There are two types of flashbacks in *Dolores Claiborne*. The first is the conventional sort that Deleuze discusses in *Cinema 2*, and that which lacks cinematic sophistication because "[i]t is like a sign with the words 'watch out! recollection' (sic.)" and remains "analogous to a sensory-motor determinism, and despite its circuits, only confirms the progression of a linear narration" (Deleuze 1989:48). This conventional flashback is announced by either a dissolve or voice-over according to causal narrative determinations. This flashback is delineated from the present narrative trajectory and signals a deviation from the narrative course. In short, the conventional flashback functions to fill in the back-story or narrative gaps, for instance, in the places where Dolores recounts the extensive back-story of her long relationship with Vera and the circumstances surrounding the latter's death. The other type of flashback in *Dolores Claiborne*, however, infiltrates the present and privileges the past in relation to the present. It signals the significance of the past on the present course of action and in effect suspends the causal functioning of the narrative's present, clearly as an innovation on classic realism's textual operation. More significantly, it exceeds Deleuze's understanding of the flashback as it works across the film's narrative level to impinge on *Dolores Claiborne's* cinematic dimensions and rid the narrative of Oedipal hauntings.

Selena's inability to remember the past causes the rift with Dolores as she heaps the blame of her father's death on her mother. This process of remembering the past to redeem the present situation necessitates the past to become present, as it were, and disrupts the perspective of time as linearity. The past that she fails to remember hinders Selena's attempt to move on in her own life and explains her self-destructive behavioural patterns. The film resolves this suspension of Selena's life by the family secrets involving violence, abuse, and incest by making present and available Dolores' memories that rectify the present situation. The sequences wherein the past infiltrates the present have in common the consistency of space that although present, does not confine. Spatiality takes a back seat in a film that simultaneously registers the importance of, and relegates to secondary status, the significance of space in the cinematic manifestations of the gothic and the neo-gothic. The consistency of space in *Dolores Claiborne* allows for the playing out of time and memory, the co-existence of past and present, and the freeing of the past from psychoanalytic repression. The flashback sequences where past and present interact relate to Selena's failure to remember. *Dolores Claiborne* is past Oedipal hauntings and the family romance. While the undercurrent of the young Selena's affections for the father and suspicions of her mother is evident, the film denounces this Electral complex and instead exposes Selena's delusions about her father. When past and present exist together, the past no longer remains a realm for family secrets and hauntings; instead, it creates an outlet for the exorcism of such hauntings.

The past's infiltration of the present in *Dolores Claiborne*'s exorcism of Oedipal hauntings is most evident at the points where the past intersects with the present course of action. The first of such sequences begin when Dolores and Selena arrive at the house from the sheriff's office. As Selena struggles with the lock on the front door, Dolores looks around the porch and the past encroaches on the present for the first time. The warm and glowing colours become brighter as details of the flashback are superimposed onto the present landscape as voices, from what is later established as the search party for the missing Joe, begin to emerge. A younger Dolores appears in her own recollection, in a bright dress, standing in the exact same position as the present older Dolores. This sequence also introduces, in a quick close-up, the young Selena as Dolores barks orders at her to get into the house. Dolores only snaps out of this recollection when Selena's voice interrupts Dolores' thoughts as she commands her mother to get indoors with the exact same words as in the flashback. However, despite snapping back to the present, the past only relinquishes its hold on the present reluctantly. The brighter colours of the flashback recedes very gradually as the shot dims, the last bits of which fade away in Dolores' close-up, as her bright orange collar becomes duller and fades into the darker colours of the tartan shirt she is wearing in the present.

These flashbacks are particularly significant because of the ways in which they exceed conventional, and Deleuze's, understanding of their cinematic function. The encroaching past in the sequence described above possesses a quality that undermines the privilege of Dolores' subjective point of view. For Deleuze, the conventional flashback that triggers memory speaks through the "voice as memory [that] frames the flashback," in that "what the latter 'shows', and what the former reports, are more voices: characters and décors which are of course meant to be seen, but are in essence speaking and of sound" (Deleuze 1989:51). The richness of the voices in, and the texture of, *Dolores Claiborne*'s first flashback is derived from the film's materiality that, in the first place, enables their manifestations. Although flashbacks emerge out of a character's memory, this first recollection undermines Dolores' voice as the sequence's primary perspective in the way that the voice-over would function in a conventional flashback. The voices, the sound, and the visual complexity of this recollection-image exceed Dolores' perspective and al-low the past, as a recollection-image, to possess a level of complexity not otherwise possible if the past remains within the remit of a particular sub-ject's point of view and through the subject's voice-over as in many classic realist films of the 1930s and 1940s. Such an understanding of the flashback's potential as a cinematic device undermines the importance of the cinematic subject as predicated on identification with the protagonist's point of view. Dolores' first recollection provides more in visual and narrative terms than a mere re-telling of family secrets on film would.

These infiltrations of the past into the present become ever more signifi-cant as Selena struggles with the trauma of re-learning the past and undoing the damage of wholesale belief in the Oedipal scenario. The interaction between Dolores and Selena becomes more intense and strained as their conflicting memories of the past hinder the possibility of their reconcilia-tion. As Dolores recounts the incident where she fights her husband after he hits her by challenging him with an axe, Joe literally comes into the same frame as Selena. The realness of Dolores' recollection confuses even her as she expresses shock when Joe appears in the background of the shot of Selena getting herself drunk at the table in the foreground of the frame. The brighter colour scheme of the past does not encroach on the present directly, as in the reverse situation. As Joe appears in the frame, he is in the dull colour scheme of the present. Apart from the knowledge that Joe is dead, the only clue at this point of the film that this is a recollection-image comes from the glow emanating from without. This glow from outside the house gets shut out as Joe closes the door and walks further into the house. The camera, at this point to the left of Dolores' position in the frame, dollies across behind her, and as it rounds to Dolores' right, it uses the close-up of the back of her head as a wipe into the past scenario where Joe comes home from work and hits his wife for no reason at all. From this point on, the recollection-image functions as a conventional flashback until the sequence wipes back to a tearful Selena, in the present, and still sitting at the table. We then learn that Dolores has just given an accurate rendition of a piece of the past to her daughter.

The past continues to encroach on the present throughout the rest of the film. Everything in the present triggers the incursion of the past. Sickened by her mother's ostracism by the rest of the island folks and the harassment of the posse, of which Dolores remains defiant, Selena breaks down watch-ing her mother deal with the mob who have come to hurl abuses from a lorry. She crouches at the bathroom sink and pops pills while Dolores looks on at her daughter in despair. At this moment, as Selena begs for time to recompose herself, Dolores alternates between looking at her daughter at one side and the phone on the other. The phone starts ringing, although the narrative has established from the beginning that the phone no longer works. The shot cuts to a close-up of the phone and a hand picks up the receiver. The next shot shows the young Selena's trauma as she listens to the taunting on the other end of the line, presumably about her parents. The young Selena subsequently tries to slit her own throat, an act that foreshadows the self-destructive behaviour in her adult life. In another instance, realising that her daughter has no clue of what her father did to her, Dolores resolves to tell Selena about the incest. Forcing Selena to sit, Dolores pushes a shot of whiskey across the table at her. However, the hand that reaches out to receive the glass of whiskey is Joe's rough hand with unkempt nails, gripping an almost burnt out rolled-up cigarette between his fingers, thereby rendering the back-story of how Joe was interfering with his daughter.

As time comes into active play in *Dolores Claiborne*, space remains a constant. Although the neo-gothic space of the family home triggers the incursion of the past into the present, the film makes clear that spatiality alone, gothic or otherwise, does not occupy a privileged discursive position. The film piles flashback upon flashback. In the flashback sequence that affirms the relationship between Dolores and Vera, Dolores tells Vera of her confrontation with Selena on the ferry, where she discovers the pendant that Joe has given to Selena, thereby confirming her suspicions of incest. In this flashback within a flashback, the young Selena slaps her mother as Dolores pushes her to tell on Joe. At this point, as Dolores registers the slap on her face, the close-up cuts to present, where the older Selena screams "you crazy, lying bitch" at her mother and runs up the stairs. The layers of Dolores' recollection merge with the present, pivoting not only on space, but also on the emotional ties that Dolores has with both Vera and Selena. The conflict between mother and daughter is that which allows the incursion of the past, evident in the links the film makes between present action and past incursions, as much as the neo-gothic space that seems to prompt such irruptions.

The final flashback sequence in *Dolores Claiborne* is Selena's. As she attempts to get away from the past by hopping onto the ferry and getting away physically from her mother, the past comes to her. The extraordinary sequence on the ferry where past and present co-exist on the same plane is that which achieves the final exorcism. The sequence begins when Selena buys a cup of coffee on the boat. Scrutinising the paper cup she holds in her hands, Selena begins to feel a sense of *déjà vu* as the vendor announces her purchase, "one coffee one dollar." Beside her, out of frame, someone else is buying drinks as well. The vendor's voice-over announces the beverages: "one coffee, one hot cocoa, sixty-cents," a combination of beverages that suggests the drinks are meant for an adult and a child, the pre-inflation price of which indicates a discrepancy of time between the two purchases. With no conversion into the colour scheme of the past, Selena sees her father appear beside her, grabbing the drinks and walking out onto the deck. As he gets onto the deck, she spies him from a window, and the view from the window changes into the warm glowing colours of this film's flashbacks. She follows him out onto the deck, and into the colour tones of the past, while being subsumed in her own recollection-images. Selena rounds the corner, stands off-frame at a side, and watches herself as a child being coerced to masturbate her father. She continues watching in horror and a hand appears in the close-up of her watching and interrupts her thoughts by tapping her on the shoulder. It then cuts to a close-up of the drinks vendor, framed in the tonality of the present's dullness, with Selena's change in his hands.

That Selena is able to recall the details of the ride on the ferry with her father in effect reconciles the present with past hauntings. This ability to finally remember allows the resumption of the film's narrative causality that brings *Dolores Claiborne* towards its conclusion, a conclusion that because the film functions to exorcise Oedipal hauntings, does not end with the requisite heterosexual romance or the re-establishment of the father figure. Instead, the film ends by reinstating the legitimacy of female anger and defiance. The hauntings of *Dolores Claiborne* has nothing to do with dead and/or mad former wives. Husbands, dead through mysterious circumstances, litter the film. Two, to be precise, and by all accounts, deserving of their ends. Doing away with Freud and Lacan would, in a similar way, free feminist film theory from submitting to the paternal metaphor.

Notes

1. A shorter version of this paper was delivered at the Screen conference at the University of Glasgow in July 2003. It also forms a chapter in my PhD thesis entitled *Transgressing sexual difference: Sustaining feminist politics in film theory* (Norwich: University of East Anglia, 2003). I am grateful to Yvonne Tasker, Sadie Wearing, Patricia Zimmermann, as well as the editors of this anthology for their constructive comments at various stages of writing.

2. The notion of a feminist backlash refers to the discourse that Susan Faludi's *Backlash: The undeclared war against American women* (New York: Crown, 1991) opens up.

References

Braidotti, R. (2002). *Metamorphoses: Towards a materialist theory of becoming*. Cambridge: Polity Press.

Brontë, E. (1985). *Wuthering heights*. London: Penguin.

Creed, B. (1993). The Monstrous-feminine: Film, feminism, psychoanalysis. London and New York: Routledge.

Deleuze, G. (1989). *Cinema 2: The Time-image*. H. Tomlinson & R. Galeta (Trans.). London: The Athlone Press.

Faludi, S. (1991). *Backlash: The undeclared war against American women*. New York: Crown.

Grindstaff, L. (2001). Sometimes being a bitch is all a woman has to hold on to: Memory, haunting, and revenge in *Dolores Claiborne*. In M. McCaughey & N. King (Eds.), *Reel knockouts: Violent women in the movies* (pp. 147- 71). Austin: University of Texas Press.

Halberstam, J. (2001). Imagined violence/queer violence: Representations of rage and resistance. In M. McCaughey & N. King (Eds.), *Reel knockouts: Violent women in the movies* (pp. 244-266). Austin: University of Texas Press.

Kristeva, J. (1982). *Powers of horror: An essay on abjection*. L. S. Roudiez (Trans.). New York: Columbia University Press.

Smelik, A. (1998). *And the mirror cracked: Feminist cinema and film theory*. Basingstoke and London: Macmillian.

The Authors

Walter Alesci is a Ph.D. Student at Autonomous University of Barcelona. His academic research interests are in women's studies, gender and queer theory on Latin American television. He is a writer and has worked in journalism and television in Argentina and Spain, where he has been able to link academic focus with the communication media.

Anne Gjelsvik is Assistant Professor at the Department of Art and Media Studies, Faculty of Arts, Norwegian University of Science and Technology. She finished her Ph.D. thesis entitled *Ethical Judgments of Fiction Film* in 2004. She is the author of *Mørkets Øyne. Filmkritikk, analyse og vurdering* [Eyes of Darkness. Film Reviewing, Analysis and Judgements] Universitetsforlaget, 2001, and chief editor of the Norwegian media journal *Norsk medietidsskrift.*

Ingrid Lindell is Ph.D. and Senior Lecturer at the Department of Literature, University of Gothenburg, Sweden, and finished her Ph. D. thesis entitled *Att se och synas. Filmutbud, kön och modernitet* [To see and be seen. Cinema, gender and modernity] in 2004. The central question is how film studies should deal with social and ethical issues when analysing works of art. She teaches popular culture at the Centre for Cultural Studies, University of Gothenburg.

Deneka C. MacDonald is a post doctorate Research Assistant with Glasgow University Initiative in Distance Education and an Associate Lecturer with the Open University of Scotland. Her interests and current research areas include contemporary fantasy in television and film, emotional and gendered geographies, and women's writing. She is currently publishing in popular culture; feminist, media and film studies; as well as humanities computing.

Maja Mikula is Coordinator of the Italy major in the International Studies program at the University of Technology Sydney and subject coordinator for the Italian Language and Culture subjects. Her research interests are in the areas of (trans)nationalism, gender and the new media. Current research projects include: Stretching Boundaries: Women, Revolt and Social Change; Nation, State and Political Leadership in Cyberspace; and 'Living in the Trees': the Italian Intellectuals in the New Millennium.

Wencke Mühleisen is Researcher in Media Studies, Centre for Feminist Research, University of Oslo. Her Ph.D. thesis is *Kjønn i uorden: Iscenesettelse av kjønn og seksualitet i eksperimentell talkshow underholdning på norsk fjernsynet* [Gender Disorder: Representations of Gender and Sexuality in Experimental Talkshow Entertainment in Norwegian Television, 2002]. She is the author of *Kjønn og Sex på Tv: Norske medier i postfeminismens tid* [Gender and Sexuality in Television. Norwegian Media in the Age of Postfeminism, 2003]. Her research is on popular culture (film, television and art), queer theory, gender and sexuality. She currently works with artist Christel Sverre leading the co-project "Sex(Y) Art" for artists and researchers, a series of seminars resulting in an exhibition 2006.

Mervi Pantti is Ph.D. and Research Fellow in the Department of Communication, University of Helsinki. Currently she is visiting scholar at ASCoR, Amsterdam School of Communications Studies. She has published several books in Finnish and articles in Finnish and English. Research interests include reality television, teen films and -shows, popular television and culture, national identity and media, and mediatized emotions. She also works as a freelance television critic for *Helsingin Sanomat*.

Rikke Schubart is Ph.D., Associate Professor and Director of studies at the Center for Media Studies, University of Southern Denmark. She has published several books in Danish, two on the horror movie and one on the American action movie: *Med vold og magt. Actionfilm fra Dirty Harry til The Mission* [Mission Complete. The Action Movie from Dirty Harry to The Matrix, 2002]. She has edited an anthology on contemporary American cinema with Heidi Jørgensen, *Made in America: Tendencies in American Cinema* (2003). Her research is on popular film genres and gender, and her current research project is "Woman In a Man's World: A Study of Heroines in Male Film Genres", funded by the Danish Research Council for the Humanities. She is chief editor of the Danish media journal *MedieKultur*.

Yvonne Tasker is Professor of Film and Television Studies at the University of East Anglia, UK. She is the author of *Spectacular Bodies. Gender, genre and action cinema* (1993) and *Working Girls: Gender and Sexuality in Popular Cinema* (1998). Most recently she has edited an anthology, *Action and Adventure Cinema*, which will be published by Routledge in 2004. She is currently working on a study of military women in cinema and television since WWII.

Sharon Lin Tay is a Lecturer in Film Studies at Middlesex University, London, UK. Her recently completed doctoral thesis explores the applicability of Deleuze to feminist film theory while her new research project considers the incorporation of digitality and new media into film theory. She also writes on world cinema and women filmmakers.

Kim Walden is Senior Lecturer in Digital Culture and Discourse in the Faculty of Art and Design, University of Hertfordshire. She has an MA in Film and Television from University of London. Her research interests fall into two areas: media education, visual literacy and the impact of the digital information environment on teaching, and, secondly, the relationship between new media and film. She has published numerous articles, teaching materials and contributed to anthologies. Kim's three daughters have provided invaluable support in helping her get to grips with the complexities of the Sony PlayStation and antics of Lara Croft.

Karma Waltonen is a Writer, currently pursuing her doctorate in literature at the University of California, Davis. She teaches at UC Davis, American River College, and Sacramento City College. She specializes in gender, film, and theatre. Though her periods and genres seem disparate, she always tends to be writing about 'bad girls'.